PARADIGM
EDUCATION SOLUTIONS

BENCHMARK SERIES

Microsoft®

Access®

2016

Level 2

Davidson

PARADIGM
EDUCATION SOLUTIONS

St. Paul

Senior Vice President	Linda Hein
Editor in Chief	Christine Hurney
Director of Production	Timothy W. Larson
Production Editor	Jen Weaverling
Cover and Text Designer	Valerie King
Copy Editors	Communicáto, Ltd.
Senior Design and Production Specialist	Jack Ross
Design and Production Specialist	PerfecType
Assistant Developmental Editors	Mamie Clark, Katie Werdick
Testers	Janet Blum, Fanshawe College; Traci Post
Instructional Support Writers	Janet Blum, Fanshawe College; Brienna McWade
Indexer	Terry Casey
Vice President Information Technology	Chuck Bratton
Digital Projects Manager	Tom Modl
Vice President Sales and Marketing	Scott Burns
Director of Marketing	Lara Weber McLellan

Trademarks: Microsoft is a trademark or registered trademark of Microsoft Corporation in the United States and/or other countries. Some of the product names and company names included in this book have been used for identification purposes only and may be trademarks or registered trade names of their respective manufacturers and sellers. The authors, editors, and publisher disclaim any affiliation, association, or connection with, or sponsorship or endorsement by, such owners.

We have made every effort to trace the ownership of all copyrighted material and to secure permission from copyright holders. In the event of any question arising as to the use of any material, we will be pleased to make the necessary corrections in future printings.

Cover Photo Credits: © Photomall/Dreamstime.com.

Paradigm Publishing is independent from Microsoft Corporation, and not affiliated with Microsoft in any manner. While this publication may be used in assisting individuals to prepare for a Microsoft Office Specialist certification exam, Microsoft, its designated program administrator, and Paradigm Publishing do not warrant that use of this publication will ensure passing a Microsoft Office Specialist certification exam.

ISBN 978-0-76386-956-4 (print)
ISBN 978-0-76386-957-1 (digital)

© 2017 by Paradigm Publishing, Inc.
875 Montreal Way
St. Paul, MN 55102
Email: educate@emcp.com
Website: ParadigmCollege.com

Printed in the United States of America

23 22 21 20 19 18 17 16   1 2 3 4 5 6 7 8 9 10 11 12

Brief Contents

Contents

Preface

Benchmark Series: Microsoft® Access 2016 is designed for students who want to learn how to use this feature-rich data management tool to track, report, and share information. After successfully completing a course using this textbook and digital courseware, students will be able to:

- Create database tables to organize business or personal records
- Modify and manage tables to ensure that data is accurate and up to date
- Perform queries to assist with decision making
- Plan, research, create, revise, and publish database information to meet specific communication needs
- Given a workplace scenario requiring the reporting and analysis of data, assess the information requirements and then prepare the materials that achieve the goal efficiently and effectively

Upon completing the text, students can expect to be proficient in using Access to organize, analyze, and present information.

Well-designed textbook pedagogy is important, but students learn technology skills through practice and problem solving. Technology provides opportunities for interactive learning as well as excellent ways to quickly and accurately assess student performance. To this end, this textbook is supported with SNAP 2016, Paradigm's web-based training and assessment learning management system. Details about SNAP as well as additional student courseware and instructor resources can be found on page xiv.

Achieving Proficiency in Access 2016

Since its inception several Office versions ago, the *Benchmark Series* has served as a standard of excellence in software instruction. Elements of the *Benchmark Series* function individually and collectively to create an inviting, comprehensive learning environment that produces successful computer users. The following visual tour highlights the structure and features that comprise the highly popular *Benchmark* model.

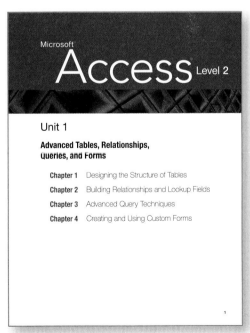

Microsoft

Access Level 2

Unit 1

Advanced Tables, Relationships, Queries, and Forms

Chapter 1   Designing the Structure of Tables

Chapter 2   Building Relationships and Lookup Fields

Chapter 3   Advanced Query Techniques

Chapter 4   Creating and Using Custom Forms

Unit Openers display the unit's four chapter titles. *Access Level 2* contains two units; each unit concludes with a comprehensive unit performance assessment.

Student Textbook and eBook

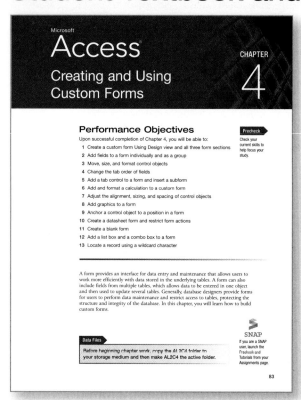

Chapter Openers present the performance objectives and an overview of the skills taught.

Precheck quizzes allow students to check their current skills before starting chapter work.

Data Files are provided for each chapter from the ebook. A prominent note reminds students to copy the appropriate chapter data folder and make it active.

Students with SNAP access are reminded to launch the Precheck quiz and chapter tutorials from their SNAP Assignments page.

Projects Build Skill Mastery within Realistic Context

Multipart Projects provide a framework for instruction and practice on software features. A project overview identifies tasks to accomplish and key features to use in completing the work.

Preview Finished Project shows how the file will look after students complete the project.

Tutorials provide interactive, guided training and measured practice.

Quick Steps provide feature summaries for reference and review.

Hint margin notes offer useful tips on how to use features efficiently and effectively.

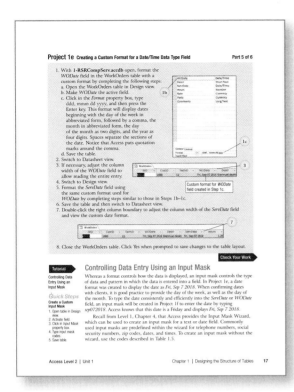

Step-by-Step Instructions guide students to the desired outcome for each project part. Screen captures illustrate what the screen should look like at key points.

Magenta Text identifies material to type.

Check Your Work allows students to confirm they have completed the project activity correctly.

Typically, a file remains open throughout all parts of the project. Students save their work incrementally. At the end of the project, students save and then close the file.

Between project parts, the text presents instruction on the features and skills necessary to accomplish the next section of the project.

Chapter Review Tools Reinforce Learning

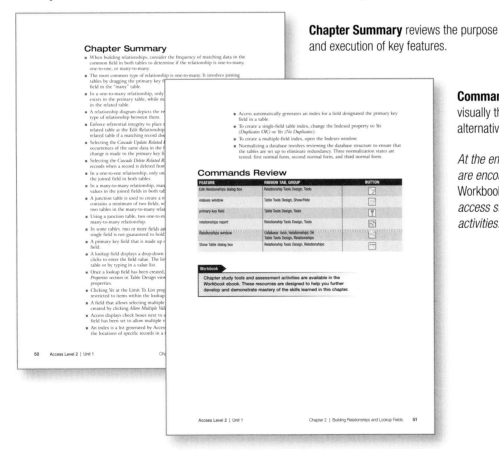

Chapter Summary reviews the purpose and execution of key features.

Commands Review summarizes visually the major features and alternative methods of access.

At the end of each chapter, students are encouraged to go to the Workbook pages of the ebook to access study tools and assessment activities.

Workbook eBook Activities Provide a Hierarchy of Learning Assessments

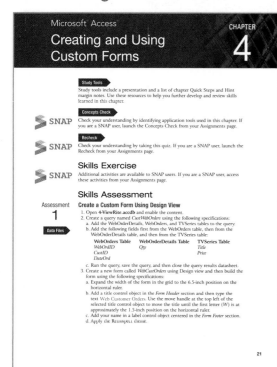

Study Tools are presentations with audio support and a list of chapter Quick Steps and Hint margin notes designed to help students further develop and review skills learned in the chapter.

Concepts Check is an objective completion exercise that allows students to assess their comprehension and recall of application features, terminology, and functions.

Recheck concept quizzes for each chapter enable students to check how their skills have improved after completing chapter work.

Skills Exercises are available to SNAP 2016 users. SNAP will automatically score student work, which is preformed live in the application, and provide detailed feedback.

Skills Assessment exercises ask students to develop both standard and customized types of databases without how-to directions.

Visual Benchmark assessments test problem-solving skills and mastery of application features.

Case Study requires analyzing a workplace scenario and then planning and executing a multipart project.

Students search the web and/or use the program's Help feature to locate additional information required to complete the Case Study.

Unit Performance Assessments Deliver Cross-Disciplinary, Comprehensive Evaluation

Assessing Proficiency exercises check mastery of features.

Writing Activities involve applying application skills in a communication context.

Internet Research projects reinforce research and information processing skills.

Job Study at the end of Unit 2 presents a capstone assessment requiring critical thinking and problem solving.

SNAP Training and Assessment

SNAP is a web-based training and assessment program and learning management system (LMS) for learning Microsoft Office 2016. SNAP is comprised of rich content, a sophisticated grade book, and robust scheduling and analytics tools. SNAP courseware supports the *Benchmark Series* content and delivers live-in-the-application assessments for students to demonstrate their skills mastery. Interactive tutorials increase skills-focused moments with guided training and measured practice. SNAP provides automatic scoring and detailed feedback on the many activities, exercises, and quizzes to help identify areas where additional support is needed, evaluating student performance both at an individual and course level. The *Benchmark Series* SNAP course content is also available to export into any LMS system that supports LTI tools.

Paradigm Education Solutions provides technical support for SNAP through 24-7 chat at ParadigmCollege.com. In addition, an online User Guide and other SNAP training tools for using SNAP are available.

Student eBook

The student ebook, available through SNAP or online at Paradigm.bookshelf.emcp.com, provides access to the *Benchmark Series* content from any device (desktop, tablet, and smartphone) anywhere, through a live Internet connection. The versatile ebook platform features dynamic navigation tools including a linked table of contents and the ability to jump to specific pages, search for terms, bookmark, highlight, and take notes. The ebook offers live links to the interactive content and resources that support the print textbook, including the student data files, Precheck and Recheck quizzes, and interactive tutorials. The *Workbook* pages of the ebook also provide access to presentations with audio support and to end-of-chapter Concept Check, Skills Assessment, Visual Benchmark, Case Study, and end-of-unit Performance Assessment activities.

Instructor eResources eBook

All instructor resources are available digitally through a web-based ebook at Paradigm.bookshelf.emcp.com. The instructor materials include these items:

- Planning resources, such as lesson plans, teaching hints, and sample course syllabi
- Presentation resources, such as PowerPoint slide shows with lecture notes
- Assessment resources, including live and annotated PDF model answers for chapter work and workbook activities, rubrics for evaluating student work, and chapter-based exam banks

Microsoft® Access® Level 2

Unit 1

Advanced Tables, Relationships, Queries, and Forms

Microsoft®

Access®

Designing the Structure of Tables

Performance Objectives

Precheck

Check your current skills to help focus your study.

Upon successful completion of Chapter 1, you will be able to:

1 Design the structure of a table

2 Select field data type based on an analysis of the source data

3 Disallow blank field values

4 Allow and disallow zero-length strings in fields

5 Create custom formats for Short Text, Number, and Date/Time data type fields

6 Restrict data entry using input masks

7 Enable rich text formatting in a Long Text data type field

8 Maintain a history of changes for a Long Text data type field

9 Define and use an Attachment data type field with multiple attachments

Designing tables in Access is the most important task when creating a database because all the other objects are based on tables. All queries, forms, and reports rely on tables as the sources of their data. Designing a new database involves planning the number of tables needed, the fields to be included in each table, and the methods to be used to check and/or validate new data as it is entered. In this chapter, you will learn the basic steps involved in planning a new database by analyzing existing data. You will also learn to select appropriate data types and use field properties to control, restrict, or otherwise validate data.

In order to complete the projects in this chapter, you will already need to know the steps in creating a new table, including changing the data type and field size and assigning the primary key field. Readers are also assumed to know the meanings of the terms *field*, *record*, *table*, and *database*.

SNAP

If you are a SNAP user, launch the Precheck and Tutorials from your Assignments page.

Data Files

Before beginning chapter work, copy the AL2C1 folder to your storage medium and then make AL2C1 the active folder.

Preview Finished Project

Tutorial

Review: Creating
a Table in Design
View

Designing Tables and
Fields for a New Database

Most databases encountered in the workplace have been created by database
designers. Even so, understanding the process involved in creating a new database
will help users make sense of how objects are organized and related. Creating a new
database from scratch involves careful planning.

Database designers spend considerable time analyzing existing data and asking
questions of users and managers. Designers want to know how data will be used
so they can identify the forms, queries, and reports that will need to be generated.
Often designers begin by modeling a required report from the database to see the
data used to populate the report. The designer then compiles a data dictionary,
which is a list of fields as well as the attributes of each field. The designer uses the
data dictionary to map out the number of required tables.

A sample work order for RSR Computer Services is analyzed in Project 1. RSR
started as a small computer service company and the owners used Excel worksheets
to enter information from service records and to produce revenue reports. The
company's success has created the need for a relational database to track customer
information. The owners want to be able to generate queries and reports that will
help them in decision making. Examine the data in the sample work order shown
in Figure 1.1. The work order that the technicians have been filling out at the
customer site will be used as the input source document for the database.

Figure 1.1 Sample Work Order for RSR Computer Services

Designers analyze all the input documents and output requirements to capture the entire set of data elements that needs to be created. Once all the data has been identified, the designer maps out the number of tables required to hold it. During the process of mapping out the tables and fields to be associated with each table, the designer follows these guidelines and techniques:

- Consider each table an entity that describes a single person, place, object, event, or other subject. Each table should store facts related only to that entity.

- Segment the data until it is in its smallest unit. For example, in the work order shown in Figure 1.1, the customer's name and address should be split into separate fields for first name, last name, street address, city, state, and zip code. Using this approach provides maximum flexibility for generating other objects and allows the user to sort or filter by any individual data element.

- Do not include fields that can be calculated using data from other fields. For example, the total labor and total due amounts in the work order can be calculated using other elements of numeric data.

- Identify fields that can be used to answer questions from the data. Queries and reports can be designed to extract information based on the results of a conditional expression (sometimes referred to as Boolean logic). For example, in the work order in Figure 1.1, the technician indicates whether the customer has a service contract. Providing a field that stores a *Yes* or *No* (true or false) condition for the service contract data element allows the business to generate reports of customers that have subscribed to a service contract (true condition) and customers that have not subscribed to a service contract (false condition).

- Identify a field in each table that will hold the data that uniquely identifies each record. This field becomes the primary key field. If the data that the database is designed to organize do not reveal a logical unique identifier, it is possible to use the ID field that Access automatically generates with the AutoNumber data type for each record as the primary key field.

- Identify each table that will relate to another table and the field that will be used to join the two tables when the relationships are created. Identifying relationships at this stage helps determine whether a field needs to be added to a related table to allow the tables to be joined.

- Keep in mind that relational databases are built on the concept that data redundancy should be avoided, except for fields that will be used to join tables in a relationship. (The term *data redundancy* means that data in one table is repeated in another table.) Repeating fields in multiple tables wastes storage space, promotes inefficiency and inconsistency, and increases the likelihood of errors being made when adding, updating, and deleting field values.

The database design process may seem time consuming but creating a well-designed database will save time later. A poorly designed database often contains logical and structural errors that require redefining data or objects after live data has been entered.

Diagramming a Database

Recall from Level 1, Chapter 1 that designers often create a visual representation of the structure of a database in a diagram similar to the one shown in Figure 1.2. In the database diagram, each table is represented in a box with the table name at the top. Within each box, the fields that will be stored in the table are listed with the field names that will be used when the table is created. The

Figure 1.2 Diagram of Table Structure for RSR Computer Services Database

Customers
*CustID
FName
LName
Street
City
State
ZIP
HPhone
CPhone
ServCont

ServiceContracts
*CustID
SCNo
StartDate
EndDate
FeePd

WorkOrders
*WO
CustID
TechID
WODate
Descr
ServDate
Hours
Rate
Parts
Comments

Technicians
*TechID
SSN
FName
LName
Street
City
State
ZIP
HPhone
CPhone

💡 **Hint** Words such as *Name* and *Date* are reserved words in Access and cannot be used as field names. A prompt will appear when trying to save a table containing field names that use reserved words.

primary key field is denoted with an asterisk. Tables that will be joined are connected with lines at their common fields. The database represented in Figure 1.2 will be built in the remainder of this chapter and the relationships will be created in Chapter 2.

Notice that many of the field names in the diagram are abbreviated. Although a field name can contain up to 64 characters, using field names that are short enough to be understood is recommended; they are easier to manage and to type into expressions. For abbreviated field names, the Caption property is used to display descriptive headings that contain spaces and/or longer words when viewing the data in a datasheet, form, or report.

Also notice that none of the field names contains spaces. Spaces are allowed in field names but most database designers avoid using them. Instead, designers indicate a space between words by changing the case, using an underscore character (_), or using a hyphen (-).

Assigning Data Types

Designers assign each field a data type based on the types of entries that will be allowed into the field and the operations that will be used to manipulate the data. Selecting the appropriate data type is important because restrictions will be placed on a field based on its data type. For example, in a field designated with the Number data type, only numbers, a period to represent a decimal point, and a plus or minus symbol (+ or −) can be entered into the field in a datasheet or form. Table 1.1 identifies the available data types.

Table 1.1 Data Types

Data Type	Description
Short Text	Alphanumeric data up to 255 characters—for example, a name, an address, or a value such as a telephone number or social security number that is used as an identifier and not for calculating.
Long Text	Alphanumeric data longer than 255 characters; up to 65,535 characters can be stored in a field, although only 64,000 can be displayed. These fields are used to store longer passages of text in a record. Rich text formatting can be added such as bold, italic, or font color.
Number	Positive or negative values that can be used in calculations; not to be used for monetary amounts (see Currency).
Date/Time	Used to ensure dates and times are entered and sorted properly.
Currency	Values that involve money; Access will not round off during calculations.
AutoNumber	Used to automatically number records sequentially (increments of 1); each new record is numbered as it is typed.
Yes/No	Data in the field is restricted to conditional logic of *Yes* or *No*, *True* or *False*, *On* or *Off*.
OLE Object	Used to embed or link objects in other Office applications.
Hyperlink	Used to store a hyperlink, such as a URL.
Attachment	Used to add file attachments to a record such as a Word document or Excel workbook.
Calculated	Used to display the Expression Builder dialog box, where an expression is entered to calculate the value of the calculated column.
Lookup Wizard	Used to enter data in a field from another existing table or to display a list of values in a drop-down list from which the user chooses.

Using the Field Size Property to Restrict Field Length

By default, a Short Text data type field is set to a width of 255 characters in the Field Size property. Access uses only the amount of space needed for the data entered, even when the field size allows for more characters. Even so, it can be helpful to change this property to a smaller value.

One reason to change the Field Size property to a smaller value is that it allows restricting the length of the data that can be entered into the field. For example, assume that RSR Computer Services has developed a four-character numbering system for customer numbers. Setting the field size for the *CustID* field to four characters will ensure that no one enters a longer customer number by accident. Access will disallow any character typed after the fourth character.

Figure 1.3 shows the table structure diagram for the RSR Computer Services database expanded to include the data type and Field Size property for each field. Use this diagram to create the tables in Project 1a.

Figure 1.3 Expanded Table Structure Diagram with Data Types and Field Sizes for Project 1a

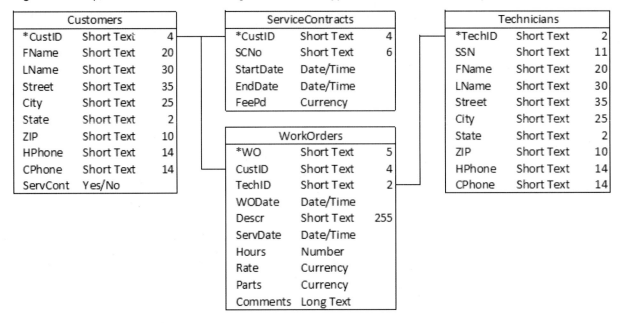

Customers		
*CustID	Short Text	4
FName	Short Text	20
LName	Short Text	30
Street	Short Text	35
City	Short Text	25
State	Short Text	2
ZIP	Short Text	10
HPhone	Short Text	14
CPhone	Short Text	14
ServCont	Yes/No	

ServiceContracts		
*CustID	Short Text	4
SCNo	Short Text	6
StartDate	Date/Time	
EndDate	Date/Time	
FeePd	Currency	

WorkOrders		
*WO	Short Text	5
CustID	Short Text	4
TechID	Short Text	2
WODate	Date/Time	
Descr	Short Text	255
ServDate	Date/Time	
Hours	Number	
Rate	Currency	
Parts	Currency	
Comments	Long Text	

Technicians		
*TechID	Short Text	2
SSN	Short Text	11
FName	Short Text	20
LName	Short Text	30
Street	Short Text	35
City	Short Text	25
State	Short Text	2
ZIP	Short Text	10
HPhone	Short Text	14
CPhone	Short Text	14

Project 1a Creating Tables in Design View

1. Start Access.
2. At the Access 2016 opening screen, complete the following steps to create a new database to store the work orders for RSR Computer Services:
   a. Click the *Blank desktop database* template.
   b. At the Blank desktop database window, click the Browse button and navigate to the AL2C1 folder on your storage medium. Select the current text in the *Filename* text box, type 1-RSRCompServ, and then click OK.

   c. Click the Create button below the *File Name* text box.
3. Close the Table1 blank table datasheet that displays. Design view will be used to access all the field properties available for fields.
4. Click the Create tab and then click the Table Design button in the Tables group. Create the fields shown in the Customers table in Figure 1.3, including the data type and field size settings, by completing the following steps:

   a. Type CustID and then press the Tab key. Short Text is the default data type.
   b. Double-click *255* in the *Field Size* property box in the *Field Properties* section and then type 4.
   c. Click in the blank *Field Name* text box directly under the last field name entered.
   d. Enter the rest of the field names, data types, and field sizes for the Customers table shown in Figure 1.3 by completing steps similar to those in Steps 4a–c. For the *ServCont* data type, type y or click the *Data Type* list box arrow and then select *Yes/No*.

5. Select the *CustID* field and then click the Primary Key button in the Tools group.
6. Click the Save button on the Quick Access Toolbar, type Customers in the *Table Name* text box, and then click OK.

7. Close the table.
8. Create the ServiceContracts, WorkOrders, and Technicians tables shown in Figure 1.3 by completing steps similar to those in Steps 4–7. Assign the primary key field in each table using the fields denoted with asterisks in Figure 1.3.
9. Make sure all the tables are closed.

Check Your Work

Tutorial

Controlling Data Entry

Controlling Data Display and Data Entry Using Field Properties

What properties are available for a field depend on the field's data type. For example, a Yes/No data type field has 7 properties, whereas a Short Text data type field has 14 and a Number data type field has 11.

Use the options available in the *Field Properties* section in Design view to place restrictions on or control data accepted into a field and ensure that data is entered and displayed consistently. Field properties carry over when objects such as queries, forms, and reports are created if the properties are defined before the other objects are created. Taking the time to define the properties when the table is created reduces the number of changes needed if the properties are modified later.

When entering field properties, it is important to select the appropriate field and enter the properties correctly. If properties are applied to the wrong field or entered incorrectly, Access may not be able to save the table or enter the data.

Adding Captions

In Level 1, captions were entered using the Caption property in the Name & Caption dialog box when a new table was created using Datasheet view. The same property appears in Design view in the *Field Properties* section. Recall that the Caption property allows the user to enter a more descriptive title for a field if the field name has been truncated or abbreviated.

The words in field name captions should be separated using spaces, rather than the underscore or hyphen characters used in the field names themselves. In the absence of a caption, Access displays the field name in datasheets, queries, forms, and reports.

Quick Steps

Add a Caption to an Existing Field
1. Open table in Design view.
2. Select field.
3. Click in *Caption* property box.
4. Type descriptive text.
5. Save table.

Require Data in a Field
1. Open table in Design view.
2. Select field.
3. Double-click in *Required* property box.
4. Save table.

Requiring Data in a Field

Hint Set the *Required* field to *Yes* and *Allow Zero Length* to *No* to make sure a field value (and not a space) will be entered when the record is added.

Use the Required property to make sure that a certain field is never left empty when a new record is added. By default, the Required property is set to *No*. Change this value to *Yes* to make sure data is typed into the field when a new record is added. For example, setting the Required property to *Yes* will force all new records to have zip code entries. A field defined as a primary key field already has this property set to *Yes* because a primary key field cannot be left empty.

Using and Disallowing Zero-Length Strings

Quick Steps
Disallow a Zero-Length String in a Field
1. Open table in Design view.
2. Activate a field.
3. Double-click in *Allow Zero Length* property box.
4. Save table.

Hint Press the spacebar to insert a zero-length string.

A zero-length field can be used to indicate that a value will not be entered into the field because the field does not apply to the current record. When a new record is entered and a field is left blank, Access records a null value in the field. For example, assume that a new record for a customer is being entered and the cell phone number is not known; leave the field empty with the intention of updating it later. Access will record a null value in the field. Alternatively, assume that if there is no home phone number; enter a zero-length string in the field to indicate that no field value applies to this record.

To enter a zero-length string, type two double quotation marks with no space between them (""). It is impossible to distinguish between a field with a null value and a field with a zero-length string when viewing the field in a datasheet, query, form, or report; both display as blanks. To help distinguish between the two, create a control in a form or report that returns a user-defined message in a blank field. For example, display the word *Unknown* in a field with a null value and the phrase *Not applicable* in a field with a zero-length string.

By default, Short Text, Long Text, and Hyperlink data type fields allow zero-length strings. Change the Allow Zero Length property to *No* to disallow zero-length strings.

Project 1b **Modifying Field Properties to Add Captions and Disallow Blank Values in a Field**

Part 2 of 6

1. With **1-RSRCompServ.accdb** open, add captions to the fields in the Customers table by completing the following steps:
   a. Right-click *Customers* in the Tables group in the Navigation pane and then click *Design View* at the shortcut menu.
   b. With *CustID* the active field, click in the *Caption* property box in the *Field Properties* section and then type Customer ID.
   c. Click in the *FName* field row to activate the field, click in the *Caption* property box in the *Field Properties* section, and then type First Name.
   d. Add captions to the following fields by completing the step similar to Step 1c:

LName	Last Name
Street	Street Address
HPhone	Home Phone
CPhone	Cell Phone
ServCont	Service Contract?

---

e. Click the Save button on the Quick Access Toolbar.

f. Click the View button (not the button arrow) to switch to Datasheet view and then select all the columns in the datasheet. If necessary, click the Shutter Bar Open/Close button (the two left-pointing chevrons at the top of the Navigation pane) to minimize the Navigation pane.

g. Click the More button in the Records group on the Home tab, click *Field Width* at the drop-down list, and then click the Best Fit button at the Column Width dialog box to adjust the column widths to fit the longest entries.

h. To deselect the columns, click in the *Customer ID* field in the first row of the datasheet.

1h

2. Switch to Design View and then click the Shutter Bar Open/Close button (the two right-pointing chevrons) to redisplay the Navigation pane if the pane was minimized in Step 1f.

3. Ensure that no record is entered without an entry in the *ZIP* field and disallow blank values in the field, including zero-length strings, by completing the following steps:

a. Click in the *ZIP* field row to select the field.

b. Click in the *Required* property box in the *Field Properties* section (which displays *No*), click the down arrow that appears, and then click *Yes* at the drop-down list.

3b

c. Double-click in the *Allow Zero Length* property box (which displays *Yes*) to change the *Yes* to *No*.

d. Save the changes to the table design.

Required	Yes	
Allow Zero Length	No	3c
Indexed	No	
Unicode Compression	Yes	
IME Mode	No Control	

4. Use a new record to test the restrictions on the *ZIP* field by completing the following steps:

a. Switch to Datasheet view.

b. Add the following data in the fields indicated:

Customer ID	1000
First Name	Jade
Last Name	Fleming
Street Address	12109 Woodward Avenue
City	Detroit
State	MI

c. At the *ZIP* field, press the Tab key to move past the field, leaving it blank.

d. Type 313-555-0214 in the *Home Phone* field.

e. Type 313-555-3485 in the *Cell Phone* field.

f. Press the spacebar in the *Service Contract?* field to insert a check mark in the check box.

g. Press the Enter key. Access displays an error message because the record cannot be saved without an entry in the *ZIP* field.

h. Click OK at the Microsoft Access message box.

i. Click in the *ZIP* field, type 48203-3579, and then press the Enter key four times to move to the *Customer ID* field in the second row of the datasheet.

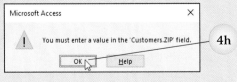

5. Double-click the right boundaries of the *Street Address* and *ZIP* columns to adjust the column widths so that the entire field values can be read.

6. Close the Customers table. Click Yes when prompted to save changes to the layout of the table.

Check Your Work

Tutorial

Creating a Custom Format for a Short Text Field

Quick Steps

Format a Short Text Field

1. Open table in Design view.
2. Activate field.
3. Click in *Format* property box.
4. Type format codes.
5. Save table.

Creating a Custom Format for a Short Text Data Type Field

The Format property controls how data is displayed in the field in the datasheet, query, form, or report. What formats are available depends on the data type of the field. Predefined formats are available for some data types and can be selected from a drop-down list in the *Format* property box. No predefined formats exist for Short Text and Long Text data type fields. If no predefined format exists or the predefined format options are not suitable, then a custom format can be created. Table 1.2 displays commonly used format codes for Short Text and Long Text data type fields.

The Format property does not control how data is entered into the field. Rather, formatting a field controls the display of accepted field values. Refer to the section on input masks (which begins on page 17) to learn how to control new data as it is being entered.

Table 1.2 Format Codes for Short Text and Long Text Data Type Fields

Code	Description	Format Property Example
@	Used as a placeholder, one symbol for each character position. An unused position in a field value is replaced with a blank space to the left of the text entered into the field.	@@@@ Field value entered is *123*. Access displays one blank space followed by *123*, left-aligned in the field.
!	Placeholder positions are filled with characters from left to right instead of the default right to left sequence.	!@@@@ Field value entered is *123*. Access displays *123* left-aligned in the field with one blank space after the *3*.
>	All text is converted to uppercase.	> Field value entered is *mi*. Access displays *MI* in the field.
<	All text is converted to lowercase.	< Field value entered is *Jones@EMCP.NET*. Access displays *jones@emcp.net* in the field.
[color]	Text is displayed in the font color specified. Available colors are black, blue, cyan, green, magenta, red, yellow, and white.	[red]@@@@@-@@@@ Field value entered is *482033579*. Access displays *48203-3579*.

1. With **1-RSRCompServ.accdb** open, format the *State* field in the Customers table to ensure that all the text is displayed in uppercase letters by completing the following steps:
   a. Right-click *Customers* in the Tables group in the Navigation pane and then click *Design View* at the shortcut menu.
   b. Click in the *State* field row to activate the field.
   c. Click in the *Format* property box and then type >.
   d. Save the table.

General	Lookup	
Field Size	2	
Format	>	1c
Input Mask		

2. Format the *ZIP* field to fill it with characters from left to right, display the text in red, and provide for the five-plus-four-character US zip code (with the two sets of characters, each separated by a hyphen) by completing the following steps:
   a. Click in the *ZIP* field row to activate the field.
   b. Click in the *Format* property box and then type ![red]@@@@@-@@@@.
   c. Save the table.

General	Lookup	
Field Size	10	
Format	![red]@@@@@-@@@@	2b
Input Mask		

3. Test the custom formats in the *State* and *ZIP* fields using a new record by completing the following steps:
   a. Switch to Datasheet view.
   b. Add the following data in a new record. Type the text for the *State* field as indicated in lowercase text. Notice that Access automatically converts the lowercase text to uppercase when moving to the next field. As you type the *ZIP* field text, notice that it displays in red. Since no field values are entered for the last four characters of the *ZIP* field, Access displays blank spaces in these positions.

Customer ID	1005
First Name	Cayla
Last Name	Fahri
Street Address	12793 Riverdale Avenue
City	Detroit
State	mi
ZIP	48223
Home Phone	313-555-6845
Cell Phone	313-555-4187
Service Contract?	Press spacebar for *Yes*

4. Look at the data in the *ZIP* field for the first record. This data was entered before the *ZIP* field was formatted. Since a hyphen was typed when the data was entered in Project 1b and the field is now formatted to automatically add the hyphen, two hyphen characters appear in the existing record. Update the record by editing the *ZIP* field value for record 1 to remove the extra hyphen.

5. Display the datasheet in Print Preview. Change to landscape orientation. Set the top margin to 1 inch and the bottom, left, and right margins to 0.25 inch. Print the datasheet and then close Print Preview.
6. Close the Customers table.

Check Your Work

Creating a Custom Format for a Numeric Data Type Field

Access provides predefined formats for Number, AutoNumber, and Currency data type fields that include options for displaying a fixed number of digits past the decimal point, a comma separator, and a currency symbol. Table 1.3 displays format codes that can be used to create custom formats. Use the placeholders shown in Table 1.3 in combination with other characters (such as the dollar symbol, comma, and period) to create the desired custom numeric format.

Quick Steps

**Format a Numeric
Field**

1. Open table in Design
   view.
2. Activate field.
3. Click in *Format*
   property box.
4. Type format codes
   or select from
   predefined list.
5. Save table.

Specify up to four formats for a numeric data type field to include different options for displaying positive values, negative values, zero (0) or null values, and zero-length values. Examine the following custom format code:

> #,###.00;-#,###.00[red];0.00;"Unknown"

Notice that the four sections are separated with semicolons (;). The first section, *#,###.00*, defines the format for positive values. It includes a comma in thousands values and two digits past the decimal point; zeros are used if no decimal value is entered. The second section, *-#,###.00[red]*, defines negative values. It includes the same placeholders as used with positive values but starts the field with a minus symbol and displays the numbers in red. The third section, *0.00*, instructs Access to show *0.00* in the field if a zero is entered or nothing is entered. Finally, a field value that is a zero-length value (the spacebar is pressed) will display the text *Unknown* (italic used here for emphasis only) in the field. Text to be directly entered into the field is enclosed in quotation marks.

Table 1.3 Format Codes for Numeric Data Type Fields

Code	Description	Format Property Example
#	Used as a placeholder to display a number.	*#.##* Field value entered is *123.45*. Access displays *123.45* in the field. Notice that the number of placeholder positions does not restrict the data entered into the field.
0	Used as a placeholder to display a number. Access displays a *0* in place of a position for which no value is entered.	*000.00* Field value entered is *55.4*. Access displays *055.40* in the field.
%	Value is multiplied times 100 and a percent symbol is added.	*#.0%* Field value entered is *.1246*. Access displays *12.5%* in the field. Field value entered is *.1242*. Access displays *12.4%* in the field. Having only one digit past the decimal point causes rounding up or down to occur.

Project 1d Create a Custom Format and Use a Predefined Format for Numeric Data Type Fields

1. With **1-RSRCompServ.accdb** open, format the *Rate* field in the WorkOrders table with a custom format by completing the following steps:
   a. Open the WorkOrders table in Design view.
   b. Make the *Rate* field active.
   c. Click in the *Format* property box, delete the current entry, and then type #.00[blue];;;"Not Available". Notice that three semicolons are typed after the first custom format option, *#.00[blue]*. When a custom format for negative or zero values is not needed, include the semicolon to indicate that there is no format setting. Since an hourly rate is never a negative or zero value, do not use custom formats in these situations.
   d. Save the table.

2. Format the *Hours* field using a predefined format and change the field size by completing the following steps:
   a. Make the *Hours* field active.
   b. Click in the *Field Size* property box, click the down arrow that appears, and then click *Double* at the drop-down list. The default setting for a Number data type field is *Long Integer*, which stores only whole numbers. (This means that a decimal value entered into the field is rounded.) Changing the *Field Size* property box to *Double* allows decimal values to be stored.
   c. Click in the *Format* property box, click the down arrow that appears, and then click *Standard* at the drop-down list.
   d. Click in the *Decimal Places* property box, click the down arrow that appears, and then click *2* at the pop-up list.
   e. Save the table.

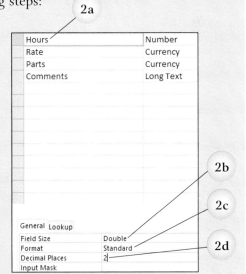

3. Switch to Datasheet view.
4. Add the following data in a new record to test the custom format and the predefined format. Notice that when you move past the *Rate* field, the value is displayed in blue. Compare your data entry to the screen image on the next page and notice the new format for the *Hours* and *Rate* fields.

WO	65012
CustID	1000
TechID	11
WODate	09-07-2018
Descr	Biannual desktop computer cleaning and maintenance
ServDate	09-07-2018
Hours	1.25
Rate	30
Parts	15.15
Comments	"H" key is sticking; cleaning did not resolve. Customer is considering buying a new keyboard.

ServDate	Hours	Rate	Parts	Comments
9/7/2018	1.25	30.00	$15.15	"H" key is stick
	0.00	.00	$0.00	

The *Hours* field is formatted to *Standard* with two digits after the decimal point.

The custom format in the *Rate* field displays *.00* in all blank fields.

The custom format in the *Rate* field displays positive values in blue with two digits after the decimal point.

5. Close the WorkOrders table.

Check Your Work

Tutorial

Creating a Custom Format for a Date/Time Field

Creating a Custom Format for a Date/Time Field

Access provides predefined formats for fields with a Date/Time data type. These formats provide a variety of combinations of month, day, and year options for dates and hour and minute display options for time. If the predefined display formats are not suitable, custom formats can be created using a combination of the codes described in Table 1.4, along with symbols (such as hyphens and slashes) between parts of the date. If a format option for a Date/Time data type field is not chosen, Access displays the date in the format *m/d/yyyy*. For example, in Project 1d, the date entered into the *WODate* field displays as *9/7/2018*.

A custom format for a Date/Time data type field can contain two sections separated by a semicolon. The first section specifies the format for displaying dates. To add a format for displaying times, type a semicolon and then add the format codes.

Quick Steps

Format a Date/Time Field

1. Open table in Design view.
2. Activate field.
3. Click in *Format* property box.
4. Type format codes or select from predefined list.
5. Save table.

Table 1.4 Format Codes for Date/Time Data Type Fields

Code	Description
d or dd	displays the day of the month as one digit (*d*) or two digits (*dd*)
ddd or dddd	displays the day of the week abbreviated (*ddd*) or in full (*dddd*)
m or mm	displays the month as one digit (*m*) or two digits (*mm*)
mmm or mmmm	displays the month abbreviated (*mmm*) or in full (*mmmm*)
yy or yyyy	displays the year as the last two digits (*yy*) or all four digits (*yyyy*)
h or hh	displays the hour as one digit (*h*) or two digits (*hh*)
n or nn	displays the minutes as one digit (*n*) or two digits (*nn*)
s or ss	displays the seconds as one digit (*s*) or two digits (*ss*)
AM/PM	displays 12-hour clock values followed by *AM* or *PM*

1. With **1-RSRCompServ.accdb** open, format the *WODate* field in the WorkOrders table with a custom format by completing the following steps:
   a. Open the WorkOrders table in Design view.
   b. Make *WODate* the active field.
   c. Click in the *Format* property box, type ddd, mmm dd yyyy, and then press the Enter key. This format will display dates beginning with the day of the week in abbreviated form, followed by a comma, the month in abbreviated form, the day of the month as two digits, and the year as four digits. Spaces separate the sections of the date. Notice that Access puts quotation marks around the comma.
   d. Save the table.

WODate	Date/Time
Descr	Short Text
ServDate	Date/Time
Hours	Number
Rate	Currency
Parts	Currency
Comments	Long Text

1b

1c

General Lookup
Format   ddd', 'mmm dd yyyy
Input Mask

2. Switch to Datasheet view.
3. If necessary, adjust the column width of the *WODate* field to allow reading the entire entry.
4. Switch to Design view.
5. Format the *ServDate* field using the same custom format used for *WODate* by completing steps similar to those in Steps 1b–1c.
6. Save the table and then switch to Datasheet view.
7. Double-click the right column boundary to adjust the column width of the *ServDate* field and view the custom date format.

WorkOrders

WO	CustID	TechID	WODate	Descr
65012	1000	11	Fri, Sep 07 2018	Biannual deskt

3

Custom format for *WODate* field created in Step 1c.

WorkOrders

WO	CustID	TechID	WODate	Descr	ServDate	Hours
65012	1000	11	Fri, Sep 07 2018	Biannual deskt	Fri, Sep 07 2018	1.25

7

8. Close the WorkOrders table. Click Yes when prompted to save changes to the table layout.

Check Your Work

Tutorial

Controlling Data Entry Using an Input Mask

Quick Steps

Create a Custom Input Mask
1. Open table in Design view.
2. Activate field.
3. Click in *Input Mask* property box.
4. Type input mask codes.
5. Save table.

Controlling Data Entry Using an Input Mask

Whereas a format controls how the data is displayed, an input mask controls the type of data and pattern in which the data is entered into a field. In Project 1e, a date format was created to display the date as *Fri, Sep 7 2018*. When confirming dates with clients, it is good practice to provide the day of the week, as well as the day of the month. To type the date consistently and efficiently into the *ServDate* or *WODate* field, an input mask will be created in Project 1f to enter the date by typing *sep072018*. Access knows that this date is a Friday and displays *Fri, Sep 7 2018*.

Recall from Level 1, Chapter 4, that Access provides the Input Mask Wizard, which can be used to create an input mask for a text or date field. Commonly used input masks are predefined within the wizard for telephone numbers, social security numbers, zip codes, dates, and times. To create an input mask without the wizard, use the codes described in Table 1.5.

Table 1.5 Commonly Used Input Mask Codes

Code	Description
0	Required digit.
9	Optional digit.
#	Digit, space, plus or minus symbol. If no data is typed at this position, Access leaves a blank space.
L	Required letter.
?	Optional letter.
A	Required letter or digit.
a	Optional letter or digit.
&	Required character or space.
C	Optional character or space.
!	Field is filled from left to right instead of right to left.
\	Character is displayed that immediately follows in the field.

> **Hint** If you create a custom input mask for a date field that also contains a custom format, make sure the two properties do not conflict. For example, a format code that displays dates with the year first followed by the month and then the day will be confusing if the input mask requires the date to be entered as the month first followed by the day and then the year.

An input mask can contain up to three sections, with each section separated by a semicolon. The first section contains the input mask codes for the data entry in the field. The second section instructs Access to store or not store the display characters used in the field, such as hyphens, slashes, or brackets). A zero indicates that Access should store the characters. Leaving the second section blank means the display characters will not be stored. The third section specifies the placeholder character to display in the field when it becomes active for data entry.

The following is an example of an input mask to store a four-digit customer identification number with a pound symbol (#) as the placeholder: *0000;;#*. The first section, *0000*, contains the four required digits for the customer identification number. Since the mask contains no display characters (hyphens, slashes, etc.), the second section is blank. The pound symbol after the second semicolon is the placeholder character.

In addition to the symbols in Table 1.5, use the format code > to force characters to be uppercase or the format code < to force characters to be lowercase. Decimal points, hyphens, slashes, and other punctuation symbols can also be used.

Project 1f Controlling Data Entry Using Custom Input Masks   Part 6 of 6

1. With **1-RSRCompServ.accdb** open, create a custom input mask for the work order numbers in the WorkOrders table by completing the following steps:
   a. Open the WorkOrders table in Design view.
   b. With *WO* the active field, click in the *Input Mask* property box and then type 00000;;_. This mask requires a five-digit work order number to be entered. The underscore is used as the placeholder character that displays when the field becomes active.
   c. Save the table.

General	Lookup	
Field Size		5
Format		
Input Mask		00000;;_
Caption		

1b

2. Create an input mask to require the two date fields to be entered as three characters for the month, followed by two digits for the day and four digits for the year by completing the following steps:

   a. Make *WODate* the active field.

   b. Click in the *Input Mask* property box and then type >L<LL\ 00\ 0000;0;_. This mask requires three letters for the month; the first letter is converted to uppercase and the remaining two letters are converted to lowercase. The backslash symbol (\ ) followed by the space instructs Access to display a space after the month as data is entered. Two digits are required for the day, followed by another space and then four digits for the year. The *0* after the first semicolon instructs Access to store the display characters. At the end of the mask, the underscore character is used again as the placeholder character.

2b

   c. Make *ServDate* the active field, click in the *Input Mask* property box, and then type >L<LL\ 00\ 0000;0;_.

   d. Save the table.

3. Switch to Datasheet view.

4. Test the input masks using a new record by completing the following steps:

   a. Click the New button in the Records group on the Home tab.

   b. Type 6501. Notice that as soon as the first character is typed, the placeholders appear in the field.

   c. Press the Tab key to move to the next field in the datasheet. Since the mask contains five zeros (indicating five required digits), Access displays a message box stating that the value entered is not appropriate for the input mask.

   d. Click OK at the Microsoft Access message box.

4d

e. Type 3 in the last position in the *WO* field and then press the Tab key to move to the next field.

f. Type 1000 in the *CustID* field and then press the Tab key.

g. Type 10 in the *TechID* field and then press the Tab key.

h. Type sep072018 in the *WODate* field and then press the Tab key. Notice that the placeholder characters and spaces appear as soon as the first letter is typed. Notice also that the first character is converted to uppercase and that the spaces do not need to be typed; Access moves automatically to the next position after the month and day are typed.

i. Type Replace keyboard in the *Descr* field and then press the Tab key.

j. Type sep102018 in the *ServDate* field and then press the Tab key.

k. Complete the remainder of the record as follows:

Hours	.5
Rate	28.50
Parts	47.25
Comments	Serial Number AWQ-982358

l. Double-click the right column boundary to adjust the column width of the *ServDate* field.

4e-4l

Notice that once the date is accepted into the field, the custom Format property controls how the date is presented in the datasheet; the abbreviated day of the week is at the beginning of the field and spaces are between the month, day, and year instead of hyphens.

5. Display the datasheet in Print Preview. Change the orientation to landscape. Set the top and bottom margins to 1 inch and the left and right margins to 0.25 inch. Print the datasheet and then close Print Preview.

6. Close the WorkOrders table. Click Yes when prompted to save changes to the table layout.

Check Your Work

Tutorial

Review: Modifying Field Properties in Design View

Other field properties that promote accuracy when entering data and that should be considered when designing database tables include the Default Value, Validation Rule, and Validation Text properties. Use the Default Value property to populate the field in a new record with the field value that is used most often. For example, when most employees live in the same city and state, use default values for these fields to ensure consistent spelling and capitalization within the table. The text appears automatically in the fields when new records are added to the table. The user can accept the default value by pressing the Tab key or the Enter key to move past the field or type new data in the field. In Level 1, default values were created using the Default Value button in the Properties group on the Table Tools Fields tab. In Design view, the Default Value property is located below the Caption property.

Tutorial

Review: Applying a Validation Rule in Design View

Use the Validation Rule and Validation Text properties to enter conditional statements that are checked against new data entered into the field. Invalid entries that do not meet the conditional statement test are rejected. For example, a validation rule on a field used to store labor rates can check that a minimum labor rate value is entered in each record. In Level 1, a validation rule was added in Design view. The Validation Rule and Validation Text properties are located just above the Required property.

You will edit properties for a Long Text data type field, apply rich text formatting to text, and attach files to records using an Attachment data type field.

Preview Finished Project

Tutorial

Working with a
Long Text Field

Q̃uick Steps

Enable Rich Text Formatting in a Long Text Field
1. Open table in Design view.
2. Select field defined as Long Text.
3. Double-click in *Text Format* property box.
4. Click Yes.
5. Save table.

Track Changes in a Long Text Data Type Field
1. Open table in Design view.
2. Select field defined as Long Text.
3. Double-click in *Append Only* property box.
4. Click Yes.
5. Save table.

Working with a Long Text Data Type Field

By default, Access formats a Long Text data type field as plain text. However, formatting attributes can be applied to text by enabling rich text formatting. Enabling rich text formatting in a Long Text data type field allows the user to change the font, apply bold or italic formatting, or add font color to text, among other formatting options. To enable rich text formatting, change the Text Format property to *Rich Text*.

The Append Only property for a Long Text data type field is set to *No* by default. Change the property to *Yes* to track changes made to the field value in the datasheet. Scroll down the General tab in the *Field Properties* section to locate the Append Only property. When this property is set to *Yes*, Access maintains a history of additions to the field, which can be viewed in the datasheet. Changing the Append Only property to *No* causes Access to delete any existing history.

In Project 2a, the text format of the *Comments* field is changed from *Plain Text* to *Rich Text* and then bold red formatting is applied to the serial number of the new keyboard. These formatting changes make it easier to find important information in the *Comments* field—in this case, the serial number. Changing the Append Only property from *No* to *Yes* allows the user to keep track of the dates for any comments entered into the field.

Project 2a **Working with Rich Text Formatting and Maintaining a History of Changes in a Long Text Data Type Field**   **Part 1 of 2**

1. With **1-RSRCompServ.accdb** open, enable rich text formatting and turn on tracking of history in a field defined as a Long Text data type field by completing the following steps:
   a. Open the WorkOrders table in Design view.
   b. Make *Comments* the active field.
   c. Double click in the *Text Format* property box (displays *Plain Text*). It should now read *Rich Text*.
   d. At the Microsoft Access message box indicating that the field will be converted to rich text, click Yes.

IME Sentence Mode	None
Text Format	Rich Text
Text Align	General
Append Only	No

1c

Microsoft Access   ✕

⚠ **This field will be converted to Rich Text, and all the data it contains will be HTML encoded.**

If your data already contains valid HTML Rich Text, you can remove any extra HTML encoding by using the PlainText function in an update query.

Do you want to convert the column to Rich Text?

[Yes]   [No]

1d

e. If necessary, scroll down the General tab in the *Field Properties* section to locate the *Append Only* property box.

f. Double-click in the *Append Only* property box to change *No* to *Yes*.

g. Save the table.

2. Switch to Datasheet view.

3. Minimize the Navigation pane and then adjust all the column widths except the *Descr* and *Comments* columns to best fit.

4. Change the column width of the *Comments* field to 25 characters.

5. Select the serial number text *AWQ-982358* in the second record in the *Comments* field and then apply bold formatting and the standard red font color using the buttons in the Text Formatting group on the Home tab. Click at the end of the serial number to deselect the text.

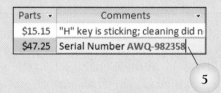

6. Click in the *Comments* field in the first record. Press the End key to move the insertion point to the end of the existing text. Press the spacebar, update the record by typing Microsoft wireless keyboard was recommended., and then press the Enter key to save the changes and move to the next row.

7. Right-click in the *Comments* field of the first record and then click *Show column history* at the shortcut menu.

8. Click OK after reading the text in the History for Comments dialog box.

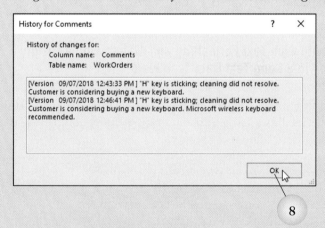

9. Click in the *Comments* field of the first record. Press the End key to move the insertion point to the end of the current text. Press the spacebar, type See work order 65013 for replacement keyboard request., and then press the Enter key.

10. Right-click in the *Comments* field of the first record and then click *Show column history* at the shortcut menu.

11. Click OK after reading the text in the History for Comments dialog box.
12. Display the datasheet in Print Preview. Change to landscape orientation. Set the top and bottom margins to 1 inch and the left and right margins to 0.25 inch. Print the datasheet and then close Print Preview.
13. Close the WorkOrders table. Click Yes if prompted to save changes to the table layout and then redisplay the Navigation pane.

Check Your Work

Tutorial

Creating an Attachment Field

Creating an Attachment Data Type Field and Attaching Files to Records

Use an Attachment data type field to store several files in a single field attached to a record. The attachments can be opened within Access and viewed in the program from which the document originated. For example, attach a Word document to a field in a record. Opening the attached file in the Access table causes Microsoft Word to start and the document to display. A file that is attached to a record cannot be larger than 256 megabytes (MB).

An Attachment data type field displays with a paper clip in Datasheet view. To manage the attached files, double-click the paper clip to open the Attachments dialog box, shown in Figure 1.4. A field that is created with an Attachment data type cannot be changed. Multiple files can be attached to a record, as long as the combined size of all the files does not exceed 2 gigabytes (GB).

Any file created within the Microsoft Office suite can be attached to a record or an image file (.bmp, .jpg, .gif, .png), a log file (.log), a text file (.txt), or a compressed file (.zip). Some files, such as any file ending with *.com* or *.exe*, are considered potential security risks and therefore blocked by Access.

Quick Steps

Create an Attachment Field
1. Open table in Design view.
2. Click in first blank field row.
3. Type field name.
4. Click in *Data Type* column.
5. Click down arrow.
6. Click *Attachment*.
7. Save table.

Attach Files to a Record
1. Open table in Datasheet view.
2. Double-click paper clip in record.
3. Click Add button.
4. Navigate to drive and/or folder location.
5. Double-click file name.
6. Click OK.

View an Attached File
1. Open table in Datasheet view.
2. Double-click paper clip in record.
3. Double-click file name.
4. View file contents.
5. Exit source program.
6. Click OK.

Figure 1.4 Attachments Dialog Box

Project 2b Creating an Attachment Data Type Field, Attaching Files to a Record, and Viewing the Contents of Attached Files

Part 2 of 2

1. With **1-RSRCompServ.accdb** open, create a new field in the Technicians table to store file attachments by completing the following steps:

   a. Open the Technicians table in Design view.

   b. Click in the blank row below *CPhone*, type Attachments, and then press the Tab key.

   c. Click the down arrow in the *Data Type* column and then click *Attachment* at the drop-down list.

   d. Save the table.

2. Switch to Datasheet view.

3. Add the following data in the first row of the datasheet:

TechID	10
SSN	000-43-5789
FName	Kelsey
LName	Eastman
Street	550 Montclair Street
City	Detroit
State	MI
ZIP	48214-3274
HPhone	"" (Recall that double quotation marks indicate a zero-length field.)
CPhone	313-555-6315

4. Attach two files to the record for Kelsey Eastman by completing the following steps:

   a. Double-click the paper clip in the first row of the datasheet. An Attachment data type field displays a paper clip in each record in a column and has a paper clip in the field name row. The number in brackets next to the paper clip indicates the number of files attached to the record.

   b. At the Attachments dialog box, click the Add button.

   c. At the Choose File dialog box, navigate to the AL2C1 folder on your storage medium.

   d. Click the file named *EastmanResume.docx*.

   e. Press and hold down the Ctrl key, click the file named *KelseyEastman.jpg*, and then release the Ctrl key.

   f. Click the Open button.

   g. Click OK. Access closes the Attachments dialog box and displays *(2)* next to the paper clip in the first record.

5. Open the attached files by completing the following steps:

   a. Double-click the paper clip in the first row of the datasheet to open the Attachments dialog box.

b. Double-click ***EastmanResume.docx*** in the *Attachments* list box to open the Word document.

c. Read the resume in Microsoft Word and then exit Word.

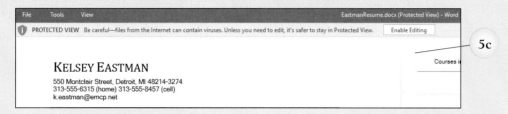

d. Double-click ***KelseyEastman.jpg*** in the *Attachments* list box to open the picture file.

e. View the picture and then exit the photo viewer program.

f. Click OK to close the Attachments dialog box.

6. Adjust all the column widths to best fit.

7. Display the datasheet in Print Preview. Change the orientation to landscape, print the datasheet, and then close Print Preview.

8. Close the Technicians table. Click Yes when prompted to save changes to the table layout.

9. Close **1-RSRCompServ.accdb**.

Check Your Work

Saving an Attached File to Another Location

To save a copy of an attachment outside Access, select the file and then click the Save As button in the Attachments dialog box. At the Save Attachment dialog box, navigate to the drive and/or folder in which the duplicate copy is to be saved, click the Save button, and then click OK to close the Attachments dialog box.

Editing an Attached File

Access 2016 provides two options for editing an attachment. The first option is to save the attached file to another location, as noted above. After the necessary changes are made, save the file, remove the original attachment from the database, and then attach the edited file. The second option is to open the attachment directly in Access. After making the necessary changes in the source program (for example, Word), respond to the message asking you to save the file to your OneDrive or computer. Go back into Access, remove the attachment from the database, and then reattach the file to the field.

Removing an Attached File

To remove a file attached to a record in a database, open the Attachments dialog box in the record containing the file attachment, click the file name for the file to be removed, click the Remove button, and then click OK to close the Attachments dialog box.

Chapter Summary

- Database designers plan the tables for a new database by analyzing sample data, input documents, and output requirements to generate the entire set of data elements needed.

- Once all the data has been identified, the designer maps out the number of tables required.

- Each table holds data only for a single entity (topic). Data is split into the smallest unit that will be manipulated.

- Designers also consider the relationships that will be created. Doing so in the planning stage helps determine if a field needs to be added to a table to join tables.

- Data redundancy should be avoided. This means that fields should not be repeated in another table, except those fields needed to join tables in a relationship.

- A diagram of a database portrays the database tables, providing field names, data types, field sizes, and notation of the primary key fields.

- A field is assigned a data type by selecting a type appropriate for the kind of data that will be accepted into the field.

- Changing the Field Size property is one way to restrict entries in the field to a maximum length. This prevents having longer entries added to the field by accident.

- Add field properties before creating queries, forms, and reports as the properties carry over to these objects.

- Change the Required property to *Yes* to make sure data is typed into the field when a new record is added to the table.

- A zero-length field is entered into a record by typing two double quotation marks with no space between them. This method is used to indicate that a field value does not apply to the current record.

- Disallow zero-length strings by changing the Allow Zero Length property to *No*.

- The Format property controls the display of data in a field. Custom formats can be created by typing the appropriate format codes in the *Format* property box.

- A custom numeric format can contain four sections: one for positive values, one for negative values, one for zero or empty values, and one for zero-length values.

- Use an input mask to control the type and pattern of data entered into the field.

- Create a custom input mask for a Short Text or Date/Time data type field by typing the appropriate input mask codes in the *Input Mask* property box.

- A Long Text data type field can be formatted using rich text formatting options in the Text Formatting group on the Home tab. To enable rich text formatting, change the Text Format property to *Rich Text*.

- Change the Append Only property of a Long Text data type field to *Yes* to track changes made to field values.

- An Attachment data type field can be used to store files in a single field attached to a record.

- Double-click the paper clip in the Attachment data type field for a record to add, view, save, or remove a file attachment.

Commands Review

FEATURE	RIBBON TAB, GROUP	BUTTON	KEYBOARD SHORTCUT
create table in Design view	Create, Tables		
minimize Navigation pane		≪	F11
redisplay Navigation pane		≫	F11
switch to Datasheet view from Design view	Table Tools Design, Views		
switch to Design view from Datasheet view	Home, Views		

Microsoft®
Access®

Building Relationships and Lookup Fields

Performance Objectives

Upon successful completion of Chapter 2, you will be able to:

1　Create and edit relationships between tables, including one-to-many, one-to-one, and many-to-many relationships

2　Define a table with a multiple-field primary key field

3　Create and modify a lookup field to populate records with data from another table

4　Create a lookup field that allows having multiple values in records

5　Create single-field and multiple-field indexes

6　Define the term *normalization*

7　Determine if a table is in first, second, or third normal form

Precheck

Check your current skills to help focus your study.

Once the table design has been completed, the next step is to establish relationships and relationship options between tables. This involves analyzing the type of relationship that exists between two tables. Some database designers draw a relationship diagram to depict the primary table and the matching record frequency of the related table. In this chapter, you will create and edit relationships and lookup fields, multiple-field primary key fields, multiple-value fields, and indexes. The concept of database normalization and three forms of normalization will be introduced to complete the examination of database design fundamentals.

Data Files

Before beginning chapter work, copy the AL2C2 folder to your storage medium and then make AL2C2 the active folder.

SNAP

If you are a SNAP user, launch the Precheck and Tutorials from your Assignments page.

Project 1 Create and Edit Relationships

4 Parts

You will create relationships and edit relationship options for the tables designed to track work orders for RSR Computer Services.

Preview Finished Project

Building Relationships

Hint Are you unsure whether two tables should be related? Consider whether data will need to be extracted from both tables in the same query, form, or report. If yes, then the tables should be joined in a relationship.

After determining which tables to relate to one another, the next step in designing a database is to examine the types of relationships that exist between the tables. A relationship is based on an association between two tables. For example, in the database created in Chapter 1 for RSR Computer Services, there is an association between the Customers table and the WorkOrders table. A customer is associated with all of his or her work orders involving computer maintenance requests, and each work order is associated with the individual customer who requested the service.

When building relationships, consider the associations between tables and how these associations affect the data that will be entered into the tables. In the database diagram presented in Chapter 1, relationships were shown with lines connecting the common field name between tables. In this chapter, consider the type of relationship that should exist between the tables and the relationship options to use to place restrictions on data entry. Access provides for three types of relationships: one-to-many, one-to-one, and many-to-many. Access Level 1, Chapter 2 addressed one-to-many and one-to-one relationships. This chapter begins by reviewing these two relationship types and then discusses how to establish a many-to-many relationship.

Tutorial

Review: Creating a One-to-Many Relationship

Establishing a One-to-Many Relationship

In the computer service database in Chapter 1, the relationship between the Customers table and WorkOrders table exists because a work order involves computer maintenance for a specific customer. The customer is identified by the customer number stored in the Customers table. In the Customers table, only one record exists per customer. In the WorkOrders table, the same customer number can be associated with several work orders. This means that the relationship between the Customers table and WorkOrders table is a one-to-many relationship. This is the most common type of relationship created in Access.

 Relationships

A common field is needed to join the Customers table and WorkOrders table, so the *CustID* field is included in both tables. In the Customers table, *CustID* is the primary key field because it contains a unique identification number for each customer. In the WorkOrders table, *CustID* cannot be the primary key field because the same customer can be associated with several work orders. In the WorkOrders table, *CustID* is a type of field referred to as a *foreign key* field. A foreign key field is included in a table for the purpose of creating a relationship to a field that is a primary key field in another table. The Customers-to-WorkOrders one-to-many relationship is illustrated in Figure 2.1.

Figure 2.1 One-to-Many Relationship between the Customers Table and WorkOrders Table

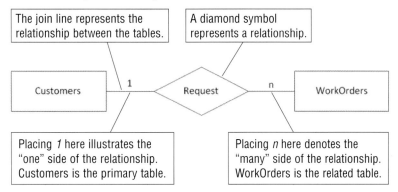

Quick Steps

Create a One-to-Many Relationship
1. Click Database Tools tab.
2. Click Relationships button.
3. Add tables from Show Table dialog box.
4. Close Show Table dialog box.
5. Drag primary key field name from primary table to foreign key field name in related table.
6. Click Create button.

When diagramming a database, designers may choose to show relationships in a separate illustration. In the diagram shown in Figure 2.1, table names are displayed in rectangles and connected with lines to a diamond symbol, which represents a relationship. Inside the diamond, a word (usually a verb) describes the action that relates the two tables. For example, in the relationship shown in Figure 2.1, the word *Request* is used to show that "Customers *request* WorkOrders." On the line connecting the rectangle to the diamond symbol (called the *join line*), a *1* is placed next to the primary table, or the "one" side of the relationship, and an *n* is placed next to the related table, or the "many" side of the relationship.

Project 1a Creating a One-to-Many Relationship

Part 1 of 4

1. Open **2-RSRCompServ.accdb**. This database has the same structure as the database created in Chapter 1. However, additional field properties have been defined and several records have been added to each table to provide data for testing relationships and lookup fields.

2. If a security warning appears in the message bar to indicate that some active content has been disabled, click the Enable Content button.

3. Create a one-to-many relationship between the Customers table and WorkOrders table by completing the following steps:

   a. Click the Database Tools tab.

   b. Click the Relationships button in the Relationships group.

   c. At the Show Table dialog box with the Tables tab active and *Customers* selected in the list box, press and hold down the Ctrl key, click *WorkOrders*, click the Add button, and then release the Ctrl key.

   d. Click the Close button to close the Show Table dialog box.

   e. Resize both table field list boxes by dragging down the bottom borders of the boxes until all the field names are visible.

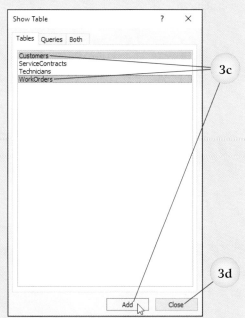

f. Drag the *CustID* field from the Customers table field list box to the *CustID* field in the WorkOrders table field list box. Be careful to drag the common field name from the primary table (Customers) to the related table (WorkOrders) and not vice versa.

g. At the Edit Relationships dialog box, notice that *One-To-Many* appears in the *Relationship Type* section. Access detected this type of relationship because the field used to join the tables is a primary key field in only one of the tables. Establishing this relationship makes *CustID* a foreign key field in the WorkOrders table. Always check that the correct table and field names are shown in the *Table/Query* and *Related Table/Query* option boxes. If the table name and/or the common field name is not shown correctly, click the Cancel button. Errors can occur if the mouse is dragged starting or ending at the wrong table or field. If this happens, click the Cancel button, return to Step 3f and then try again.

h. Click the Create button.

4. Click the Close button in the Relationships group on the Relationship Tools Design tab.

5. Click Yes at the message box asking if you want to save changes to the layout of the Relationships window.

Check Your Work

Another one-to-many relationship exists between the Technicians table and WorkOrders table. A technician is associated with each work order assigned to that technician and a work order is associated with the technician that carried out the service request. The Technicians-to-WorkOrders relationship diagram is shown in Figure 2.2.

Figure 2.2 One-to-Many Relationship between the Technicians Table and WorkOrders Table

1. With **2-RSRCompServ.accdb** open, display the Relationships window by clicking the Database Tools tab and then clicking the Relationships button in the Relationships group.
2. Click the Show Table button in the Relationships group on the Relationship Tools Design tab.
3. Double-click *Technicians* in the list box at the Show Table dialog box with the Tables tab selected. Move the Show Table dialog box, if necessary, to verify that the Technicians table has been added and then click the Close button.
4. Drag the bottom and right borders of the Technicians table field list box until all the field names are fully visible.
5. Drag the *TechID* field from the Technicians table field list box to the *TechID* field in the WorkOrders table field list box.
6. Check that the correct table and field names appear in the *Table/Query* and *Related Table/Query* option boxes. If necessary, click the Cancel button and repeat Step 5.
7. Click the Create button at the Edit Relationships dialog box.
8. Click the Close button in the Relationships group on the Relationship Tools Design tab.
9. Click Yes at the message box asking if you want to save changes to the layout of the Relationships window.

This join line represents the one-to-many relationship created between the Technicians table and the WorkOrders table in Steps 1–7.

Check Your Work

Editing a Relationship

Quick Steps

Edit a Relationship
1. Click Database Tools tab.
2. Click Relationships button.
3. Click join line between tables.
4. Click Edit Relationships button.
5. Select options.
6. Click OK.

Edit Relationships

At the Edit Relationships dialog box, shown in Figure 2.3, select relationship options and/or specify the type of join to create. To open the Edit Relationships dialog box, click the Database Tools tab, click the Relationships button, click the join line for the relationship to be edited, and then click the Edit Relationships button.

Once the Edit Relationships dialog box is open, select any of the options. The *Cascade Update Related Fields* and *Cascade Delete Related Records* options do not become active unless referential integrity is turned on. To turn on referential integrity, click the *Enforce Referential Integrity* check box to insert a check mark.

Figure 2.3 Edit Relationships Dialog Box

Selecting *Enforce Referential Integrity* places restrictions on data entry. In this example, it means that a technician cannot be assigned to a work order if the technician does not exist in the Technicians table.

Edit Relationships

Table/Query: Technicians
Related Table/Query: WorkOrders

TechID — TechID

☐ Enforce Referential Integrity
☐ Cascade Update Related Fields
☐ Cascade Delete Related Records

Relationship Type: One-To-Many

OK
Cancel
Join Type..
Create New..

Hint To enable referential integrity, the primary key and foreign key fields must be the same data type.

If an error message displays when you are attempting to enforce referential integrity, open each table in Design view and compare the data types for the fields used to join the tables.

Activating referential integrity in a one-to-many relationship is a good way of ensuring that orphan records do not occur. An orphan record is a record in a related table for which no "parent" record exists in the primary table. Assigning a technician to a work order in the WorkOrders table when there is no matching technician record in the Technicians table results in creating an orphan record in the WorkOrders table. Once referential integrity has been turned on, Access checks for the existence of a matching record in the primary table as each new record is added to the related table. If no match is found, Access does not allow the record to be saved.

For example, suppose that referential integrity has not been activated and a typing mistake is made that causes the accidental entry of an unassigned *TechID* to a work order. If the customer later has a question for the technician about the service, no one will know which technician to contact. However, if referential integrity is activated before the record is saved, Access will check the Technicians table and verify that the *TechID* exists. If the *TechID* does not exist, the error message shown in Figure 2.4 will display. Click OK at the message and then enter a *TechID* that exists in the Technicians table.

When the *Enforce Referential Integrity* check box is clicked to insert a check mark, the *Cascade Update Related Fields* and *Cascade Delete Related Records* check boxes become available. When a check mark is inserted in the *Cascade Update Related Fields* check box, Access automatically updates all the occurrences of the same data in the foreign key field in the related table when a change is made to the primary key field in the primary table. When a check mark is inserted in the *Cascade Delete Related Records* check box, deleting a record from the primary table for which related records exist in the related table results in all the related records being automatically deleted.

Join types and situations in which changing the join type is warranted will be discussed in Chapter 3.

Figure 2.4 Referential Integrity Error Message

Microsoft Access

⚠ ! You cannot add or change a record because a related record is required in table 'Technicians'.

OK   Help

1. With **2-RSRCompServ.accdb** open, edit the one-to-many relationship between the Customers table and WorkOrders table by completing the following steps:
   a. Open the Relationships window.
   b. Click to select the join line between the Customers table and WorkOrders table.
   c. Click the Edit Relationships button in the Tools group on the Relationship Tools Design tab.

   d. At the Edit Relationships dialog box, click to insert check marks in the *Enforce Referential Integrity* check box, the *Cascade Update Related Fields* check box, and the *Cascade Delete Related Records* check box.
   e. Click OK at the Edit Relationships dialog box. The *1* at the primary table (the "one") side of the join line and the infinity symbol (∞) at the related table (the "many" side) of the join line indicate that referential integrity has been activated.

2. Edit the one-to-many relationship between the Technicians table and WorkOrders table by completing the following steps:
   a. Double-click the join line between the Technicians table and WorkOrders table in the Relationships window. (Or right-click the join line and then click *Edit Relationship* at the shortcut menu.)
   b. At the Edit Relationships dialog box, click to insert check marks in the *Enforce Referential Integrity* check box, the *Cascade Update Related Fields* check box, and the *Cascade Delete Related Records* check box.
   c. Click OK.
3. Notice with referential integrity turned on, the 1 and the infinity symbol (∞) display on the join lines.
4. Close the Relationships window.

With referential integrity turned on, the 1 and the infinity symbol (∞) display on the join lines.

Check Your Work

Creating a One-to-One Relationship

In the database for RSR Computer Services, a table is used to store service contract information for each customer. That table, ServiceContracts, is associated with the Customers table. Only one record exists for a customer in the Customers table and each customer subscribes to only one service contract in the ServiceContracts table. This means that the two tables have a one-to-one relationship, as shown in Figure 2.5.

When a new customer is added to the database, the customer's name and contact information are entered into the Customers table first and then the service contract information (including start date, end date, and fee paid) is entered into the ServiceContracts table. When creating the relationship, drag the primary key field name from the table in which the data is entered into the database first (Customers table) to the primary key field name from the table in which the data is entered second (ServiceContracts table). When the relationship is established, the Customers table is placed in the *Table/Query* option box and the ServiceContracts table is placed in the *Related Table/Query* option box; otherwise, when data is being entered, an error message will appear, as shown in Figure 2.4.

To print the relationship, first create the Relationship Report by clicking the Relationship Report button in the Tools group. When Access displays the report in Print Preview, click the Print button on the Print Preview tab.

Figure 2.5 One-to-One Relationship between the Customers Table and ServiceContracts Table

Project 1d Creating a One-to-One Relationship

Part 4 of 4

1. With **2-RSRCompServ.accdb** open, create a one-to-one relationship between the Customers table and ServiceContracts table by completing the following steps:
   a. Open the Relationships window.
   b. Click the Show Table button in the Relationships group.
   c. Double-click *ServiceContracts* in the list box at the Show Table dialog box with the Tables tab selected and then click the Close button.
   d. Drag the *CustID* field from the Customers table field list box to the *CustID* field in the ServiceContracts table field list box.
   e. At the Edit Relationships dialog box, check that the correct table and field names appear in the *Table/Query* and *Related Table/Query* option boxes. If necessary, click the Cancel button and repeat Step 1d.
   f. Notice that *One-To-One* appears in the *Relationship Type* section. Access detected this type of relationship because the field used to join the tables is a primary key field in both tables.
   g. Click to insert check marks in the *Enforce Referential Integrity* check box, the *Cascade Update Related Fields* check box, and the *Cascade Delete Related Records* check box.
   h. Click the Create button.

2. Drag the Title bar of the ServiceContracts table field list box to the approximate location in the Relationships window shown below. This makes it easier to view the join line and the *1* at each end of the join line between the Customers and ServiceContracts table field list boxes.

This join line indicates the one-to-one relationship created in Step 1.

3. Create a relationship report by clicking the Relationship Report button in the Tools group on the Relationship Tools Design tab.
4. Access displays the report in Print Preview. Click the Print button in the Print group on the Print Preview tab and then click OK at the Print dialog box.
5. Close the relationship report for **2-RSRCompServ.accdb** by clicking the Close Relationship button on the far right side of the screen. At the Microsoft Access message box, click Yes to save the report and click OK at the Save As dialog box to accept the default name.
6. Close the Relationships window.

Check Your Work

Tutorial

Creating a Many-to-Many Relationship

Creating a Many-to-Many Relationship

Consider the association between the Customers table and Technicians table in the RSR Computer Services database. Over time, any individual customer can have computer service work done by many different technicians and any individual technician can perform computer service work at many different customer locations. In other words, a record in the Customers table can be matched to many records in the Technicians table and a record in the Technicians table can be matched to many records in the Customers table. This is an example of a many-to-many relationship. A diagram of the many-to-many relationship between the Customers table and Technicians table is shown in Figure 2.6.

A many-to-many relationship is problematic because it creates duplicate records. If the same customer number is associated with many technicians and vice versa, many duplicates will occur in the two tables and Access may experience data conflicts when trying to identify unique records. To resolve the duplication and create unique entries, a third table is used to associate, or link, the many-to-many tables. That table is called a *junction table* and contains the primary key

Figure 2.6 Many-to-Many Relationship between the Customers Table and Technicians Table

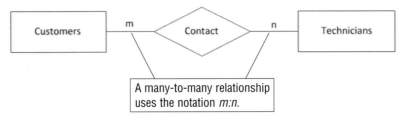

A many-to-many relationship uses the notation *m:n*.

Figure 2.7 Relationships Window Showing a Many-to-Many Relationship between the Customers Table and Technicians Table

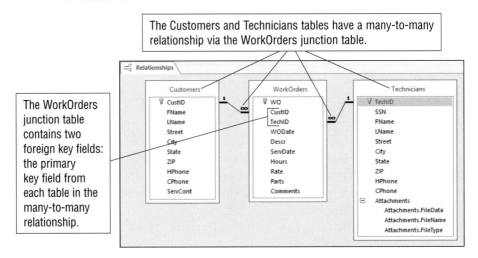

The Customers and Technicians tables have a many-to-many relationship via the WorkOrders junction table.

The WorkOrders junction table contains two foreign key fields: the primary key field from each table in the many-to-many relationship.

fields from both tables in the many-to-many relationship as its foreign key fields. Using the junction table, two one-to-many relationships are created.

In the Relationships window shown in Figure 2.7, the WorkOrders table is the junction table. Notice that the WorkOrders table contains two foreign key fields: *CustID*, which is the primary key field in the Customers table, and *TechID*, which is the primary key field in the Technicians table. One-to-many relationships exist between the Customers and WorkOrders tables and the Technicians and WorkOrders tables. These two one-to-many relationships create a many-to-many relationship between the Customers and Technicians tables.

Project 2 Create a Table with a Multiple-Field Primary Key Field and Lookup Fields   **5 Parts**

You will create a new table that requires two fields to uniquely identify each record. To restrict data entry in the table, you will create fields that each display a list from which the user selects the field value(s).

Preview Finished Project

Defining a Multiple-Field Primary Key Field

In most tables, one field is designated the primary key field. However, in some situations, a single field may not be guaranteed to hold unique data. Look at the fields in the table shown in Figure 2.8. This is a new table that will be created in the RSR Computer Services database to store computer profiles for RSR customers. The company stores the profiles as a service to clients, who sometimes forget their login information. Technicians can also access the profile data when troubleshooting at a customer's site.

A customer may have more than one computer in his or her home or office and each computer may have a different profile for each username. The *CustID* field will not serve as the primary key field if the customer has more than one record in the Profiles table. However, a combination of the three fields *CustID*, *CompID*, and *Username* will uniquely identify each record. In this table, three fields will be defined as primary key fields. A primary key field that is made up of two or more fields is called a *composite key* field.

Figure 2.8 Project 2a Profiles Table

Profiles		
*CustID	Short Text	4
*CompID	Short Text	2
*Username	Short Text	15
Password	Short Text	15
Remote	Yes/No	

Project 2a   Creating a New Table with a Multiple-Field Primary Key   Part 1 of 5

1. With **2-RSRCompServ.accdb** open, create a new table to store customer profiles by completing the following steps:
    a. Click the Create tab and then click the Table Design button in the Tables group.
    b. Type the field names, assign the data types, and change the field sizes according to the data structure shown in Figure 2.8.
2. Hover the mouse pointer over the field selector bar (the blank column left of the field names) next to *CustID* until the pointer changes to a black right-pointing arrow and then click to select the field.
3. Press and hold down the Shift key, click in the field selector bar next to *Username*, and then release the Shift key. The three adjacent fields *CustID*, *CompID*, and *Username* are now selected.
4. Click the Primary Key button in the Tools group on the Table Tools Design tab. Access displays the primary key icon next to each field name.
5. Click in any data type field to deselect the first three rows.
6. Save the table with the name *Profiles*.
7. Close the table.

Check Your Work

Tutorial

Creating a Field to
Look Up Values in
Another Table

Tutorial

Modifying Lookup
List Properties

Creating a Field to Look Up Values in Another Table

In Level 1, Chapter 4, the Lookup Wizard was used to create a lookup field where the values in the list were typed. The Lookup Wizard can also be used to create a lookup field to look up values found in records from another table. Lookup fields allow the user to enter data by pointing and clicking, rather than by typing the entry in the field.

A lookup field that draws its data from a field in another table can be useful in several ways. Data can be restricted to items within the list, which prevents orphan records, data entry errors, and spelling inconsistencies from occurring. The lookup field can also provide more information to help the user select the correct option. For example, suppose that a lookup field requires the user to select a customer's identification number. If the lookup field displays a drop-down list of identification numbers, identifying the correct number will be difficult. However, if the lookup field displays the identification number along with the customer's name, the correct entry will be easy to identify. When the user chooses the field entry based on the name, Access automatically enters the correct identification number.

When using the Lookup Wizard to create a lookup field, make sure to do so before the relationships are created. If a relationship already exists between the table for the lookup field and the source data table, Access will display a message stating that the relationship needs to be deleted before the Lookup Wizard can run.

Use the Lookup tab in the *Field Properties* section to change the *Limit to List* property from *No* to *Yes*. A user will not be able to type in an entry that is not in the list.

Quick Steps

Create a Lookup Field to Another Table

1. Open table in Design view.
2. Click in column of lookup field.
3. Click down arrow.
4. Click *Lookup Wizard*.
5. Click Next.
6. Choose table and click Next.
7. Choose fields to display in column.
8. Click Next.
9. Choose field by which to sort.
10. Click Next.
11. If necessary, expand column widths.
12. Clear *Hide key column*.
13. Click Next.
14. Choose field value to store in table.
15. Click Next.
16. Click Finish.
17. Click Yes.

Project 2b Creating a Field to Look Up Values in Another Table   Part 2 of 5

1. With **2-RSRCompServ.accdb** open, open the Profiles table in Design view.
2. Create a lookup field to select and enter a customer's identification number from a list of customers in the Customers table by completing the following steps:

    a. With *CustID* the active field, click in the *Data Type* column, click the down arrow that appears, and then click *Lookup Wizard* at the drop-down list.

    b. At the first Lookup Wizard dialog box with *I want the lookup field to get the values from another table or query* selected, click the Next button.

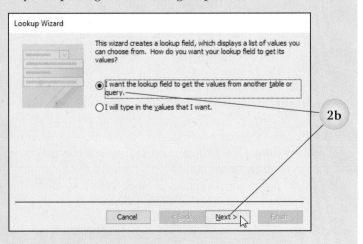

c. At the second Lookup Wizard dialog box with *Table: Customers* already selected in the *Which table or query should provide the values for your lookup field?* list box, click the Next button.

d. At the third Lookup Wizard dialog box, double-click *FName* in the *Available Fields* list box to move the field to the *Selected Fields* list box.

e. Double-click *LName* in the *Available Fields* list box to move the field to the *Selected Fields* list box and then click the Next button.

f. At the fourth Lookup Wizard dialog box, click the first sort option box arrow, click *LName* at the drop-down list, and then click the Next button. Notice that up to four sort keys can be defined to sort the lookup list and that an Ascending button appears next to each *Sort* option box. You can change the sort order from Ascending to Descending by clicking the Ascending button.

g. At the fifth Lookup Wizard dialog box, expand the column widths if necessary to display all the data. Scroll down the list of entries in the dialog box. Notice that the column widths are sufficient to show all the text.

h. To view the customer identification numbers with the names while the list is open in a record, click the *Hide key column (recommended)* check box to remove the check mark. Removing the check mark displays the *CustID* field values as the first column in the lookup list.

i. Click the Next button.

j. At the sixth Lookup Wizard dialog box, choose the field value to be stored in the table when an entry is selected in the drop-down list. With *CustID* already selected in the Available Fields list box, click the Next button.

k. At the last Lookup Wizard dialog box, click the Finish button to accept the existing field name for the lookup field of *CustID*.

l. At the Lookup Wizard message box stating that the table must be saved before relationships can be created, click Yes to save the table. Access automatically creates a relationship between the Customers table and Profiles table based on the *CustID* field used to create the lookup field.

3. Close the Profiles table.

Project 2c Modifying Lookup List Properties and Using a Lookup List Field in a Record

Part 3 of 5

1. With **2-RSRCompServ.accdb** open, open the Profiles table in Design view.
2. Type the following text in the *Caption* property box for each of the following fields:

CustID	Customer ID
CompID	Computer ID
Remote	Remote Access?

3. Modify the lookup field properties to restrict entries in new records to items within the list by completing the following steps:
   a. Make *CustID* the active field.

b. Click the Lookup tab in the *Field Properties* section.

c. Look at the entries in all the property boxes for the Lookup tab. These entries were created by the Lookup Wizard.

d. Double-click in the *Limit To List* property box to change *No* to *Yes*. This means that the field will accept data only from existing customer records. A user will not be able to type in an entry that is not in the list.

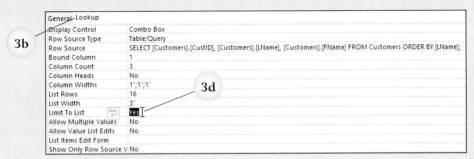

e. Save the table.

4. Switch to Datasheet view.

5. With *Customer ID* in the first row of the datasheet as the active field, click the down arrow in the field and then click *Jade Fleming* at the drop-down list. Notice that Access inserts *1000* as the field value in the first column since that is the customer number associated with the selected name.

6. Type the remaining data as indicated:

 Computer ID D1
 Username jade
 Password P$ck7
 Remote Access? (Leave blank to indicate *No*.)

7. Best fit the width of each column.

8. Print and then close the Profiles datasheet. Click Yes when prompted to save changes to the table layout.

Check Your Work

Tutorial

Creating a Field
That Allows
Multiple Values

💡**Hint** Multiple-value fields should be used when more than one choice from a small list needs to be stored. This makes it unnecessary to create an advanced database design.

Creating a Field That Allows Multiple Values

The industry certifications that a technician has achieved could be organized by creating a separate field for each certification. A more efficient approach is to create a single field that displays a list of certifications with check boxes to indicate whether they have been attained.

Look at the fields in the table structure shown in Figure 2.9. For each technician, a list in the *Certifications* field is opened and the check box next to the applicable certification title is checked if the technician has obtained that specific certification. In the *OperatingSys* field, another list can be used to keep track of the operating systems for which the technician is considered an expert.

Create a Multiple-Value Lookup Field
1. Open table in Design view.
2. Start Lookup Wizard for desired field.
3. Create list by typing values or binding data to field in another table.
4. At last Lookup Wizard dialog box, insert check mark in *Allow Multiple Values* check box.
5. Click Finish.
6. Click Yes.

Figure 2.9 Project 2d TechSkills Table

TechSkills		
*TechID	Short Text	2
Certifications	Short Text	20
OperatingSys	Short Text	20
NetworkSpc	Yes/No	
WebDesign	Yes/No	
Programming	Yes/No	

Use the Lookup Wizard to create a field to store multiple values. Choose to look up the values in a field in another table or create a custom value list. At the last Lookup Wizard dialog box, make sure to click the *Allow Multiple Values* check box to insert a check mark.

Project 2d Creating Fields That Allow Multiple Values in a New Table

1. With **2-RSRCompServ.accdb** open, create a new table to store technician competencies by completing the following steps:
   a. Create a new table using Design view.
   b. Type the field names and assign the data types according to the data structure shown in Figure 2.9.
   c. Assign the field denoted with an asterisk in Figure 2.9 as the primary key field.
   d. Save the table with the name *TechSkills*.
2. Create a lookup field to select a technician from a list of names in the Technicians table by completing the following steps:
   a. Click in the *Data Type* column for the *TechID* field, click the down arrow that appears, and then click *Lookup Wizard*.
   b. Click the Next button at the first Lookup Wizard dialog box.
   c. Click *Table: Technicians* and then click the Next button.
   d. Double-click *FName* in the *Available Fields* list box to move the field to the *Selected Fields* list box.
   e. Double-click *LName* in the *Available Fields* list box and then click the Next button.
   f. Sort by *LName* and then click the Next button.
   g. With a check mark in the *Hide key column (recommended)* check box, click the Next button to accept the current column widths. (In this lookup example, you are electing not to show the technician's ID field value. Although you will view and select by name, Access stores the primary key field's value in the table. *TechID* is considered the bound field and *FName* and *LName* are considered display fields).
   h. Click the Finish button and then click Yes to save the table.

3. Create a lookup field that allows multiple values for certification information by completing the following steps:

a. Click in the *Data Type* column for the *Certifications* field, click the down arrow that appears, and then click *Lookup Wizard*.

b. Click *I will type in the values that I want* and then click the Next button.

c. At the second Lookup Wizard dialog box, type the following entries in *Col1*:

    CCNA Cloud
    CCNA Wireless
    Comp TIA A+
    Microsoft MCT
    MOS Master

d. Click the Next button.

e. At the last Lookup Wizard dialog box, click the *Allow Multiple Values* check box to insert a check mark and then click the Finish button.

f. At the message box indicating that once the field is set to store multiple values, the action cannot be undone, click Yes to change the *Certifications* field to multiple values.

3c

3d

3e

3f

4. Complete steps similar to those in Steps 3a–3f to create a lookup list to store multiple values in the *OperatingSys* field using the following value list:

    Windows 10
    Windows 8
    Windows 7
    Linux
    Unix

5. Save and then close the TechSkills table.

Check Your Work

1. With **2-RSRCompServ.accdb** open, open the TechSkills table in Design view.
2. Type the following text in the *Caption* property box for each field as indicated:

TechID	Technician ID
OperatingSys	Operating Systems
NetworkSpc	Network Specialist?
WebDesign	Design Web Sites?
Programming	Programming?

3. Save the table and then switch to Datasheet view.
4. Add a new record to the table by completing the following steps:

    a. With the insertion point positioned in the *Technician ID* column, click the down arrow and then click *Kelsey Eastman* at the drop-down list. Notice that Access displays the technician's first name in the column. *FName* is considered a display field for this column but the identification number associated with the name *Kelsey Eastman* is stored in the table.

    b. Press the Tab key and then click the down arrow in the *Certifications* column.

    c. Since *Certifications* is a multiple-value field, the drop-down list displays with check boxes next to all the items. Click the *CCNA Cloud* check box and the *Microsoft MCT* check box to insert check marks and then click OK.

    d. Press the Tab key and then click the down arrow in the *Operating System* column.

    e. Click the *Windows 10*, *Windows 8*, and *Linux* check boxes to insert check marks and then click OK.

    f. Press the Tab key and then press the spacebar to insert a check mark in the *Network Specialist?* check box.

    g. Press the Tab key three times to finish the record, leaving the check boxes blank in the *Design Web Sites?* and *Programming?* columns.

5. Best fit the width of each column.
6. Print the TechSkills table in landscape orientation with left and right margins of 0.25 inch.
7. Close the TechSkills table. Click Yes when prompted to save changes to the layout.

Check Your Work

You will create indexes to speed up database processing.

Creating an Index

Quick Steps

Create a Single-Field Index
1. Open table in Design view.
2. Make field active.
3. Click in *Indexed* property box.
4. Click down arrow.
5. Click *Yes (Duplicates OK)* or *Yes (No Duplicates)*.
6. Save table.

Create a Multiple-Field Index
1. Open table in Design view.
2. Click Indexes button.
3. Click in first blank row in *Index Name* column.
4. Type name for index.
5. Press Tab.
6. Click down arrow in *Field Name* column.
7. Click field.
8. If necessary, change sort order.
9. Click in *Field Name* column in next row.
10. Click down arrow.
11. Click field.
12. If necessary, change sort order.
13. Repeat Steps 9–12 until finished.
14. Close Indexes window.

 Indexes

 Hint An index cannot be generated for fields with a data type of OLE Object or Attachment.

An index is a list created by Access containing pointers that direct Access to the locations of specific records in a table. A database index is very similar to an index found at the end of a book. Search the book's index for a keyword associated with the topic being searched, and the index gives the page number(s) in the book that contains information on that topic. Using a book's index allows information to be retrieved quickly and efficiently. Although the information in an Access index cannot be seen, it operates in much the same way, reducing the amount of time it takes to find a particular record.

Access automatically generates an index for a field designated the primary key field in a table. In a database with a large number of records, it is useful to identify fields other than the primary key field that are often sorted or searched and to create indexes for these fields to speed up sorting and searching. For example, in the Customers table in the RSR Computer Services database, creating an index for the *LName* field is a good idea because the table data will frequently be sorted by a customer's last name.

An index can be created to restrict the data in a field to unique values. This creates a field similar to a primary key field in that Access will not allow two records to hold the same data. For example, an email field in a table that is frequently searched is a good candidate for an index. To avoid data entry errors in a field that should contain unique values (and is not the primary key field), set up the index so it will not accept duplicates.

Create a multiple-field index if a large table is frequently sorted by two or more fields at the same time. In Table Design view, click the Indexes button to open the Indexes window, as shown in Figure 2.10. Create an index for a combination of up to 10 fields.

Figure 2.10 Indexes Window

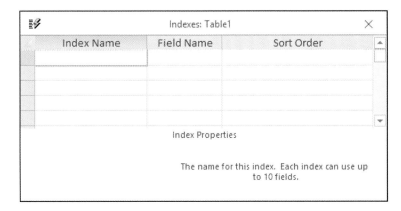

1. With **2-RSRCompServ.accdb** open, open the Customers table in Design view.
2. Create a single-field index for the *ZIP* field by completing the following steps:
   a. Make *ZIP* the active field.
   b. Double-click in the *Indexed* property box to change *No* to *Yes (Duplicates OK)*.
   c. Save the table.
3. Create a multiple-field index for the *LName* and *FName* fields by completing the following steps:
   a. Click the Indexes button in the Show/Hide group on the Table Tools Design tab.
   b. At the Indexes: Customers window, click in the first blank row in the *Index Name* column (below *ZIP*) and then type Names.
   c. Press the Tab key, click the down arrow that appears in the *Field Name* column, and then click *LName* at the drop-down list. The sort order for *LName* defaults to *Ascending*.

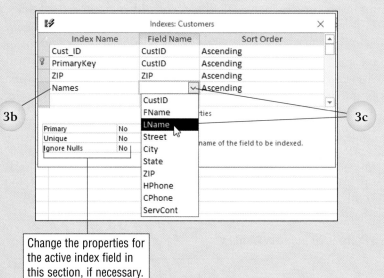

Change the properties for the active index field in this section, if necessary.

   d. In the *Field Name* column, click in the row below *LName*, click the down arrow that appears, and then click *FName*.
   e. Close the Indexes: Customers window.
   f. Save the table.
4. Close the Customers table.
5. Close **2-RSRCompServ.accdb**.

Normalizing a Database

Normalizing a database involves reviewing the database structure to ensure that the tables are set up to eliminate redundancy. If data redundancy is discovered, the process of normalization often involves splitting fields into smaller units and/or breaking down larger tables into smaller tables and creating relationships to remove repeating groups of data. Three normalization states are tested: first normal form, second normal form, and third normal form.

Checking First Normal Form

A table meets first normal form when it does not contain any fields that can be broken down into smaller units and when it does not have similar information stored in several fields.

For example, a table that contains a single field called *TechnicianName* that stores the technician's first and last names in the same column violates first normal form. To correct the structure, split *TechnicianName* into two fields, such as *TechLastName* and *TechFirstName*.

A table that has multiple fields and in which each field contains similar data—such as *Week1*, *Week2*, *Week3*, and *Week4*—also violates first normal form. To correct this structure, delete the four week fields and replace them with a single field named *WeekNumber*.

Checking Second Normal Form

Meeting second normal form is of concern only for a table that has a multiple-field primary key field (composite key field). A table with a composite key field meets second normal form when it is in first normal form and when all of its fields are dependent on all the fields that form the primary key field.

Hint If a field cannot relate to the individual fields of a composite key field, then it should be included in a different table.

For example, assume that a table is defined with two fields that form the primary key field: *CustID* and *ComputerID*. Also assume that a field in the same table is titled *EmailAdd*. The contents of the *EmailAdd* field are dependent on the customer only (not the computer). Since *EmailAdd* is not dependent on both *CustID* and *ComputerID*, the table is not in second normal form. To correct the structure, delete the *EmailAdd* field. (The *EmailAdd* field belongs in another table in the database.)

Checking Third Normal Form

Meeting third normal form applies to a table that has a single primary key field and is in first normal form. If a field exists in the table for which the field value is not dependent on the field value of the primary key field, the table is not in third normal form.

For example, assume that a table is defined with a single primary key field titled *TechnicianID*. Also assume that fields in the same table are titled *PayCode* and *PayRate*. Finally, assume that a technician's pay rate is dependent on the pay code assigned to him or her. Since the pay rate is dependent on the field value in the pay code field and not on the technician's identification number, the table is not in third normal form. To convert the table to third normal form, delete the *PayRate* field from the table. (The *PayRate* field belongs in another table in the database.)

Chapter Summary

- When building relationships, consider the frequency of matching data in the common field in both tables to determine if the relationship is one-to-many, one-to-one, or many-to-many.

- The most common type of relationship is one-to-many. It involves joining tables by dragging the primary key field from the "one" table to the foreign key field in the "many" table.

- In a one-to-many relationship, only one record for a matching field value exists in the primary table, while many records for the same value can exist in the related table.

- A relationship diagram depicts the two tables joined in the relationship and the type of relationship between them.

- Enforce referential integrity to place restrictions on new data entered into a related table at the Edit Relationships dialog box. A record is not allowed in the related table if a matching record does not already exist in the primary table.

- Selecting the *Cascade Update Related Fields* option automatically updates all the occurrences of the same data in the foreign key field in the related table when a change is made to the primary key field in the primary table.

- Selecting the *Cascade Delete Related Records* option automatically deletes related records when a record is deleted from the primary table.

- In a one-to-one relationship, only one record exists that has a matching value in the joined field in both tables.

- In a many-to-many relationship, many records can exist that have matching values in the joined fields in both tables.

- A junction table is used to create a many-to-many relationship. A junction table contains a minimum of two fields, which are the primary key fields from the two tables in the many-to-many relationship.

- Using a junction table, two one-to-many relationships are joined to form a many-to-many relationship.

- In some tables, two or more fields are used to create the primary key field if a single field is not guaranteed to hold unique data.

- A primary key field that is made up of two or more fields is called a *composite key* field.

- A lookup field displays a drop-down list in a field, in which the user points and clicks to enter the field value. The list can be generated from records in a related table or by typing in a value list.

- Once a lookup field has been created, options at the Lookup tab in the *Field Properties* section in Table Design view can be selected to modify individual properties.

- Clicking *Yes* at the Limit To List property box allows entries in the field to be restricted to items within the lookup list.

- A field that allows selecting multiple entries from a drop-down list can be created by clicking *Allow Multiple Values* at the final Lookup Wizard dialog box.

- Access displays check boxes next to all the items in the drop-down list if the field has been set to allow multiple values.

- An index is a list generated by Access containing pointers that direct Access to the locations of specific records in a table.

- Access automatically generates an index for a field designated the primary key field in a table.
- To create a single-field table index, change the Indexed property to *Yes (Duplicates OK)* or *Yes (No Duplicates)*.
- To create a multiple-field index, open the Indexes window.
- Normalizing a database involves reviewing the database structure to ensure that the tables are set up to eliminate redundancy. Three normalization states are tested: first normal form, second normal form, and third normal form.

Commands Review

FEATURE	RIBBON TAB, GROUP	BUTTON
Edit Relationships dialog box	Relationship Tools Design, Tools	
indexes window	Table Tools Design, Show/Hide	
primary key field	Table Tools Design, Tools	
relationships report	Relationship Tools Design, Tools	
Relationships window	Database Tools, Relationships OR Table Tools Design, Relationships	
Show Table dialog box	Relationship Tools Design, Relationships	

Workbook

Chapter study tools and assessment activities are available in the *Workbook* ebook. These resources are designed to help you further develop and demonstrate mastery of the skills learned in this chapter.

Microsoft®

Access®

Advanced Query Techniques

Performance Objectives

Precheck

Check your current skills to help focus your study.

Upon successful completion of Chapter 3, you will be able to:

1 Save a filter as a query

2 Create and run a parameter query to prompt for criteria

3 Create an inner join, left outer join, and right outer join to modify query results

4 Add tables to and remove tables from a query

5 Create a self-join query to match two fields in the same table

6 Assign an alias to a table name

7 Create a query that includes a subquery

8 Create a query that uses conditional logic

9 Select records using a multiple-value field in a query

10 Create a new table using a make table query

11 Remove records from a table using a delete query

12 Add records to a table using an append query

13 Modify records using an update query

In this chapter, you will create, save, and run queries that incorporate advanced query features, such as saving a filter as a query, prompting for criteria on single and multiple fields, modifying join properties to view alternative query results, and using action queries to perform operations on groups of records. In addition, you will create an alias for a table and incorporate subqueries to manage multiple calculations.

Data Files

Before beginning chapter work, copy the AL2C3 folder to your storage medium and then make AL2C3 the active folder.

SNAP

If you are a SNAP user, launch the Precheck and Tutorials from your Assignments page.

Project 1 **Select Records Using Filtered Criteria and Prompted Criteria**

3 Parts

You will create queries to select records by saving the criteria for a filter and creating a query that prompts the user for the criteria when the query is run.

Preview Finished Project

Extracting Records Using Select Queries

A select query is the type of query most often used in Access. It extracts records that meet specified criteria from a single table or multiple tables. The subset of records that a query returns can be edited, viewed, and/or printed. In Query Design view, the criteria used to select records are entered by typing expressions in the *Criteria* row for the required field(s). Access also provides other methods for specifying query criteria.

Tutorial

Saving a Filter as a Query

Saving a Filter as a Query

A filter is used in a datasheet or form to temporarily hide records that do not meet specified criteria. For example, filter a WorkOrders datasheet to display only those work orders completed on a specified date. The subset of records can then be edited, viewed, and/or printed. Use the Filter by Form feature to filter a datasheet by multiple criteria using a blank datasheet. A filter is active until it is removed or the datasheet or form is closed. A filter can be saved when the table is closed but when the worksheet is reopened, all the records redisplay. Click the Toggle Filter button to reapply the filter.

If these steps are being repeated often, save the filtered datasheet as a query. Some users are more comfortable using filters to select records than with typing criteria expressions in Query Design view. To save a filter as a query, click the Advanced button in the Sort & Filter group on the Home tab and then click *Filter By Form* at the drop-down list to display the criteria. Click the Advanced button again and then click *Save As Query* at the drop-down list. Type a query name at the Save As Query dialog box and then press the Enter key or click OK. Saving a filter as a query means that all the columns in the table display in the query results datasheet. Use the Hide Fields feature to remove a field(s) from the results.

Quick Steps

Save a Filter as a Query
1. Open table.
2. Filter table as needed.
3. Click Advanced button.
4. Click *Filter By Form.*
5. Click Advanced button.
6. Click *Save As Query.*
7. Type query name.
8. Click OK.

 Advanced

Project 1a **Saving a Filter as a Query**

Part 1 of 3

1. Open **3-RSRCompServ.accdb** and enable the content.
2. Use the Filter by Form feature to display only those service calls that required two or more hours of labor by technicians billed at $35.00 per hour by completing the following steps:
   a. Open the WorkOrders table in Datasheet view.
   b. Minimize the Navigation pane.
   c. Hide the *Comments* field by right-clicking the *Comments* column heading in the datasheet and then clicking *Hide Fields* at the shortcut menu.

d. Click the Advanced button in the Sort & Filter group on the Home tab and then click *Filter By Form* at the drop-down list.

e. Click in the empty record in the *Hours* column. Type >=2 and then press the Tab key.

f. With the insertion point positioned in the *Rate* column, click the down arrow that appears and then click *35* at the drop-down list.

g. Click the Toggle Filter button (which displays the ScreenTip *Apply Filter*) in the Sort & Filter group on the Home tab. The records that meet the filter conditions display.

3. Review the nine filtered records in the datasheet.

4. Click the Toggle Filter button (which displays the ScreenTip *Remove Filter*) to redisplay all the records.

5. Click the Advanced button and then click *Filter By Form* at the drop-down list. Notice that the filter criteria in the *Hours* and *Rate* columns are intact.

6. Save the filter as a query so the criteria can be reused by completing the following steps:

a. Click the Advanced button and then click *Save As Query* at the drop-down list.

b. At the Save As Query dialog box, type WO2orMoreRate35 in the *Query Name* text box and then click OK.

c. Click the Advanced button and then click *Close* at the drop-down list to close the Filter By Form datasheet.

d. Close the WorkOrders table. Click No when prompted to save changes to the table design.

7. Expand the Navigation pane.

8. Double-click the query object *WO2orMoreRate35* to open the query and then review the results.

9. Hide the *Comments* column in the query results datasheet.

10. Print the datasheet in landscape orientation with the left and right margins set to 0.5 inch.

11. Switch to Design view. Notice that the query design grid for a query created from a filter includes columns only for those columns for which criteria have been defined.

12. Close the query. Click Yes when prompted to save changes to the query layout.

Check Your Work

Creating a Parameter Query

In a parameter query, specific criteria for a field are not stored with the query design. Instead, the field(s) used to select records has a prompt message that displays when the query is run. The prompt message instructs the user to type the criteria to be used in selecting records.

Figure 3.1 shows the Enter Parameter Value dialog box, which displays when a parameter query to select by a technician's name is run. The message shown in the dialog box is created in the field for which the criterion will be applied. When the query is run, the user types the criterion at the Enter Parameter Value dialog box and Access selects the records based on the entry. If more than one field contains a parameter, Access prompts the user one field at a time.

A parameter query is useful if a query is run several times on the same field but different criteria are used each time. For example, suppose that a list of each technician's work orders is needed. Normally, a separate query would be made for each technician, resulting in several query objects being displayed in the Navigation pane. Creating a parameter query that prompts the user to enter the technician's name means that only one query is created.

To create a parameter query, start a new query in Design view and then add the desired tables and fields to the query design grid. Type a message enclosed in square brackets to prompt the user for the required criterion in the *Criteria* row of the field to be used to select records. Access does not allow punctuation at the end of the message. The text inside the square brackets is displayed in the Enter Parameter Value dialog box when the query is run. Figure 3.2 displays the entry in the *Criteria* row of the *FName* field that generated the Enter Parameter Value message shown in Figure 3.1.

Figure 3.1 Enter Parameter Value Dialog Box

Figure 3.2 Criterion to Prompt for the Name in the *FName* Field

Type a message enclosed in square brackets to prompt the user for the criterion to use in selecting records.

Project 1b Creating a Parameter Query to Prompt for Technician Names   Part 2 of 3

1. With **3-RSRCompServ.accdb** open, create a query in Design view to select records from the Technicians table and WorkOrders table by completing the following steps:
   a. Click the Create tab and then click the Query Design button in the Queries group.
   b. At the Show Table dialog box, add the Technicians table and WorkOrders table to the query.

c. Close the Show Table dialog box.

d. At the top of the query, drag down the bottom borders of both table field list boxes until all the field names are visible.

e. Double-click the following field names in the Technicians table field list box and WorkOrders table field list box to add the fields to the query design grid (click the field names in the order indicated): *WO, FName, LName, ServDate, Hours, Rate*.

These fields are added to the query design grid in Step 1e.

Field:	WO	FName	LName	ServDate	Hours	Rate	
Table:	WorkOrders	Technicians	Technicians	WorkOrders	WorkOrders	WorkOrders	
Sort:							
Show:	☑	☑	☑	☑	☑	☑	

2. Click the Run button in the Results group on the Query Tools Design tab to run the query.

3. Add parameters to select records by a technician's first and last names by completing the following steps:

a. Switch to Design view.

b. Click in the *Criteria* row in the *FName* column in the query design grid, type [Type the technician's first name], and then press the Enter key.

c. Position the mouse pointer on the vertical line between *FName* and *LName* in the gray field selector bar above the field names until the pointer changes to a left-and-right-pointing arrow with a vertical line in the middle. Double-click to expand the width of the *FName* column so the entire criterion entry can be seen.

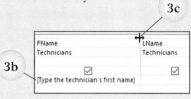

d. With the insertion point positioned in the *Criteria* row in the *LName* column, type [Type the technician's last name] and then press the Enter key.

e. Expand the width of the *LName* column so the entire criterion entry can be seen.

4. Click the Save button on the Quick Access Toolbar, type PromptedTechLabor in the *Query Name* text box at the Save As dialog box, and then click OK.

5. Close the query.

6. Run the parameter query and extract a list of work orders for the technician named *Pat Hynes* by completing the following steps:

a. Double-click the query named *PromptedTechLabor* in the Navigation pane.

b. Type pat at the first Enter Parameter Value dialog box, which displays the message *Type the technician's first name*, and then click OK. (Note that Access is not case-sensitive for text strings.)

c. Type hynes at the second Enter Parameter Value dialog box, which displays the message *Type the technician's last name*, and then click OK.

7. Review the records in the query results datasheet.

8. Print the query results datasheet.

9. Close the query.

Check Your Work

1. With **3-RSRCompServ.accdb** open, create a parameter query in Design view to prompt the user for the starting and ending dates for selecting records in the WorkOrders table by completing the following steps:
   a. Click the Create tab and then click the Query Design button in the Queries group.
   b. At the Show Table dialog box, add the WorkOrders table to the query and then close the dialog box.
   c. Drag down the bottom border of the table field list box until all the field names are visible.
   d. Add the following fields to the query design grid in this order: *WO, CustID, Descr, ServDate, Hours, Rate, Parts*.
   e. Click in the *Criteria* row in the *ServDate* column, type the entry Between [Type starting date] And [Type ending date], and then press the Enter key.

   f. Expand the width of the *ServDate* column until the entire criterion entry is visible.
2. Save the query, type PromptedServiceDate at the Save As dialog box, and then click OK.
3. Close the query.
4. Double-click *PromptedServiceDate* in the Navigation pane. At the first Enter Parameter Value dialog box with *Type starting date* displayed, type October 1, 2018 and then click OK. At the second Enter Parameter Value dialog box with *Type ending date* displayed, type October 13, 2018 and then click OK.

PromptedServiceDate					
Work Order ▾	Customer ID ▾	Description ▾	Service Date ▾	Rate ▾	Parts ▾
65027	1010	Replace hard drive	Tue, Oct 02 2018	35.00	$375.50
65028	1030	Reinstall operating system	Tue, Oct 02 2018	35.00	$0.00
65029	1035	Set up automatic backup	Wed, Oct 03 2018	25.00	$0.00
65030	1000	Clean malware from system	Sat, Oct 06 2018	20.00	$0.00
65031	1045	Customer reports noisy hard drive	Sat, Oct 06 2018	35.00	$0.00
65032	1008	Install second hard drive	Sat, Oct 13 2018	35.00	$425.75
65033	1000	Install Windows 10	Sat, Oct 13 2018	35.00	$335.75

Records within the date range October 1, 2018 to October 13, 2018 are selected in Step 4.

5. Print the query results datasheet in landscape orientation.
6. Close the query.

Check Your Work

Project 2 **Modify Query Results by Changing the Join Property** **4 Parts**

You will create and modify queries that obtain various results based on changing the join properties for related tables.

Preview Finished Project

Modifying Join Properties in a Query

The term *join properties* refers to how Access matches the field values in the common field between the two tables in a relationship. The method used determines how many records are selected for inclusion in the query results datasheet. Access provides for three join types in a relationship: an inner join, a left outer join, and a right outer join. By default, Access uses an inner join between the tables; records are selected for display in a query only when a match on the joined field value exists in both tables. If a record exists in either table with no matching record in the other table, the record is not displayed in the query results datasheet. This means that in some cases, not all the records are seen from both tables when a query is run.

Specifying the Join Type

Double-click the join line between tables in a query to open the Join Properties dialog box, shown in Figure 3.3. By default, option *1*, referred to as an *inner join*, is selected. In an inner join, only those records are displayed for which the primary key field value in the primary table matches a foreign key field value in the related table.

Options *2* and *3* are referred to as *outer joins*. Option *2* is a left outer join. In this type of join, the primary table (referred to as the *left table*) displays all the rows, whereas the related table (referred to as the *right table*) displays only rows with matching values in the foreign key field. For example, examine the query results datasheet shown in Figure 3.4. This query was created with the Technicians table and TechSkills table. All the technician records are shown in the datasheet. However, notice that some technician records display with empty field values for the columns from the TechSkills table. These records reflect the technicians for which no information has yet been entered in the TechSkills table. In a left outer join, all the records from the primary table in the relationship are shown in the query results datasheet

Figure 3.3 Join Properties Dialog Box

Figure 3.4 Left Outer Join Example

First Name	Last Name	Certifications	Operating Systems	Network Specialist?	Design Websites?	Programming?
Pat	Hynes	CCNA Cloud, CCNA Wireless, Microsoft MCT	Linux, Unix, Windows 7, Windows 8	☑	☐	☑
Hui	Chen	CCNA Cloud, Comp TIA A+	Linux, Unix, Windows 10, Windows 7, Windows 8	☑	☑	☐
Kayla	Blewett			▣	▣	▣
Mihir	Patel	Comp TIA A+, Microsoft MCT	Unix, Windows 10, Windows 8	☐	☐	☑
Madir	Sadiku	Comp TIA A+, Microsoft MCT	Mac OS X, Windows 10, Windows 7, Windows 8	☐	☐	☐
Brody	Stewart			▣	▣	▣
Ana	Takacs	CCNA Wireless	Windows 8	☑	☐	☑
Marty	O'Leary	CCNA Wireless	Linux, Unix	☑	☑	☐
Armando	Colacci	CCNA Wireless, MOS Master	Windows 10, Windows 7, Windows 8	☐	☐	☑
Kelsey	Eastman	Comp TIA A+, MOS Master	Linux, Windows 7, Windows 8	☑	☑	☐
Dana	Westman			▣	▣	▣

Left outer join query results show blank related *TechSkills* fields for those technicians for which records have not yet been entered in the TechSkills table.

Quick Steps

Create a Query with a Right Outer Join

1. Create new query in Design view.
2. Add tables to query window.
3. Double-click join line between tables.
4. Select option *3*.
5. Click OK.
6. Add fields to query design grid.
7. Save and run query.

Option *3* is a right outer join. In this type of join, the related table (right table) shows all the rows, whereas the primary table (left table) shows only rows with matching values in the common field. For example, examine the partial query results datasheet shown in Figure 3.5. This datasheet illustrates 15 of the 39 records in the query results datasheet from the Technicians table and WorkOrders table. Notice that the first four records have no technician first or last names. These are the work orders that have not yet been assigned to a technician. In a right outer join, all the records from the related table in the relationship are shown in the query results datasheet. In a left or right outer join, Access displays an arrow at the end of the join line pointing to the table that shows only matching rows.

To illustrate the difference in query results when no change is made to the join type, examine the query results datasheet shown in Figure 3.6. This is the datasheet created in Project 2a. In this project, a list of technician names and qualifications will be created. Compare the number of records shown in Figure 3.6 with the number of records shown in Figure 3.4. Notice that fewer records display in the datasheet in Figure 3.6. Since an inner join displays only those records for which matching entries exists in both tables, records from either table that do not have matching records in the other table are not displayed. Understanding that an inner join (the default join type) may not display all the records that exist in the tables when a query is run is important.

Figure 3.5 Right Outer Join Example

Right outer join query results show blank related technician fields for those work orders that have not yet been assigned to a technician.

First Name	Last Name	Work Order	WO Date	Description
		65047	Sat, Oct 27 2018	Set up automatic backup
		65048	Mon, Oct 29 2018	Replace LCD monitor
		65049	Tue, Oct 30 2018	Set up dual monitor system
		65050	Tue, Oct 30 2018	Reinstall Windows 10
Pat	Hynes	65020	Mon, Sep 17 2018	Troubleshoot noisy fan
Pat	Hynes	65033	Fri, Oct 12 2018	Install Windows 10
Pat	Hynes	65038	Fri, Oct 19 2018	Install last version of Windows
Hui	Chen	65014	Mon, Sep 10 2018	Replace power supply
Hui	Chen	65019	Sat, Sep 15 2018	Upgrade to new Windows
Hui	Chen	65026	Sat, Sep 29 2018	Upgrade memory
Hui	Chen	65032	Fri, Oct 12 2018	Install second hard drive
Hui	Chen	65035	Sun, Oct 14 2018	Office 2016 training
Kayla	Blewett	65023	Sat, Sep 22 2018	Upgrade RAM
Kayla	Blewett	65036	Mon, Oct 15 2018	Set up home network
Kayla	Blewett	65041	Mon, Oct 22 2018	Biannual computer maintenance

Figure 3.6 Inner Join Example

First Name	Last Name	Certifications	Operating Systems	Network Specialist?	Design Websites?	Programming?
Pat	Hynes	CCNA Cloud, CCNA Wireless, Microsoft MCT	Linux, Unix, Windows 7, Windows 8	☑	☐	☑
Hui	Chen	CCNA Cloud, Comp TIA A+	Linux, Unix, Windows 10, Windows 7, Windows 8	☑	☑	☐
Mihir	Patel	Comp TIA A+, Microsoft MCT	Unix, Windows 10, Windows 8	☐	☐	☑
Madir	Sadiku	Comp TIA A+, Microsoft MCT	Mac OS X, Windows 10, Windows 7, Windows 8	☐	☐	☐
Ana	Takacs	CCNA Wireless	Windows 8	☑	☐	☑
Marty	O'Leary	CCNA Wireless	Linux, Unix	☑	☑	☐
Armando	Colacci	CCNA Wireless, MOS Master	Windows 10, Windows 7, Windows 8	☐	☐	☑
Kelsey	Eastman	Comp TIA A+, MOS Master	Linux, Windows 7, Windows 8	☑	☑	☐

An inner join displays a record from either table only when a matching value in the joined field exists in the other table. No blank records appear in the query results. However, notice that not all the records in the Technicians table display.

Project 2a Selecting Records in a Query Using an Inner Join
Part 1 of 4

1. With **3-RSRCompServ.accdb** open, create a query in Design view to display a list of technicians that notes each individual's skill specialties by completing the following steps:
   a. Create a new query in Design view. At the Show Table dialog box, add the Technicians table and TechSkills table. Close the Show Table dialog box and then drag down the bottom borders of both table field list boxes until all the field names are visible.
   b. Double-click the join line between the two tables to open the Join Properties dialog box.

   c. At the Join Properties dialog box, notice that option *1* is selected by default. Option *1* selects records only when the joined fields from both tables are equal. This represents an inner join. Click OK.

   d. Add the following fields to the query design grid in order: *FName, LName, Certifications, OperatingSys, NetworkSpc, WebDesign, Programming*.
   e. Run the query.
2. Save the query and type TechSpecialties as the query name.
3. Close the query.

Check Your Work

1. With **3-RSRCompServ.accdb** open, modify the TechSpecialties query to a left outer join to check whether information for any technicians has not yet been entered in the TechSkills table by completing the following steps:

    a. Right-click the *TechSpecialties* query and then click *Design View* at the shortcut menu.

    b. Right-click the join line between the two tables and then click *Join Properties* at the shortcut menu.

    c. At the Join Properties dialog box, click option *2*. Option *2* includes all the records from the Technicians table and only those records from the TechSkills table for which the joined fields are equal. The left table (Technicians) is the table that will show all the records. If there is not a matching record for a technician in the other table, the columns display empty fields next to the technician's name.

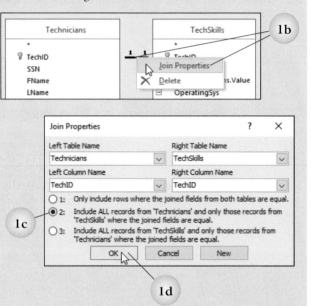

    d. Click OK.

    e. Notice that the join line between the two tables now displays with an arrow pointing to the joined field in the TechSkills table.

    f. Run the query.

2. Minimize the Navigation pane and then compare your results with the query results datasheet displayed in Figure 3.4. Notice that 11 records display in this datasheet, whereas only 8 records display in the query results from Project 2a.

3. Click the File tab and then click the *Save As* option. At the Save As backstage area, click *Save Object As* in the *File Types* section and then click the Save As button. At the Save As dialog box, type AllTechSkills in the *Save 'TechSpecialties' to* text box and then click OK.

4. Close the query.

5. Expand the Navigation pane.

Check Your Work

> Do not assume that a left join always occurs with the table that is the left table in the query window. Although Technicians was the left table in the Project 2b query window, the term *left* refers to the table that represents the "one" side (primary table) in the relationship.

Adding Tables to and Removing Tables from a Query

Show Table

Open a query in Design view to add a table to a query. Click the Show Table button in the Query Setup group on the Query Tools Design tab and then add the desired table using the Show Table dialog box. Close the Show Table dialog box when finished.

To remove a table from a query, click any field within the table field list box to activate the table in the query window and then press the Delete key. The table is removed from the window and all the fields associated with the table that were added to the query design grid are automatically removed. A table can also be removed by right-clicking the table in the query window and then clicking *Remove Table* at the shortcut menu.

Project 2c Selecting Records in a Query Using a Right Outer Join

1. With **3-RSRCompServ.accdb** open, modify an existing query to create a new query to check for work orders that have not been assigned to a technician by completing the following steps:
   a. Open the TechSpecialties query in Design view.
   b. Right-click the *TechSkills* table name in the table field list box in the query window and then click *Remove Table* at the shortcut menu. Notice that the last five columns are removed from the query design grid along with the table.

   c. Click the Show Table button in the Query Setup group on the Query Tools Design tab.
   d. At the Show Table dialog box, double-click *WorkOrders*, click the Close button, and then drag down the bottom border of the WorkOrders table field list box until all the fields are visible.
   e. Double-click the join line between the two tables.
   f. At the Join Properties dialog box, click option *3*. Option *3* includes all the records from the WorkOrders table and only those records from the Technicians table for which the joined fields are equal. The right table (WorkOrders) is the table that will show all the records. If a work order does not have a matching record in the other table, the columns display empty fields for the technician names.
   g. Click OK.
   h. Notice that the join line between the two tables now displays with an arrow pointing to the joined field in the Technicians table.
   i. Add the following fields from the WorkOrders table to the query design grid in this order: *WO, WODate, Descr*.
2. Click the File tab and then click the *Save As* option. At the Save As backstage area, click *Save Object As* in the *File Types* section and then click the Save As button. At the Save As dialog box, type UnassignedWO in the *Save 'TechSpecialties' to* text box and then click OK.
3. Run the query.

4. Compare your results with the partial query results datasheet shown in Figure 3.5. Notice that the first four records in the query results datasheet have empty fields in the *First Name* column and *Last Name* column.
5. Double-click the right boundary of the *Description* column to adjust the width and then print the query results datasheet with the right margin set to 0.5 inch.
6. Close the query. Click Yes to save the changes.

Check Your Work

Do not assume that a right join always occurs with the table that is the right table in the query window. Although WorkOrders was the right table in the Project 2c query window, the term *right* refers to the table that represents the "many" side (related table) in the relationship.

Creating a Self-Join Query

Tutorial

Creating a Self-Join Query and Assigning Aliases

Hint In a self-join query, the two fields joined must have the same data type.

Quick Steps

Create a Self-Join Query and Assign Aliases
1. Create query in Design view.
2. Add two copies of table to query.
3. Right-click second table name.
4. Click *Properties*.
5. Click in *Alias* property box and delete existing table name.
6. Type alias table name.
7. Close Property Sheet.
8. Drag field name from left table to field name with matching values in right table.
9. Add fields to query design grid.
10. Save and run query.

Assume that a table has two fields that contain similar field values. For example, look at the *Technician ID* column and *Tier 2 Supervisor* column in the Technicians table datasheet, shown in Figure 3.7. Notice that each column contains a technician's ID number. Tier 2 supervisors are senior technicians who are called in when a work order is too complex for a regular technician to solve. The ID number in the *Tier 2 Supervisor* column is the ID of the senior technician who is assigned to the technician.

Viewing the list of technicians with the Tier 2 supervisors' last names may be more informative than viewing the list with the supervisors' ID numbers. If a table has matching values in two separate fields, create a self-join query; this creates a relationship between fields in the same table. To create a self-join query, add two copies of the same table to the query window. The second occurrence of the table is named using the original table name with *_1* added to the end. Assign an alias to the second table to provide it with a more descriptive name in the query. To join the two tables, drag the field with matching values from one table field list to the other. Add the required fields to the query design grid and then run the query.

Creating an Alias for a Table

An alias is an additional name that can be used to reference a table in a query. The alias is temporary and applies only to the query. Generally, the reason for creating an alias is to assign a shorter name to a table (or a more descriptive name, in the case of a self-join query). For example, one of the tables used in the query in Project 2d is named *Technicians_1*. Assign the table a more descriptive name, such as *Supervisors*, to more accurately describe its role in the query.

To assign an alias to a table, right-click the table name in the query window and then click *Properties* at the shortcut menu to open the Property Sheet task pane. Click in the *Alias* property box, delete the existing table name, and then type the reference name of the table. Access replaces all the occurrences of the table name in the query design grid with the alias.

Figure 3.7 Technicians Table Datasheet with the Fields Used in a Self-Join Query

Technician ID	SSN	First Name	Last Name	Street Address	City	State	ZIP Code	Home Phone	Cell Phone	📎	Tier 2 Supervisor
⊞ 01	000-45-5368	Pat	Hynes	206-31 Woodland Street	Detroit	MI	48202-1138	313-555-6874	313-555-6412	📎(1)	03
⊞ 02	000-47-3258	Hui	Chen	12905 Hickory Street	Detroit	MI	48205-3462	313-555-7468	313-555-5234	📎(1)	06
⊞ 03	000-62-7468	Kayla	Blewett	1310 Jarvis Street	Detroit	MI	48220-2011	313-555-3265	313-555-6486	📎(1)	
⊞ 04	000-33-1485	Mihir	Patel	8213 Elgin Street	Detroit	MI	48234-4092	313-555-7458	313-555-6385	📎(1)	11
⊞ 05	000-48-7850	Madir	Sadiku	8190 Kenwood Street	Detroit	MI	48220-1132	313-555-6327	313-555-8569	📎(1)	03
⊞ 06	000-75-8412	Brody	Stewart	3522 Moore Place	Detroit	MI	48208-1032	313-555-7499	313-555-3625	📎(1)	
⊞ 07	000-55-1248	Ana	Takacs	14902 Hampton Court	Detroit	MI	48215-3616	313-555-6142	313-555-4586	📎(0)	11
⊞ 08	000-63-1247	Marty	O'Leary	14000 Vernon Drive	Detroit	MI	48237-1320	313-555-9856	313-555-4125	📎(0)	11
⊞ 09	000-84-1254	Armando	Colacci	17302 Windsor Avenue	Detroit	MI	48224-2257	313-555-9641	313-555-8796	📎(0)	06
⊞ 10	000-43-5789	Kelsey	Eastman	550 Montclair Street	Detroit	MI	48214-3274	313-555-6315	313-555-7411	📎(2)	06
⊞ 11	000-65-4185	Dana	Westman	18101 Keeler Streeet	Detroit	MI	48223-1322	313-555-5488	313-555-4158	📎(0)	
✳										📎(0)	

> These two fields contain technician ID numbers. Tier 2 supervisors are senior-level technicians who are assigned to handle complex cases for regular technicians.

Project 2d Creating a Self-Join Query

Part 4 of 4

1. With **3-RSRCompServ.accdb** open, create a self-join query to display the last name of the Tier 2 supervisor instead of his or her ID number by completing the following steps:
   a. Create a new query in Design view.
   b. At the Show Table dialog box, double-click *Technicians* two times to add two copies of the Technicians table to the query and then close the Show Table dialog box. Notice that the second copy of the table is named *Technicians_1*.
   c. Drag down the bottom borders of both table field list boxes until all the field names are visible.
   d. Create an alias for the second table by completing the following steps:
      1) Right-click the *Technicians_1* table name and then click *Properties* at the shortcut menu.
      2) Select the current name in the *Alias* property box in the Property Sheet task pane and then type Supervisors.
      3) Close the Property Sheet task pane.

e. Drag the field named *Tier2Supv* from the Technicians table field list box at the left to the field named *TechID* in the Supervisors table field list box at the right. This creates a join line between the two tables.

f. Add the *FName* and *LName* fields from the Technicians table to the query design grid.

g. Add the *LName* field from the Supervisors table to the query design grid.

2. Run the query. The last names displayed in the second *Last Name* column represent the *Tier2Supv* names.

3. Switch to Design view.

4. Right-click the second *LName* in the *Field* row (from the Supervisors table) in the query design grid and then click *Properties* at the shortcut menu. Click in the *Caption* property box in the Property Sheet task pane, type Tier 2 Supervisor, and then close the Property Sheet task pane.

5. Save the query. Type Tier2Supervisors at the Save As dialog box and then click OK.

6. Run the query.

7. Double-click the right boundary of the *Tier 2 Supervisor* column to adjust the width and then compare your results with the datasheet shown at the right.

8. Close the query. Click Yes to save changes.

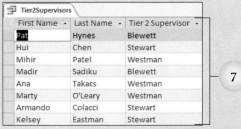

Check Your Work

Running a Query with No Established Relationship

If a query is created from two tables for which no join has been established, Access will not know how to relate the records in the tables. When there is no relationship, Access produces a datasheet representing every possible combination of records between the two tables. For example, if one table contains 20 records, the other table contains 10 records, and no join has been established between the tables, Access produces a query results datasheet containing 200 records (20 × 10). This type of query is called a *cross product query* or *Cartesian product query*. In most cases, the results of such a query provide data that serves no purpose.

If two tables are added to a query and no join line appears, create a join by dragging a field from one table field list box to a compatible field in the other table field list box. The two fields should contain the same data type and be logically related in some way. If no join can logically be established and a many-to-many relationship exists between the tables, add a junction table to the query.

<table>
<tr><td>

Project 3 Calculate Work Order Totals

</td><td>

3 Parts

</td></tr>
</table>

You will use a subquery nested within another query to calculate the total amount earned from each work order. You will also use conditional logic to apply a discount if certain criteria are met.

Preview Finished Project

Tutorial

Creating and
Using Subqueries

Tutorial

Review: Performing
Calcuations in a
Query

Creating and Using Subqueries

When performing multiple calculations based on numeric fields, a user may decide to create a separate query for each individual calculation and then use subqueries to generate the final total. The term *subquery* is used to refer to a query nested inside another query. Using subqueries to break calculations into individual objects allows a calculated field to be reused in multiple queries.

For example, assume that the total amount for each work order needs to be calculated. The WorkOrders table contains fields with the number of hours for each service call, the labor rate, and the total value of the parts used. To find the total for each work order, the total labor needs to be calculated. This is done by multiplying the hours times the rate and then adding the parts value to the total labor value. However, the total labor value should be in a separate query so that other calculations can be performed, such as finding the average, maximum, and minimum labor on work orders. To be able to reuse the total labor value, create the calculated field in its own query.

Quick Steps

Create a Subquery
1. Start new query in Design view.
2. At Show Table dialog box, click Queries tab.
3. Double-click query to be used as subquery.
4. Add other queries or tables as required.
5. Close Show Table dialog box.
6. Add fields as required.
7. Save and run query.

 Builder

Once the query is created to calculate the total labor, nest the query inside another query to add the labor to the parts and then calculate the total for each work order. Creating subqueries provides flexibility in reusing calculations, thus avoiding duplication of effort and reducing the potential for calculation errors.

Level 1, Chapter 3 demonstrated how to insert a calculated field in a query. Recall that the format for inserting an equation in a query is to type in a blank *Field* row the new field name followed by a colon and then the equation with the field names in square brackets—for example, *Total:[Sales]+[SalesTax]*.

Project 3a Creating a Query to Calculate Total Labor

Part 1 of 3

1. With **3-RSRCompServ.accdb** open, create a query to calculate the total labor for each work order by completing the following steps:
   a. Create a new query in Design view. At the Show Table dialog box, add the WorkOrders table to the query window and then close the Show Table dialog box.
   b. Drag down the bottom border of the WorkOrders table field list box until all the fields are visible.
   c. Add the following fields to the query design grid in this order: *WO, ServDate, Hours, Rate*.
   d. Click in the blank *Field* row next to *Rate* in the query design grid and then click the Builder button in the Query Setup group on the Query Tools Design tab.
   e. In the Expression Builder dialog box, type TotalLabor:[Hours]*[Rate].
   f. Click OK.

f. Expand the width of the calculated column until the entire formula in the *Field* row can be seen.
2. Run the query and view the query results. Notice that the *TotalLabor* column does not display a consistent number of decimal values.
3. Switch to Design view.
4. Format the *Total Labor* column by completing the following steps:
   a. Activate the field by clicking in the *Total Labor* field row.
   b. Click the Property Sheet button in the Show/Hide group on the Query Tools Design tab.
   c. Click in the *Format* property box in the Property Sheet task pane, click the option box arrow that appears, and then click *Standard* at the drop-down list.
   d. Type Total Labor in the *Caption* property box.
   e. Close the Property Sheet task pane.
5. Save the query. Type TotalLabor at the Save As dialog box and then click OK.
6. Run the query. Notice that the last four rows contain no values because the service calls have not yet been completed.
7. Switch to Design view. Click in the *Criteria* row in the *Hours* column, type >0, and then press the Enter key.
8. Save the revised query and then run it.
9. Close the query.

Check Your Work

Project 3b Creating a Subquery

Part 2 of 3

1. With **3-RSRCompServ.accdb** open, create a new query to calculate the total value of each work order using the TotalLabor query as a subquery by completing the following steps:
   a. Create a new query in Design view.
   b. At the Show Table dialog box, click the Queries tab.
   c. Double-click *TotalLabor* in the queries list box.
   d. Click the Tables tab.
   e. Double-click *WorkOrders* and then close the Show Table dialog box. Notice that Access automatically joins the two objects at the *WO* field.

subquery object

Access automatically joins the two objects at the *WO* field.

2. Add fields from the TotalLabor subquery and WorkOrders table by completing the following steps:

a. Double-click the asterisk (*) at the top of the TotalLabor table field list box. Access adds the entry *TotalLabor.** to the first column in the query design grid. This entry adds all the fields from the query. Individual columns do not display in the grid but when the query is run, the datasheet will show all the fields.

b. Run the query. Notice that the query results datasheet shows all five columns from the TotalLabor query.

c. Switch to Design view. Apply the Currency format to the *Total Labor* column in this new query. To do this, add the column to the query design grid as an individual field and not as a group by completing the following steps:

  1) Right-click in the field selector bar (the gray bar above the *Field* row) for the *TotalLabor.** column and then click *Cut* at the shortcut menu to remove the column from the query design grid.

  2) Add the following fields from the TotalLabor query field list box to the query design grid in this order: *WO, ServDate, TotalLabor.*

  3) Format the *TotalLabor* column by applying the Currency format.

d. Drag down the bottom border of the WorkOrders table field list box until all the fields are visible and then double-click *Parts* to add the field to the query design grid.

3. Create a calculated field to add the total labor and parts by completing the following steps:

a. Click in the blank *Field* row next to *Parts* in the query design grid, type TotalWorkOrder:[TotalLabor]+[Parts], and then press the Enter key.

b. Expand the width of the *TotalWorkOrder* column until the entire formula is visible.

c. Format the *TotalWorkOrder* column by applying the Currency format.

d. Type Total Work Order in the *Caption* property box.

e. Close the Property Sheet task pane.

4. Save the query. Type TotalWorkOrders at the Save As dialog box and then click OK. Run the query.

5. Double-click the right boundary for the *TotalWorkOrder* column to adjust the width.

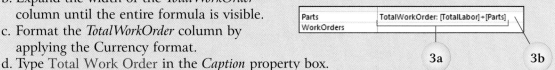

6. Close the query. Click Yes to save changes.

Check Your Work

Hint Subqueries are not restricted to use in nested calculations. Use a subquery for any combination of fields that you want to reuse in multiple queries.

Small queries and subqueries are useful because they are easier to build and troubleshoot than large queries. Subqueries are also useful when creating a complex query. They can be created to build and test sections individually and then combined into the final larger query.

Creating a Query Using Conditional Logic

Using conditional logic in an Access query is similar to using a logical formula in Excel. Using conditional logic requires Access to perform a calculation based on the outcome of a logical or conditional test. One calculation is performed if the test proves true and another calculation is performed if the test proves false. The structure of the IF function is =IIF(logical_test,value_if_true,value_if_false). Access uses an *Immediate IF* (IIF) function to differentiate between this function and the Visual Basic for Applications (VBA) IF function. VBA is discussed further in Chapter 7. Logical functions are also similar to calculated fields in Access in that the new field name is followed by a colon and field names are enclosed in square brackets.

In Project 3c, a 2% discount will be processed on the total cost of the work order if the cost of the labor is greater than $80. The following IF function will be used to calculate this discount, where *Labor>80* in the field that will store the discounted total: *Labor>80:IIF([TotalLabor]>80,[TotalWorkOrder]-([TotalWorkOrder]*.02),[TotalWorkOrder])*.

To determine whether a discount should be provided, Access first tests the value of the record in the *TotalLabor* field to see if it is greater than $80. If the condition proves true, Access populates the *Labor>80* field with the value from the *TotalWorkOrder* field minus 2%. This is the discounted total that the customer owes. If the value in the *TotalLabor* field is not greater than $80, the condition proves false. Access populates the *Labor>80* field with the same value that appears in the *TotalWorkOrder* field since the work order did not qualify for a discount.

Figure 3.8 shows the TotalWorkOrders query after the IF function has been applied. For work order 65021, the value in the *TotalLabor* field is $113.75. Since this value is greater than $80, the test is true and Access returns the value_if_true value, or the value in the *TotalWorkOrder* field minus 2% of the value ($113.75 – $2.27 = $111.48). For work order 65012, the value in the *TotalLabor* field is $43.75. Since the test is false, Access returns the value_if_false value, or the value in the *TotalWorkOrder* field ($53.90).

Figure 3.8 Project 3c TotalWorkOrders Query in Datasheet View

Work Order	Service Date	Total Labor	Parts	Total Work Order	Work Order w/Disc
65012	Fri, Sep 07 2018	$43.75	$10.15	$53.90	$53.90
65013	Mon, Sep 10 2018	$16.25	$42.75	$59.00	$59.00
65014	Mon, Sep 10 2018	$61.25	$62.77	$124.02	$124.02
65015	Tue, Sep 11 2018	$78.75	$0.00	$78.75	$78.75
65016	Tue, Sep 11 2018	$35.00	$48.75	$83.75	$83.75
65017	Sat, Sep 15 2018	$18.75	$55.87	$74.62	$74.62
65018	Sat, Sep 15 2018	$25.00	$0.00	$25.00	$25.00
65019	Mon, Sep 17 2018	$87.50	$0.00	$87.50	$85.75
65020	Mon, Sep 17 2018	$37.50	$62.77	$100.27	$100.27
65021	Tue, Sep 18 2018	$113.75	$0.00	$113.75	$111.48
65022	Sat, Sep 22 2018	$52.50	$55.47	$107.97	$107.97
65023	Sun, Sep 23 2018	$43.75	$62.50	$106.25	$106.25

The caption *Work Order w/Disc* was added to the *Labor>80* field.

Since the *Total Labor* value is less than $80, Access returns the value from the *Total Work Order* field in the *Work Order w/Disc* field.

Since the *Total Labor* value is greater than $80, Access subtracts 2% from the *Total Work Order* field and displays this value in the *Work Order w/Disc* field.

1. With **3-RSRCompServ.accdb** open, open the TotalWorkOrders query in Design view.
2. Modify the TotalWorkOrders query to calculate a 2% discount if the total labor cost is greater than $80 by completing the following steps:
   a. Right-click in the blank *Field* row next to *TotalWorkOrder* in the query design grid and then click *Zoom* at the drop-down list.

   b. Type Labor>80:IIF([TotalLabor]>80,[TotalWorkOrder]-([TotalWorkOrder]*.02), [TotalWorkOrder]).
   c. Click OK.

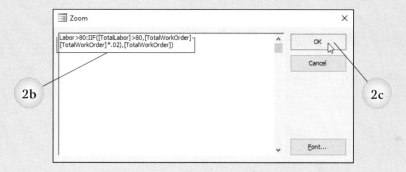

   d. Run the query. If an error message indicating that invalid syntax was entered or an Enter Parameter Value dialog box displays, close the message box and check to ensure that the formula was typed correctly.
3. Switch to Design view, open the Property Sheet task pane for the *Labor>80* column, and then make the following changes:
   a. Apply the Currency format.
   b. Type Work Order w/Disc in the *Caption* property box.
   c. Close the Property Sheet task pane.
4. Run the query.
5. Double-click the right boundary of the *Work Order w/Disc* column to adjust the width. Compare your results with the query results data displayed in Figure 3.8.
6. Print the query results datasheet with the right margin set to 0.5 inch.
7. Close the query. Click Yes to save changes.

Check Your Work

Project 4 Query a Multiple-Value Field

You will select records using a multiple-value field in a query.

1 Part

Preview Finished Project

Tutorial

Using a Multiple-
Value Field in a
Query

Quick Steps

**Show a Multiple-
Value Field in
Separate Rows in
a Query**

1. Open query in
   Design view.
2. Click in *Field* row of
   multiple-value field
   in design grid.
3. Move insertion point
   to end of field name.
4. Type period (.).
5. Press Enter to
   accept *.Value*.
6. Save query.

Using a Multiple-Value Field in a Query

Recall from Chapter 2 that a multiple-value field displays a lookup list that allows for more than one check box to be checked. In a query, a multiple-value field can display as it does in a table datasheet, with the multiple field values in the same column separated by commas. Or each field value can be shown in a separate row.

To show each value in a separate row, add *.Value* at the end of the multiple-value field name in the *Field* row in the query design grid. Figure 3.9 displays the query design grid for the query used in Project 4 that displays each entry in the *OperatingSys* field in a separate row in the datasheet.

To select records using criteria in a multiple-value field, type the criteria using the same procedures as for a single-value field. For example, in the TechSpecialties query, typing *Windows 10* in the *Criteria* row in the *OperatingSys* column causes Access to return the records of any technician with Windows 10 certification as one of the multiple field values.

Figure 3.9 Project 4 Query Design Grid

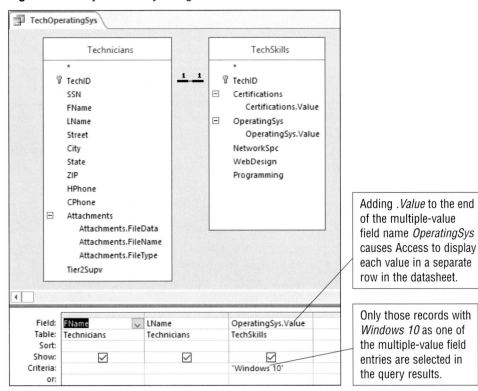

Adding *.Value* to the end of the multiple-value field name *OperatingSys* causes Access to display each value in a separate row in the datasheet.

Only those records with *Windows 10* as one of the multiple-value field entries are selected in the query results.

1. With **3-RSRCompServ.accdb** open, open the TechSpecialties query in Design view.
2. Right-click in the field selector bar above the *Certifications* field and then click *Cut* at the shortcut menu to remove the field from the query design grid.

3. Delete the *NetworkSpc*, *WebDesign*, and *Programming* columns from the query design grid. Refer to Step 2.
4. Run the query. Notice that each record in the *Operating Systems* column displays the multiple values separated by commas.
5. Switch to Design view.
6. Click in the *OperatingSys* field row in the query design grid, move the insertion point to the end of the field name, and then type a period (.). Access automatically adds *.Value* to the end of the name in the *Field* row. Press the Enter key to accept *.Value* at the end of the field name. ***Note: When creating a query from scratch, drag the multiple-value field name with the .Value property already attached from the table field list box to the query design grid.***

7. Click the File tab and then click the *Save As* option. At the Save As backstage area, click *Save Object As* in the *File Types* section and then click the Save As button. At the Save As dialog box, type TechOperatingSys in the *Save 'TechSpecialties' to* text box and then click OK.
8. Run the query. Notice that each entry in the multiple-value field now displays in a separate row.
9. Switch to Design view.
10. Click in the *Criteria* row in the *OperatingSys.Value* column in the query design grid, type Windows 10, and then press the Enter key. Access adds quotation marks around the text.
11. Run the query. Notice that the column title for the multiple-value field in the query results datasheet is now *TechSkills.OperatingSys.Value*. Change the column heading for the field by completing the following steps:
    a. Switch to Design view.
    b. Click in the *OperatingSys.Value* field row in the query design grid.
    c. Press the F4 function key to open the Property Sheet task pane.

    d. Click in the *Caption* property box, type Operating System, and then press the Enter key.
    e. Close the Property Sheet task pane.
12. Run the query.
13. Print the query results datasheet and then close the query. Click Yes to save changes.

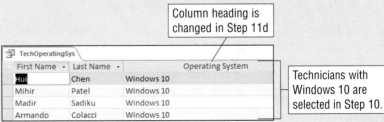

Column heading is changed in Step 11d

Technicians with Windows 10 are selected in Step 10.

Check Your Work

Project 5 **Modify Records Using Action Queries**   **4 Parts**

You will create a new table, add and delete records, and update field values using action queries.

Preview Finished Project

Performing Operations Using Action Queries

An action query is used to perform an operation on a group of records. Building an action query is similar to building a select query but with the extra step of specifying the action to perform on the group of selected records. Four types of action queries are available, as described in Table 3.1.

To create an action query, first build a select query by adding tables, fields, and criteria to the query design grid. Run the select query to make sure the correct group of records is targeted for action. After verifying the results that the proper records will be modified, change the query type using the Make Table, Append, Update, or Delete button in the Query Type group on the Query Tools Design tab, shown in Figure 3.10.

Once the query type has been changed to an action query, clicking the Run button causes Access to perform the make table, append, update, or delete operation. Once an action query has been run, the results cannot be reversed.

When you build queries, Access creates code behind the scenes using Structured Query Language (SQL). View the code by clicking the View Button arrow and then clicking *SQL View*. Three queries, the Union, Pass-Through, and Data Definition

Table 3.1 Types of Action Queries

Query Type	Description
make table	A new table is created from selected records in an existing table—for example, a new table that combines fields from two other tables in the database.
append	Selected records are added to the end of an existing table. This action is similar to performing a copy and paste.
update	A global change is made to the selected group of records based on an update expression—for example, increasing the labor rate by 10% in one step.
delete	The selected group of records is deleted from a table.

Figure 3.10 Query Type Group on the Query Tools Design Tab

Use these buttons to perform operations on a group of selected records.

These are SQL-specific queries that are created in an SQL window.

By default, new queries are select queries until another query type is chosen.

A crosstab query is used to summarize data in two fields.

queries, are created directly in the SQL view and can be initiated using buttons on the Query Tools Design tab in the Query Type group as shown in Figure 3.10.

Tutorial

Creating a Make Table Query

 Make Table

Creating a New Table Using a Query

A make table query creates a new table from selected records in the same database or another database. This type of query is useful for creating a history table before purging old records that are no longer required. The history table can be placed in the same database or in another database used as an archive copy.

Once a select query is created that will extract the records to be copied to a new table, click the Make Table button in the Query Type group on the Query Tools Design tab. This opens the Make Table dialog box, shown in Figure 3.11. Enter a table name, choose the destination database, and then click OK. Once a make table query has been run, do not double-click the query name in the Navigation pane; doing so instructs Access to run the query again. Open the query in Design view to make changes to the criteria and/or query type if the query needs to be run again.

Quick Steps

Create a Make Table Query
1. Create query in Design view.
2. Add table(s) to query.
3. Add fields to query design grid.
4. If necessary, enter criteria to select records.
5. Run query.
6. Switch to Design view.
7. Click Make Table button.
8. Type table name.
9. If necessary, select destination database.
10. Click OK.
11. Run query.
12. Click Yes.
13. Save query.

Figure 3.11 Make Table Dialog Box

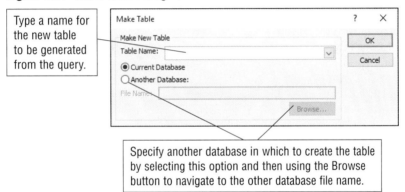

Type a name for the new table to be generated from the query.

Specify another database in which to create the table by selecting this option and then using the Browse button to navigate to the other database file name.

Project 5a Creating a New Table Using a Query   Part 1 of 4

1. With **3-RSRCompServ.accdb** open, create a select query to select all the work order records for September 1, 2018 through September 15, 2018 by completing the following steps:
   a. Create a new query in Design view. Add the WorkOrders table to the query window and then close the Show Table dialog box. Drag down the bottom border of the table field list box until all the field names can be seen.
   b. Double-click the WorkOrders table field list box title bar. This selects all the fields within the table.
   c. Position the mouse pointer within the selected field names in the table field list box and then drag the pointer to the first column in the query design grid. All the fields in the table are added to the query design grid.
   d. Click in the *Criteria* row in the *ServDate* column, type Between September 1, 2018 and September 15, 2018, and then press the Enter key.

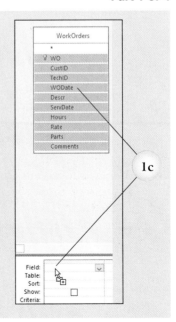

e. Run the query. The query results datasheet displays seven records.

Work Order	Customer ID	Technician ID	WO Date	Description	Service Date	Hours	Rate	Parts
65012	1000	11	Fri, Sep 07 2018	Biannual computer maintenance	Fri, Sep 07 2018	1.25	35.00	$10.15
65013	1000	10	Fri, Sep 07 2018	Replace keyboard	Mon, Sep 10 2018	0.50	32.50	$42.75
65014	1005	02	Mon, Sep 10 2018	Replace power supply	Mon, Sep 10 2018	1.75	35.00	$62.77
65015	1008	04	Mon, Sep 10 2018	Restore operating system	Tue, Sep 11 2018	2.25	35.00	$0.00
65016	1010	06	Tue, Sep 11 2018	Install upgraded video card	Tue, Sep 11 2018	1.00	35.00	$48.75
65017	1015	08	Fri, Sep 14 2018	Replace DVD drive	Sat, Sep 15 2018	0.75	25.00	$55.87
65018	1020	10	Fri, Sep 14 2018	Upgrade Office suite	Sat, Sep 15 2018	1.00	25.00	$0.00

1e

f. It has been decided not to archive the *Comments* field data. Switch to Design view and then delete the *Comments* column from the query design grid.

2. Make a new table from the selected records and store the table in a history database to be used for archiving purposes by completing the following steps:

a. If necessary, switch to Design view.

b. Click the Make Table button in the Query Type group on the Query Tools Design tab.

c. With the insertion point positioned in the *Table Name* text box, type Sept2018WO.

d. Click the *Another Database* option and then click the Browse button.

e. At the Make Table dialog box, navigate to the AL2C3 folder on your storage medium and then double-click the file named *3-RSRCompServHistory.accdb*.

Make Table dialog box:

2c — Make New Table — Table Name: Sept2018WO

2d — ○ Current Database / ⦿ Another Database:

2e — File Name: S:\AL2C3\3-RSRCompServHistory.accdb — Browse...

2f — OK / Cancel

f. Click OK.

g. Run the query.

h. Click Yes at the Microsoft Access message box indicating that seven rows are about to be pasted to a new table. You will verify that the query has run and created a table in later steps.

3. Save the query. Type Sept2018MakeTable at the Save As dialog box and then click OK.

4. Close the query.

5. Close **3-RSRCompServ.accdb**.

6. Open **3-RSRCompServHistory.accdb** and enable the content. Click OK to continue if a message appears stating that Access has to update object dependencies.

7. Open the Sept2018WO table in Datasheet view.

8. Review the records that were copied to the new table from the make table query that was run in Step 2g.

9. Close the table.

10. Close **3-RSRCompServHistory.accdb**.

Check Your Work

Creating a Delete Query

Creating a Delete
Query

Delete

A delete query is used to delete in one step a group of records that meet specified criteria. Use this action query when the records to be deleted can be selected using a criteria statement. Using a query to remove the records is more efficient and reduces the chances of removing a record in error, which can happen when records are deleted manually.

The make table query used in Project 5a created a duplicate copy of the records in the new table. The original records still exist in the WorkOrders table. The make table query used to archive the records can be changed to a delete query and then used to remove the records from the original table.

In the Navigation pane, an action query name displays with a black exclamation mark next to an icon. The icon indicates the type of action that will be performed when the query is run.

Quick Steps

Create a Delete Query
1. Create query in Design view.
2. Add table to query.
3. Add fields to query design grid.
4. Enter criteria to select records.
5. Run query.
6. Switch to Design view.
7. Click Delete button.
8. Run query.
9. Click Yes.
10. Save query.

Project 5b Deleting Records Using a Query

Part 2 of 4

1. Open **3-RSRCompServ.accdb** and enable the content.
2. Right-click *Sept2018MakeTable* in the Queries group in the Navigation pane and then click *Design View* at the shortcut menu. Do not double-click to open/run it or Access will try to make a new table.
3. Click the Delete button in the Query Type group on the Query Tools Design tab.
4. Click the File tab and then click the *Save As* option. At the Save As backstage area, click *Save Object As* in the *File Types* section and then click the Save As button. At the Save As dialog box, type Sept2018Delete in the *Save 'Sept2018MakeTable' to* text box and then click OK.
5. With the Query Tools Design tab selected, run the query.
6. At the Microsoft Access message box indicating that seven rows are about to be deleted from the table and that the action cannot be reversed, click Yes to delete the selected records.

7. Close the query.
8. Open the WorkOrders table. Notice that no records have a service date before September 15, 2018.
9. Close the table.

Check Your Work

Tutorial

Creating an
Append Query

 Append

Quick Steps

**Create an Append
Query**
1. Create query in
   Design view.
2. Add table to query.
3. Add fields to query
   design grid.
4. Enter criteria to
   select records.
5. Run query.
6. Switch to Design
   view.
7. Click Append
   button.
8. Type table name.
9. Select destination
   database.
10. Click OK.
11. Run query.
12. Click Yes.
13. Save query.

Creating an Append Query

An append query is used to copy a group of records from one or more tables to the end of an existing table. Consider using an append query when a duplicate copy of records needs to be made. For example, in Project 5a, the make table query was used to create a new table to store archived records. Once a table exists, use append queries to copy subsequent archived records to the end of the existing history table.

Click the Append button in the Query Type group on the Query Tools Design tab to open the Append dialog box. This dialog box opens with the same options as the Make Table dialog box, as shown in Figure 3.12. The receiving table should have the same structure as the query from which the records are selected.

Figure 3.12 Append Dialog Box

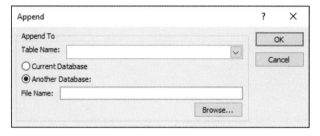

Project 5c Adding Records to a Table Using a Query   Part 3 of 4

1. With **3-RSRCompServ.accdb** open, open the Sept2018MakeTable query in Design view.
2. Modify the criteria to select work order records for the last half of September 2018 by completing the following steps:
   a. Expand the width of the *ServDate* column until the entire criteria statement can be seen.
   b. Click in the *Criteria* row in the *ServDate* field, insert and delete text as necessary to modify the criteria statement to read *Between #9/16/2018# And #9/30/2018#*, and then press the Enter key.
3. Click the Append button in the Query Type group on the Query Tools Design tab.
4. Since the query is being changed from a make table query, Access inserts the same table name and database that were used to create the table in Project 5a. Click OK to accept the table name *Sept2018WO* and the file name *3-RSRCompServHistory.accdb*.
5. Click the File tab and then click the *Save As* option. At the Save As backstage area, click *Save Object As* in the *File Types* section and then click the Save As button. At the Save As dialog box, type Sept2018Append in the *Save 'Sept2018MakeTable' to* text box and then click OK.

When appending to a table in an existing database, select the table name from this drop-down list.

6. With the Query Tools Design tab selected, run the query.
7. Click Yes at the Microsoft Access message box indicating that eight rows are about to be appended and that the action cannot be undone.
8. Close the query.
9. Close **3-RSRCompServ.accdb**.
10. Open **3-RSRCompServHistory.accdb**.
11. Open the Sept2018WO table and then print the datasheet in landscape orientation.
12. Close the table.
13. Close **3-RSRCompServHistory.accdb**.

Check Your Work

Tutorial

Creating an
Update Query

 Update

Quick Steps

Create an Update Query
1. Create query in Design view.
2. Add table to query.
3. Add fields to query design grid.
4. Enter criteria to select records.
5. Run query.
6. Switch to Design view.
7. Click Update button.
8. Click in *Update To* row in field to be changed.
9. Type update expression.
10. Run query.
11. Click Yes.
12. Save query.

Creating an Update Query

When the change needed to a group of records can be selected in a query and is the same for all the records, instruct Access to modify the data using an update query. Making a global change using an update query is efficient and reduces the potential for errors that can occur from manually editing multiple records. Increase or decrease fields such as quotas, rates, and selling prices by adding or subtracting specific amounts or by multiplying by desired percentages.

Clicking the Update button in the Query Type group on the Query Tools Design tab causes an *Update To* row to appear in the query design grid. Click in the *Update To* row in the column to be modified and then type the expression that will change the field values as needed. Run the query to make the global change.

Project 5d Changing Service Plan Rates Using an Update Query   Part 4 of 4

1. Open **3-RSRCompServ.accdb** and enable the content.
2. Open the FeesSCPlans table and review the current values in the *Rate* column. For example, notice that the current rate for Plan A's six-month term for one computer is $58.00. Close the table after reviewing the current rates.
3. Create an update query to increase the Plan A service contract rates by 4% by completing the following steps:
   a. Create a new query in Design view.
   b. Add the FeesSCPlans table to the query and then close the Show Table dialog box.
   c. Add the *Plan* field and *Rate* field to the query design grid.

d. Click in the *Criteria* row in the *Plan* column, type A, and then click in the *Criteria* row in the next column in the query design grid. ***Note: The AutoComplete feature will show a list of functions as soon as A is typed. Ignore the AutoComplete drop-down list, since a mathematical expression is not being entered for the criteria. However, pressing the Enter key causes Access to add Abs to the Criteria row. Clicking in another box in the query design grid will remove the AutoComplete drop-down list.***

Field:	Plan	Rate
Table:	FeesSCPlans	FeesSCPlans
Sort:		
Show:	☑	☑
Criteria:	"A"	
or:		

3d

e. Run the query. Review the four records shown in the query results datasheet.

Query1	
Plan ▾	Rate ▾
A	$58.00
A	$69.50
A	$169.50
A	$340.00

3e

f. Switch to Design view.

g. Click the Update button in the Query Type group on the Query Tools Design tab. Access adds a row labeled *Update To* in the query design grid between the *Table* row and *Criteria* row.

h. Click in the *Update To* row in the *Rate* column, type [Rate]*1.04, and then press the Enter key.

Field:	Plan	Rate
Table:	FeesSCPlans	FeesSCPlans
Update To:		[Rate]*1.04
Criteria:	"A"	

3h

4. Save the query. Type RateUpdate at the Save As dialog box and then click OK.

5. Run the query. Click Yes at the Microsoft Access message stating that four rows are about to be updated.

6. Close the query.

7. Open the FeesSCPlans table. Notice that the rate values for the Plan A records have increased. For example, the value in the *Rate* column for Plan A's six-month term for one computer is now $60.32. Print the datasheet.

8. Close the table and then close **3-RSRCompServ.accdb**.

Check Your Work

♀ Hint Create a backup copy of the database before running an action query.

Exercise caution when running an action query because the queries make changes to database tables. For example, in Project 5d, if the update query is run a second time, the rates for the Plan A service plans will increase another 6%. Once the rates have changed, they cannot be undone. Reversing the update would require creating and running, a mathematical expression in a new update query to remove 6% from the prices.

Chapter Summary

- Select queries extract records that meet specified criteria from a single table or multiple tables.
- A filter can be saved as a query by displaying the filter criteria in a Filter By Form window, clicking the Advanced button, and then clicking *Save As Query* at the drop-down list.
- Parameter queries prompt the user for the criteria by which to select records when the query is run.
- To create a parameter query, type a prompt message enclosed in square brackets in the *Criteria* row of the field to be used to select records.
- Changing the join property can alter the number of records that are displayed in the query results datasheet.

- An inner join displays records only if matching values are found in the joined field in both tables.

- A left outer join displays all the records from the left table and matching records from the related table. Empty fields display if no matching records exist in the related table.

- A right outer join displays all the records from the right table and matching records from the primary table. Empty fields display if no matching records exist in the primary table.

- Click the Show Table button in the Query Setup group on the Query Tools Design tab to add a table or query to the query window.

- Remove a table from a query by clicking a field within the table field list box and then pressing the Delete key or by right-clicking the table and clicking *Remove Table* at the shortcut menu.

- A self-join query is created by adding two copies of the same table to the query window and joining them by dragging the field with matching values from one table field list to the other.

- An alias is another name used to reference a table in a query.

- To assign an alias to a table, right-click the table name in the query window, click *Properties* at the shortcut menu, and then enter the alias for the table in the *Alias* property box in the Property Sheet task pane.

- A query that contains two tables that are not joined creates a cross product or Cartesian product query. This means that Access creates records for every possible combination from both tables—the results of which are generally not meaningful.

- A subquery is a query nested inside another query. Use subqueries to break down a complex query into manageable units. For example, a query with multiple calculations can be created by combining subqueries in which individual calculations are built individually.

- Another reason for using subqueries is to be able to reuse a smaller query in many other queries, avoiding the need to keep recreating the same structure.

- Using conditional logic requires Access to perform a calculation based on the outcome of a logical or conditional test.

- Create select queries on multiple-value fields using the same methods used for single-field criteria.

- Adding *.Value* at the end of a multiple-value field name in the *Field* row in the query design grid causes Access to place each field value in a separate row in the query results datasheet.

- A make table query creates a new table from selected records in the same database or another database using the structure defined in the query design grid.

- Delete a group of records in one step by creating and running a delete query.

- Add a group of records to the end of an existing table in the active database or another database by using an append query.

- An update query allows making a global change to records by entering an expression such as a mathematical formula in the query design grid.

Commands Review

FEATURE	RIBBON TAB, GROUP	BUTTON
advanced filter options	Home, Sort & Filter	
append query	Query Tools Design, Query Type	
create query in Design view	Create, Queries	
delete query	Query Tools Design, Query Type	
make table query	Query Tools Design, Query Type	
run query	Query Tools Design, Results	
show table	Query Tools Design, Query Setup	
update query	Query Tools Design, Query Type	

Workbook

Chapter study tools and assessment activities are available in the *Workbook* ebook. These resources are designed to help you further develop and demonstrate mastery of the skills learned in this chapter.

Microsoft®

Access®

Creating and Using Custom Forms

Performance Objectives

Upon successful completion of Chapter 4, you will be able to:

1 Create a custom form Using Design view and all three form sections

2 Add fields to a form individually and as a group

3 Move, size, and format control objects

4 Change the tab order of fields

5 Add a tab control to a form and insert a subform

6 Add and format a calculation to a custom form

7 Adjust the alignment, sizing, and spacing of control objects

8 Add graphics to a form

9 Anchor a control object to a position in a form

10 Create a datasheet form and restrict form actions

11 Create a blank form

12 Add a list box and a combo box to a form

13 Locate a record using a wildcard character

A form provides an interface for data entry and maintenance that allows users to work more efficiently with data stored in the underlying tables. A form can also include fields from multiple tables, which allows data to be entered in one object and then used to update several tables. Generally, database designers provide forms for users to perform data maintenance and restrict access to tables, protecting the structure and integrity of the database. In this chapter, you will learn how to build custom forms.

SNAP

If you are a SNAP user, launch the Precheck and Tutorials from your Assignments page.

You will create a custom form using Design view that includes subforms in tabbed pages to provide a single object in which data stored in four tables can be entered, viewed, and printed.

Preview Finished Project

Tutorial

Creating Forms
Using Design
View

 Form Design

Quick Steps

**Start a New Form
Using Design View**
1. Click Create tab.
2. Click Form Design
   button.

Creating Forms Using Design View

Access provides several tools that allow the user to build a form quickly, such as the Form tool, Split Form tool, and Form Wizard. A form generated using one of these tools can be modified in Layout view or Design view to customize the content, format, or layout. If several custom options are required in a form, begin in Design view and build the form from scratch. Click the Create tab and then click the Form Design button in the Forms group to begin a new form using the Design view window, shown in Figure 4.1.

In Design view, the form displays the *Detail* section, which is used to display fields from the table associated with the form. Objects are added to the form using buttons in the Controls, Header/Footer, and Tools groups on the Form Design Tools Design tab, shown in Figure 4.2.

Figure 4.1 Form Design View

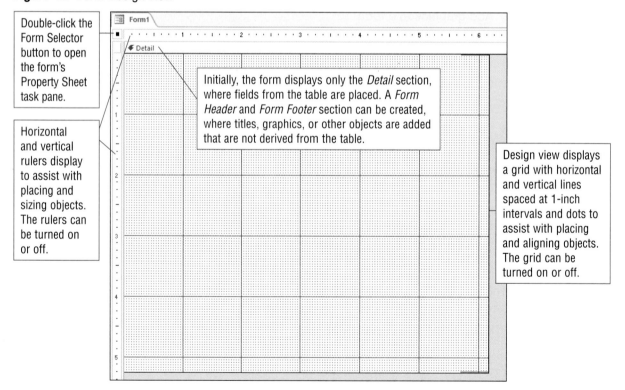

Double-click the Form Selector button to open the form's Property Sheet task pane.

Horizontal and vertical rulers display to assist with placing and sizing objects. The rulers can be turned on or off.

Initially, the form displays only the *Detail* section, where fields from the table are placed. A *Form Header* and *Form Footer* section can be created, where titles, graphics, or other objects are added that are not derived from the table.

Design view displays a grid with horizontal and vertical lines spaced at 1-inch intervals and dots to assist with placing and aligning objects. The grid can be turned on or off.

Figure 4.2 Controls, Header/Footer, and Tools Groups on the Form Design Tools Design Tab

Understanding Bound, Unbound, and Calculated Control Objects

Three types of control objects can be created in a form. A control object in a form may be bound, unbound, or calculated. A bound control object draws and displays data in the control object from the field in the table associated with the control object. In other words, the content that is displayed in the control object in Form view is drawn from a field in a record in a table. An unbound control object is used to display text or graphics and does not rely on a table for its content. For example, a control object that contains an image to enhance the visual appearance of a form or a control object that contains the hours of business for informational purposes are both unbound control objects. A calculated control object displays the result of a mathematical formula. Totals and percentages are examples of calculated control objects.

Creating Titles and Label Control Objects

Title

Label

Click the Title button in the Header/Footer group on the Form Design Tools Design tab to display the *Form Header* and *Form Footer* sections and automatically insert a label control object with the name of the form inside the *Form Header* section. Select the text inside the title control object to type new text, delete existing text, or otherwise modify the default title text. Click the Label button in the Controls group to draw a label control object within any section in the form and then type descriptive or explanatory text inside the control object.

After creating a title or label control object, format the text using buttons in the Font group on the Form Design Tools Format tab. Move and resize the control object to reposition it on the form as needed.

Use the *Form Header* section to create control objects that are to be displayed at the top of the form when scrolling through records in Form view. This section is printed at the top of the page when a record or group of records is printed from Form view. Titles and company logos are generally placed in the *Form Header* section. Use the *Form Footer* section to create control objects that are to be displayed at the bottom of the form when scrolling through records in Form view. This section is printed at the end of a printout when a record or group of records is printed from Form view. Consider adding a creation date and/or revision number in the *Form Footer* section.

1. Open **4-RSRCompServ.accdb** and enable the content.
2. Click the Create tab and then click the Form Design button in the Forms group.

3. Add a title in the *Form Header* section of the form and then center the text within the control object by completing the following steps:
   a. With the Form Design Tools Design tab active, click the Title button in the Header/Footer group. Access displays the *Form Header* section above the *Detail* section and inserts a title control object with the text *Form1* selected.

   b. With the insertion point positioned in the title control object and *Form1* selected, type Customer Data Maintenance Form. Notice that the background behind the title control object and the text of the title are both blue. The colors and fonts that appear in control objects are dependent on the current theme. The Office theme is the default for a database.

   c. Press the Enter key.
   d. With the title control object selected (as indicated by the orange border around the title text), click the Form Design Tools Format tab and then click the Center button in the Font group.
4. Scroll down the form until the *Form Footer* section is visible.
5. Position the mouse pointer at the bottom border of the form's grid until the pointer changes to an up-and-down-pointing arrow with a horizontal line in the middle and then drag down the bottom of the form to the 0.5-inch position on the vertical ruler.
6. Add one label control object at the left edge of the form footer that contains a revision number and another at the right edge of the form footer that contains your name by completing the following steps:
   a. Click the Form Design Tools Design tab and then click the Label button in the Controls group (third button from the left).
   b. Position the crosshairs with the label icon attached at the left side of the *Form Footer* section and then drag to draw a label control object of the approximate height and width shown at the right. When the mouse is released, the insertion point appears inside the label control object.

   c. Type Revision number 1.0 and then press the Enter key.

d. Create another label control object at the right side of the *Form Footer* section that is similar in height and width to the one shown below. Type your first and last names inside the label control object and then press the Enter key. Refer to Steps 6a–6c for help with this step.

e. Click in a blank area of the form to deselect the label control object.

7. Click the Save button on the Quick Access Toolbar, type CustMaintenance in the *Form Name* text box at the Save As dialog box, and then click OK.

Check Your Work

Adding Fields to a Form

Tutorial

Adding Fields to a Form

 Form Selector

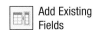 Add Existing Fields

Quick Steps

Connect a Table to a Form
1. Open form in Design view.
2. Double-click Form Selector button.
3. Click Data tab in Property Sheet task pane.
4. Click arrow in *Record Source* property box.
5. Click table.
6. Close Property Sheet task pane.

Add Fields to a Form
1. Click Add Existing Fields button.
2. Drag field name from Field List task pane to *Detail* section.
OR
1. Click first field name in Field List task pane.
2. Press and hold down Shift key.
3. Click last field name in Field List task pane.
4. Release Shift key.
5. Drag selected fields from Field List task pane to *Detail* section.

Before fields can be added to the *Detail* section, a table must be connected to the form. Specify the table that will be connected with the form using the *Record Source* property box on the Data tab of the form's Property Sheet task pane. To do this, press the F4 function key or double-click the Form Selector button above the vertical ruler and left of the horizontal ruler; this opens the Property Sheet task pane at the right side of the work area. Click the Data tab, click the down arrow in the *Record Source* property box, click the table at the drop-down list, and then close the Property Sheet task pane.

To add fields to the form, click the Add Existing Fields button in the Tools group on the Form Design Tools Design tab to open the Field List task pane. Select and drag individual or groups of field names from the Field List task pane to the *Detail* section of the form. Release the mouse button when the mouse pointer is near the location in the *Detail* section where the data will display.

For each field added to the form, Access inserts two control objects. A label control object is placed at the left of where the mouse button is released and a text box control object is placed at the right. The label control object contains the field name or a caption, if a caption was entered in the *Caption* property box. The text box control object is bound to the field and displays table data from the record in Form view. Figure 4.3 displays the fields from the Customers table that will be added to the CustMaintenance form in Project 1b.

Figure 4.3 Fields from the Customers Table Added to the CustMaintenance Form in Project 1b

If the Form Selector button does not display, click here to activate it and to select the form.

1. With **4-RSRCompServ.accdb** open and the CustMaintenance form open in Design view, scroll to the top of the form in the work area.
2. Connect the Customers table to the form by completing the following steps:

   a. Double-click the Form Selector button (which displays as a black or blue square) at the top of the vertical ruler and left of the horizontal ruler to open the form's Property Sheet task pane. *Note: If the Form Selector button does not display, click at the top of the vertical ruler and left of the horizontal ruler to display it.*

   b. Click the Data tab if necessary in the Property Sheet task pane.

   c. Click the down arrow in the *Record Source* property box and then click *Customers* at the drop-down list.

   d. Close the Property Sheet task pane.

3. Add fields individually from the Customers table to the *Detail* section of the form by completing the following steps:

   a. Click the Add Existing Fields button in the Tools group on the Form Design Tools Design tab. The Field List task pane opens at the right side of the work area.

   b. Position the mouse pointer on the right border of the form's grid until the pointer changes to a left-and-right-pointing arrow with a vertical line in the middle and then drag the right edge of the form to the 6.5-inch position on the horizontal ruler.

   c. If necessary, click *CustID* in the Field List task pane to select the field and then drag the field name to the *Detail* section. Release the mouse button when the pointer is near the top of the section at the 1-inch position on the horizontal ruler.

   d. Click to select *FName* in the Field List task pane and then drag the field to the same vertical position as *CustID* in the *Detail* section. Release the mouse button when the pointer is at the 3-inch position on the horizontal ruler.

   e. Click to select *LName* in the Field List task pane and then drag the field to the same vertical position as *CustID* in the *Detail* section. Release the mouse button when the pointer is at the 5-inch position on the horizontal ruler.

f. Drag the *Street* field from the Field List task pane to the *Detail* section below *CustID*. Release the mouse button when the pointer is at the 1-inch position on the horizontal ruler and approximately three rows of grid dots below *CustID*.

g. Drag the *City* field from the Field List task pane to the *Detail* section below *Street*. Release the mouse button when the pointer is at the 1-inch position on the horizontal ruler and approximately three rows of grid dots below *Street*.

h. Drag the *State* field from the Field List task pane to the *Detail* section at the same horizontal position as *City*. Release the mouse button when the pointer is at the 3-inch position on the horizontal ruler.

i. Drag the *ZIP* field from the Field List task pane to the *Detail* section at the same horizontal position as *City*. Release the mouse button when the pointer is at the 5-inch position on the horizontal ruler.

4. Add a group of fields from the Customers table to the *Detail* section of the form by completing the following steps:

a. Click the *HPhone* field name in the Field List task pane.

b. Press and hold down the Shift key, click the *ServCont* field name in the Field List task pane, and then release the Shift key. When the Shift key is held down, Access selects all the fields from the first field name clicked to the last field name clicked.

c. Position the mouse pointer within the selected group of fields in the Field List task pane and then drag the group to the *Detail* section below *City*. Release the mouse button when the pointer is at the 1-inch position on the horizontal ruler and approximately three rows of grid dots below *City*.

5. Click in any blank area of the form to deselect the group of fields.
6. Compare your form with the one shown in Figure 4.3.
7. Click the Save button on the Quick Access Toolbar.
8. Close the Field List task pane.

Check Your Work

Moving and Resizing Control Objects

Tutorial

Moving and
Resizing Control
Objects

Quick Steps

Move Control Objects in Design View
1. Select control object.
2. Drag using orange border or move handle to new location.

Resize Control Objects in Design View
1. Select control object.
2. Drag middle top, bottom, left, or right sizing handle to resize height or width.

OR
1. Select control object.
2. Drag corner sizing handle to resize height and width at the same time.

Toggle Snap to Grid On or Off
1. Click Form Design Tools Arrange tab.
2. Click Size/Space button.
3. Click *Snap to Grid*.

 Size/Space

Hint Do not be overly concerned with exact placement and alignment when you begin to add fields to a form. Use the alignment and spacing tools in the Form Design Tools Arrange tab to assist with layout.

Once fields in a form have been placed, control objects can be moved or resized to change the layout. As shown in Project 1b, Access places two control objects for each field in the form. A label control object, which contains the caption or field name, is placed left of a text box control object, which displays the field value from the record (or a blank entry box when a new record is added). Click the label control object or text box control object for the field to be moved or resized and the control object is surrounded by an orange border with eight handles. Access displays a large dark-gray square (called the *move handle*) at the top left of the label control object or text box control object for the selected field.

Point to the orange border around the selected control object until the mouse pointer displays with the four-headed arrow move icon attached and then drag the field to the new position on the form. Access moves both the label control and text box control objects to the new location. If a label control or text box control object is to be moved independently of its connected control object, point to the large dark-gray move handle at the top left of either control object and use it to drag the control object to the new position, as shown in Figure 4.4.

To resize a selected control object, point to one of the sizing handles (the small orange squares) on the border of the selected control object until the pointer displays with an up-and-down-pointing arrow, a left-and-right-pointing arrow, or a two-headed diagonal arrow. Drag the arrow to resize the height and/or width.

By default, the Snap to Grid feature is turned on in Design view. This feature pulls a control object to the nearest grid point when a control object is moved or resized. To move or resize a control object in small increments, turn off this feature. To do this, click the Form Design Tools Arrange tab, click the Size/Space button in the Sizing & Ordering group, and then click *Snap to Grid* at the drop-down list. Snap to Grid is a toggle feature, which means it is turned on or off by clicking the button.

Figure 4.4 Moving Control Objects

Point to the large dark-gray square (called the *move handle*) at the top left of the selected control object to move the selected *Street* text box control object independently of the *Street Address* label control object.

Point to the orange border and drag the object to the new location when the four-headed arrow move icon displays. The label control object containing the caption *Street Address* will move with the selected *Street* text box control object.

Formatting Control Objects

Quick Steps

Format Multiple Control Objects Using the Shift Key
1. In Design view, click to select first control object.
2. Shift + click remaining control objects.
3. Click formatting options.
4. Deselect controls.

Format Multiple Control Objects Using a Selection Rectangle
1. In Design view, position pointer above top left control to be formatted.
2. Drag down and right to draw rectangle around controls.
3. Release mouse.
4. Click formatting options.
5. Deselect controls.

Use the buttons in the Font group on the Form Design Tools Format tab to change the font, font size, font color, background color, or alignment and to apply bold, italic, or underline formatting to the selected control object.

Format multiple control objects at the same time by pressing and holding down the Shift key while clicking individual control objects. Select multiple control objects inside the rectangle by using the mouse pointer to draw a selection rectangle around a group of control objects.

Apply a theme to the form by clicking the Themes button on the Form Design Tools Design tab. The theme defines the default colors and fonts for control objects in the form. Change the color and fonts used in a form with the Colors and Fonts buttons in the Themes group. A theme applied to one form is applied to all the forms and reports in the database.

 Themes

Project 1c Moving and Resizing Control Objects

Part 3 of 7

1. With **4-RSRCompServ.accdb** open and the CustMaintenance form open in Design view, preview the form to determine what control objects need to be moved or resized by clicking the View button in the Views group on the Form Design Tools Design tab. (Make sure to click the button and not the button arrow.)
2. The form is displayed in Form view and data from the first record is displayed in the text box control objects. Notice that some label control objects overlap text box control objects and that the street address in the first record is not entirely displayed.
3. Click the Design View button in the view area at the right side of the Status bar.
4. Move the control objects that overlap other control objects by completing the following steps:
   a. Click the *First Name* label control object.
   b. Point to the large dark-gray move handle at the top left of the selected label control object until the pointer displays with the four-headed arrow move icon attached and then drag right to the 2-inch position on the horizontal ruler. Notice that the connected *FName* text box control object does not move because the move handle is being used while dragging.

4b

The connected *FName* text box control object does not move when the label control object is dragged using the move handle.

c. Click the *Last Name* label control object and then use the move handle to drag right to the 4-inch position on the horizontal ruler.

d. Move the *State* label control object right to the 2-inch position on the horizontal ruler.

e. Move the *ZIP Code* label control object right to the 4-inch position on the horizontal ruler.

f. Click in a blank area to deselect the *ZIP Code* label control.

5. Click the *Street* text box control object and then drag the right middle sizing handle right to the 3-inch position on the horizontal ruler.

6. Click the *State* text box control object and then drag the right middle sizing handle left to the 3.5-inch position on the horizontal ruler. (Since the *State* field displays only two characters, this control object can be made smaller.)

7. Resize the *CustID* text box control object so the right edge of the object is at the 1.5-inch position on the horizontal ruler.

8. Click the *Service Contract?* label control object. Point to the selected control object's orange border (not on a sizing handle) and then drag the control object until the left edge is at the 3-inch position on the horizontal ruler, adjacent to the *HPhone* field. Notice that both the label control object and text box control object moved because the border was dragged rather than changed with the move handle.

9. Deselect the *Service Contract?* control object.

10. Save the form.

Check Your Work

1. With **4-RSRCompServ.accdb** open and the CustMaintenance form open in Design view, click the View button to preview the form in Form view.
2. Scroll through a few records in the form and then switch back to Design view.
3. Format multiple control objects using a selection rectangle by completing the following steps:
   a. Position the arrow pointer in the top left corner of the *Detail* section (above the *Customer ID* label control object), drag down and to the right until a rectangle has been drawn around all the control objects in the section, and then release the mouse button.

   b. Notice that all the control objects contained within the rectangle are selected.

   c. Use the Font button in the Font group on the Form Design Tools Format tab to change the font to Candara.
   d. Use the Font Size button to change the font size to 10 points.
   e. Click in a blank area to deselect the control objects.
4. Apply formatting to multiple controls at once by completing the following steps:
   a. Click the *CustID* text box control object.
   b. Press and hold down the Shift key, click each of the other text box control objects in the *Detail* section, and then release the Shift key.

c. Click the Font Color button arrow in the Font group on the Form Design Tools Format tab and then click *Dark Red* at the color palette (first option in last row in the *Standard Colors* section).

d. Click the Bold button.

e. Click in a blank area to deselect the controls.

5. Click the Form Design Tools Design tab and then switch to Form view to view the formatting changes applied to the form. The zip code data remains red and does not change to dark red because of the formatting changes applied to the Format property in Chapter 1.

6. Switch to Design view and then save the form.

4c

Check Your Work

Tutorial

Changing the Tab Order of Fields

 Tab Order

Changing the Tab Order of Fields

The term *tab order* refers to the order that fields are selected when the Tab key is pressed while entering data in Form view. Data does not need to be entered into a record in the order the fields are presented. Click the Tab Order button in the Tools group on the Form Design Tools Design tab to open the Tab Order dialog box, shown in Figure 4.5.

The order of the fields in the *Custom Order* list box in the Tab Order dialog box is the order in which the fields will be selected when the Tab key is pressed in a record in Form view. To change the tab order of the fields, position the pointer in the gray field selector bar next to the field name to be moved until the pointer displays as a black right-pointing arrow and then click to select the field. Drag the selected field up or down to the appropriate position. Click OK to accept the changes and close the Tab Order dialog box. To quickly set the tab order as left-to-right and top-to-bottom, click the Auto Order button at the bottom of the Tab Order dialog box.

Quick Steps

Change the Tab Order of Fields

1. Open form in Design view.
2. Click Tab Order button.
3. Click in gray field selector bar next to field name.
4. Drag field to new location.
5. Repeat Steps 3–4 as required.
6. Click OK.

Figure 4.5 Tab Order Dialog Box

Click in the gray field selector bar next to a field and then drag the field name to the new position.

The order in which fields display in the *Custom Order* list box is the order in which they will be selected when the Tab key is pressed in a record in Form view.

Click the Auto Order button to organize the field list in a left-to-right, top-to-bottom sequence.

1. With **4-RSRCompServ.accdb** open and the CustMaintenance form open in Design view, click the View button to display the form in Form view.
2. With the insertion point positioned in the *CustID* field in the first record in the table, press the Tab key seven times. As the Tab key is pressed, notice that the fields are selected in a left-to-right, top-to-bottom sequence.
3. With the insertion point positioned in the *HPhone* field, press the Tab key. Notice that the selected field moves down to the *CPhone* field instead of right to the *ServCont* field.
4. With the insertion point in the *CPhone* field, press the Tab key to move to the *ServCont* field.
5. Switch to Design view.
6. Change the tab order of the fields so the *ServCont* field is selected after the *HPhone* field by completing the following steps:
   a. Click the Tab Order button in the Tools group on the Form Design Tools Design tab.
   b. At the Tab Order dialog box, hover the mouse pointer over the gray field selector bar next to *ServCont* until the pointer displays as a black right-pointing arrow.

   6b

   c. Click to select the field.
   d. With the pointer now displayed as a white arrow in the field selector bar, drag up *ServCont* until the black horizontal line indicating where the field will be moved is positioned between *HPhone* and *CPhone* in the *Custom Order* list and then release the mouse button.

   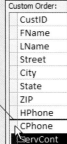

   6d

   e. Click OK. Note that since the tabs follow the left-to-right, top-to-bottom sequence, this tab order could have been created by clicking the Auto Order button in the Tab Order dialog box.
7. Switch to Form view.
8. Press the Tab key nine times to move through the fields in the first record. Notice that when the *HPhone* field is reached and the Tab key is pressed, the *ServCont* field becomes active instead of the *CPhone* field.
9. Switch to Design view.
10. Save the form.

Tutorial

Adding a Tab
Control Object to
a Form

Adding a Tab Control Object to a Form

A tab control object is an object used to add pages to a form. Each page displays with a tab at the top. When viewing the form, click the page tab to display the contents of the page within the tab control object. Add a tab control object to a form to organize fields in a large table into smaller, related groups or to insert multiple subforms that display on separate pages within the tab control object.

Examine the tab control object that will be created in Projects 1f and 1g, as shown in Figure 4.6. The tab control object contains three pages. The tabs across the top display the captions assigned to the individual pages.

In Projects 1f and 1g, a subform will be created on each page within the tab control object to display fields from a related table. When completed, the CustMaintenance form will be used to enter or view customer-related data that includes fields from four tables.

Quick Steps

Add a Tab Control Object to a Form
1. Open form in Design view.
2. Click Tab Control button.
3. Position crosshairs in *Detail* section at specified location.
4. Drag down and right to draw object.
5. Release mouse.

Change a Page Caption
1. Click tab in tab control object.
2. Click Property Sheet button.
3. Click in *Caption* property box.
4. Type text.
5. Close Property Sheet task pane.

Add a Page to a Tab Control
1. Right-click existing tab in tab control object.
2. Click *Insert Page.*

Delete a Page from a Tab Control
1. Right-click tab of page to delete.
2. Click *Delete Page.*

Tab Control

Figure 4.6 Tab Control Object with Three Pages Created in Projects 1f and 1g

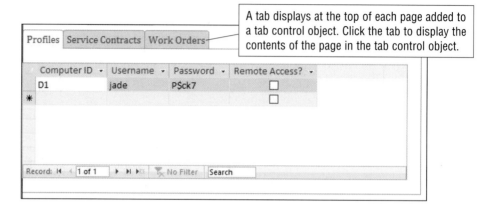

A tab displays at the top of each page added to a tab control object. Click the tab to display the contents of the page in the tab control object.

Figure 4.7 New Tab Control Object with Two Pages

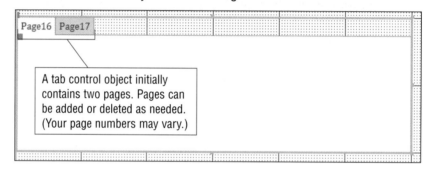

A tab control object initially contains two pages. Pages can be added or deleted as needed. (Your page numbers may vary.)

To add a tab control object to a form, click the Tab Control button in the Controls group on the Form Design Tools Design tab. Position the crosshairs with the tab control icon attached in the top left of the area of the *Detail* section where the tab control is to begin and then drag down and to the right to draw the control. When the mouse button is released, the tab control object initially displays with two pages, as shown in Figure 4.7.

Change the text displayed in the tab at the top of the page by editing the text in the *Caption* property box in the page's Property Sheet task pane. Add fields or create subforms on each page as needed. Add a page to the tab control object by right-clicking an existing tab in the tab control object and then clicking *Insert Page* at the shortcut menu. Remove a page from the tab control object by right-clicking the tab to be deleted and then clicking *Delete Page* at the shortcut menu.

Tutorial

Adding a Subform

Adding a Subform

Use the Subform/Subreport button in the Controls group on the Form Design Tools Design tab to add a subform to a form. Create a subform to display fields from another related table within the existing form. The form that a subform is created in is called the *main form*.

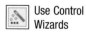
Subform/ Subreport

Adding a related table as a subform creates a control object within the main form that can be moved, formatted, and resized independently of other objects. The subform displays as a datasheet within the main form in Form view. Data can be entered or updated in the subform while the main form is being viewed. Before

Use Control Wizards

clicking the Subform/Subreport button, make sure the Use Control Wizards button in the Controls group is toggled on so the subform can be added using the Subform Wizard; the first Subform Wizard dialog box is shown in Figure 4.8. The Use Control Wizards button displays with a pink or gray background when the feature is active. In the initial release of Access 2016, the active Control Wizard button was pink. If a later Access 2016 Service Pack has been installed on your computer the active Control Wizard button will be gray.

A subform is stored as a separate object outside the main form. An additional form name (with *subform* at the end of it) will appear in the Navigation pane when the Subform Wizard is finished. Do not delete a subform object from the Navigation pane. If the subform object is deleted, the main form will no longer display the fields from the related table in the tab control object.

Figure 4.8 First Subform Wizard Dialog Box

Project 1f Adding a Tab Control Object and a Subform

Part 6 of 7

1. With **4-RSRCompServ.accdb** open and the CustMaintenance form open in Design view, add a tab control object to the form by completing the following steps:
   a. Click the Tab Control button in the Controls group on the Form Design Tools Design tab. The Tab Control button is the fifth button from the left in the Controls group.
   b. Position the crosshairs with the tab control icon attached at the left edge of the grid in the *Detail* section at the 2-inch position on the vertical ruler. Drag down to the 4-inch position on the vertical ruler and right to the 6-inch position on the horizontal ruler and then release the mouse button.

2. Change the page caption and add a subform to the first page within the tab control object by completing the following steps:

   a. Click the first tab in the tab control object that displays *Pagexx*, where *xx* is the page number to select the page. (For example, click *Page16* in the image shown above.)

   b. Click the Property Sheet button in the Tools group.

   c. Click the Format tab in the Property Sheet task pane, click in the *Caption* property box, type Profiles, and then close the Property Sheet task pane. The tab displays the caption text in place of *Pagexx*.

   d. By default, the Use Control Wizards feature is toggled on in the Controls group. Click the More button in the Controls group to expand the Controls group and view two rows of buttons and the Controls drop-down list. View the current status of the Use Control Wizards button. If the button displays with a pink or gray background, the feature is active. If the button is pink or gray, click in a blank area to remove the expanded Controls list. If the feature is not active (displays with a white background), click the Use Control Wizards button to turn it on.

   e. Click the More button in the Controls group and then click the Subform/Subreport button at the expanded Controls list.

Check the status of the Use Control Wizards button in Step 2d. When the button displays as shown (with a pink or gray background), the feature is active and the Subform Wizard can be used to create a subform.

   f. Move the crosshairs with the subform icon attached to the Profiles page in the tab control object. The background of the page turns black. Click the mouse to start the SubForm Wizard.

   g. At the first SubForm Wizard dialog box with *Use existing Tables and Queries* already selected, click the Next button.

h. At the second SubForm Wizard dialog box, select the table and fields to be displayed in the subform by completing the following steps:
   1) Click the *Tables/Queries* option box arrow and then click *Table: Profiles* at the drop-down list.
   2) Move all the fields except *CustID* from the *Available Fields* list box to the *Selected Fields* list box.
   3) Click the Next button.

i. At the third SubForm Wizard dialog box with *Show Profiles for each record in Customers using CustID* selected, click the Next button. Since a relationship has been created between two tables with *CustID* as the joined field, Access knows the field that links the records in the main form with the subform.

j. Click the Finish button at the last SubForm Wizard dialog box to accept the default subform name *Profiles subform*.

3. Access creates the subform within the active page in the tab control with a label control object above it. Click the label control object displaying the text *Profiles subform* to select the object and then press the Delete key.

4. Click the edge of the subform control object to display the orange border and sizing handles and then use the techniques learned in Project 1c to move and resize the object so that the subform fills the tab control object as shown at the right.

5. Click in a blank area outside the grid to deselect the subform control object and then switch to Form view. Notice that the subform displays as a datasheet within the tab control object in the CustMaintenance form.

6. In the field names row in the datasheet, position the mouse pointer on each boundary line that separates the columns and then double-click to adjust each column's width to best fit.

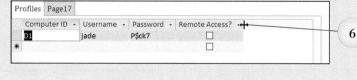

7. Notice that two sets of navigation buttons are displayed: one at the bottom of the main form (just above the Status bar) and another at the bottom of the datasheet in the subform. Use the navigation buttons at the bottom of the main form to scroll through a few records and watch the fields update in both the main form and subform upon moving to the next customer record.

8. Switch to Design view.

9. Save the form.

10. In the Navigation pane, notice that a form object exists with the name *Profiles subform*. Subforms are separate objects within the database. If the main form is closed, the subform can still be opened to edit data.

Check Your Work

In Design view, the control objects within the subform display one below another, but in Form view, the subform displays using a datasheet layout. Change the setting of the *Default View* property box in the subform's Property Sheet task pane to *Single Form* to match the layout of the controls in Design view to the layout of the fields in Form view. The fields display one below another in a single column in Form view.

To do this, open the subform's Property Sheet task pane by double-clicking the Form Selector button at the top of the vertical ruler and left of the horizontal ruler in the subform control object in Design view. Click in the *Default View* property box on the Format tab, click the down arrow, and then click *Single Form* at the drop-down list.

Project 1g Adding More Subforms and Adding a New Page to the Tab Control Object   Part 7 of 7

1. With **4-RSRCompServ.accdb** open and the CustMaintenance form open in Design view, change the caption for the second page in the tab control object to *Service Contracts* by completing steps similar to those in Steps 2a–c of Project 1f.
2. With the Service Contracts page selected in the tab control object, add a subform to display the fields from the ServiceContracts table on the page by completing the following steps:
   a. Click the More button in the Controls group and then click the Subform/Subreport button in the expanded Controls group.
   b. Click inside the selected Service Contracts page in the tab control object.
   c. Click the Next button at the first SubForm Wizard dialog box.
   d. At the second SubForm Wizard dialog box, change the table displayed in the *Tables/Queries* option box to *Table: ServiceContracts*.
   e. Move all the fields from the table except the *CustID* field to the *Selected Fields* list box.
   f. Click the Next button.
   g. At the third SubForm Wizard dialog box with *Show ServiceContracts for each record in Customers using CustID* selected, click the Next button.
   h. Click the Finish button at the last SubForm Wizard dialog box to accept the default subform name *ServiceContracts subform*.
3. Select and then delete the label control object above the subform (which displays the text *ServiceContracts subform*).
4. Click the subform control object to display the orange border and sizing handles and then move and resize the form as shown below.

5. Deselect the subform control object and then switch to Form view.

6. Click the Service Contracts tab and then adjust the width of each column in the datasheet to best fit.

7. Switch to Design view and then save the form.
8. Add a new page to the tab control object and add a subform to display selected fields from the WorkOrders table in the new page by completing the following steps:
   a. Right-click the Service Contracts tab and then click *Insert Page* at the shortcut menu.
   b. With the new page already selected, display the Property Sheet task pane, type Work Orders as the page caption, and then close the Property Sheet task pane.
   c. Click the More button in the Controls group and then click the Subform/Subreport button. Click inside the selected Work Orders page. Create a subform to display selected fields from the WorkOrders table by completing the following steps:
      1) Click the Next button at the first SubForm Wizard dialog box.
      2) At the second SubForm Wizard dialog box, change the table displayed in the *Tables/Queries* option box to *Table: WorkOrders*.
      3) Move the following fields from the *Available Fields* list box to the *Selected Fields* list box:
         WO
         WODate
         Descr
      4) Click the Next button.
      5) Click the Next button at the third SubForm Wizard dialog box.
      6) Click the Finish button at the last SubForm Wizard dialog box to accept the default subform name.
9. Select and then delete the label control object above the subform (which displays the text *WorkOrders subform*).
10. Click the subform control object to display the orange border and sizing handles and then move and resize the form as shown below.
11. Access automatically extends the width of the form and widens the tab control object if a table with many fields is added to a subform. If necessary, select the tab control object and decrease the width so the right edge of the tab control is at the 6-inch position on the horizontal ruler. If necessary, decrease the width of the form so the right edge of the grid is at the 6.5-inch position on the horizontal ruler. ***Hint: If Access resizes the tab control object to the edge of the form, the grid may have to be temporarily widened to see the middle sizing handle at the right edge of the tab control object.***

12. Deselect the subform control object and then switch to Form view.
13. While viewing the form, you decide the title would look better if it was not centered. Switch to Design view, click the Title control object in the *Form Header* section, click the Form Design Tools Format tab, and then click the Align Left button in the Font group.

14. Click the Form Design Tools Design tab and then switch to Form view.
15. Click the Work Orders tab and adjust the width of each column in the datasheet to best fit. Compare the CustMaintenance form with the one shown in Figure 4.9.
16. Print only the selected record. To do this, open the Print dialog box, click *Selected Record(s)* in the *Print Range* section, and then click OK.
17. Save and then close the CustMaintenance form.

Check Your Work

Figure 4.9 Completed CustMaintenance Form

Adding the tab control with a separate page displaying a subform for each table related to the Customers table in the CustMaintenance form allowed one object to be created that can be used to view and update fields in multiple tables.

Project 2 Create a New Form with Calculations and Graphics   5 Parts

You will create a new form using the Form Wizard, add two calculations to the form, use features that assist with alignment and spacing of multiple control objects, and add graphics to the form.

Preview Finished Project

Tutorial ▸

Adding
Calculations to a
Form

 Text Box

Quick Steps

**Add a Calculated
Control Object to a
Form**
1. Open form in
   Design view.
2. Click Text Box
   button.
3. Position crosshairs
   in *Detail* section at
   specified location.
4. Drag to create
   control object of
   required height and
   width.
5. Release mouse.
6. Click in text box
   control object.
7. Type formula.
8. Press Enter.
9. Delete text in label
   control object.
10. Type label text and
    press Enter.

Adding Calculations to a Form

To display a calculated value in a form, create a query that includes a calculated column and then create a new form based on that query. Alternatively, create a calculated control object in an existing form using Design view.

To do this, click the Text Box button in the Controls group on the Form Design Tools Design tab and then drag the crosshairs in the *Detail* section to create a control object the approximate height and width required to show the calculation. Access displays a text box control object with *Unbound* inside the object and a label control object to the left displaying *Textxx* (where *xx* is the text box control object number). A calculated control object is considered as unbound because the data displayed in the control is not drawn from a stored field value in a record. Click inside the text box control object (*Unbound* disappears) and then type the formula, beginning with an equals sign. For example, the formula *=[Hours]*[Rate]* multiplies the value in the *Hours* field times the value in the *Rate* field. The field names in a formula are enclosed in square brackets.

Edit the label control object next to the calculated control to add a descriptive name that identifies the calculated value. Open the Property Sheet task pane for the calculated control object and then apply the Fixed, Standard, or Currency format, as appropriate for the calculated value. Since the data displayed in a calculated control object is based on a formula, there is no need to tab to this control object when entering data or moving through a record. Change the *Tab Stop* property box on the Other tab of the Property Sheet task pane from *Yes* to *No* to avoid stopping at any text box control object.

Project 2a Adding and Formatting Calculated Control Objects   Part 1 of 5

1. With **4-RSRCompServ.accdb** open, use the Form Wizard to create a new form based on the WorkOrders table by completing the following steps:
   a. Click *WorkOrders* in the Tables group in the Navigation pane and then click the Create tab.
   b. Click the Form Wizard button in the Forms group.
   c. With *Table: WorkOrders* selected in the *Table/Queries* option box, complete the steps in the Form Wizard as follows:
      1) Move the *WO, Descr, ServDate, Hours, Rate,* and *Parts* fields from the *Available Fields* list box to the *Selected Fields* list box and then click the Next button.
      2) With *Columnar* selected as the layout option, click the Next button.
      3) With *WorkOrders* the default text in the *What title do you want for your form?* text box, click *Modify the form's design* at the last dialog box and then click the Finish button.
2. With the WorkOrders form displayed in Design view, change the theme and add a calculated control object to display the total labor for the work order by completing the following steps:
   a. Click the Themes button in the Themes group on the Form Design Tools Design tab and then click *Organic* (third column, second row) at the drop-down gallery.
   b. Position the pointer on the top border of the gray *Form Footer* section bar until the pointer displays as an up-and-down-pointing arrow with a horizontal line in the middle and then drag down just below the 3-inch position on the vertical ruler. (The 3-inch mark will not appear until the border is dragged below it and the mouse button is released.) Doing this creates more grid space in the *Detail* section so that controls can be added.

c. Click the Text Box button in the Controls group.

d. Position the crosshairs with the text box icon attached below the *Parts* text box control, drag to create an object of the approximate height and width shown at the right, and then release the mouse button.

e. Click in the text box control (which displays *Unbound*) and then type =[Hours]*[Rate].

f. Press the Enter key.

g. With the calculated control object selected, click the Property Sheet button in the Tools group. With the Format tab in the Property Sheet task pane active, click the option box arrow in the *Format* property box, click *Standard* at the drop-down list, and then close the Property Sheet task pane. By default, calculated values display right-aligned in Form view.

h. Click to select the label control object to the left of the calculated control object (which displays *Textxx* [where *xx* is the text box label number]). Click in the selected label control object a second time to place the insertion point. Delete *Textxx*, type Total Labor, and then press the Enter key. Notice that the label control automatically expands to accommodate the width of the typed text.

3. With the Form Design Tools Design tab selected, click the View button to display the form in Form view and then scroll through a few records to view the calculated field. Do not be concerned with the size, position, alignment, and/or spacing of the controls; the format will be fixed in a later project.

4. Switch to Design view and then save the form.

5. A calculated control object can be used as a field in another formula. To do this, reference the calculated object in the formula by its Name property enclosed in square brackets. Change the name for the calculated object created in Step 2 to a more descriptive name by completing the following steps:

a. Click the calculated control object (which displays the formula *=[Hours]*[Rate]*).

b. Click the Property Sheet button in the Tools group.

c. Click the Other tab in the Property Sheet task pane.

d. Select and delete the existing text (which displays *Textxx* [where *xx* is the text box number]) in the *Name* property box.

e. Type LaborCalc, press the Enter key, and then close the Property Sheet task pane.

6. Add another calculated control object to the form to include labor and parts and determine the total value for the work order by completing the following steps:

a. Click the Text Box button in the Controls group.

b. Position the crosshairs with the text box icon attached below the calculated control created in Step 2, drag to create an object the approximate height and width as the first calculated control, and then release the mouse button.

c. Click in the text box control (which displays *Unbound*), type =[LaborCalc]+[Parts], and then press the Enter key.

d. Apply the Currency format to the calculated control. Refer to Step 2g for assistance with this step.

e. Type Total Work Order in the label control object. Refer to Step 2h for assistance with this step.

7. Remove the tab stops from the two new calculated control objects by completing the following steps:

a. Press and hold the Shift key, use the left mouse button to click the calculated control objects that display the formulas *=[Hours]*[Rate]* and *=[LaborCalc]+[Parts]*, and then release the Shift key.

b. Click the Property Sheet button in the Tools group.

c. Click the Other tab in the Property Sheet task pane.

d. Double-click *Yes* in the *Tab Stop* property box to change it to *No*.

e. Close the Property Sheet task pane.

8. Save the form. Display the form in Form view and then scroll through a few records to view the calculations. Tab through a record and notice that when the Tab key is pressed after the *Parts* field, the insertion point does not stop at *Total Labor* or *Total Work Order* but instead moves to the next record.

9. Switch to Design view.

Check Your Work

Tutorial

Sizing, Aligning, and Spacing Multiple Control Objects

 Align

Adjusting Control Objects for Consistency in Appearance

When working in Design view, use the tools that Access provides for positioning, aligning, sizing, and spacing multiple controls to create forms with a consistent and professional appearance. Locate these tools using the Size/Space button and Align button in the Sizing & Ordering group on the Form Design Tools Arrange tab.

Aligning Multiple Control Objects

***Q**uick Steps*

Align Multiple Control Objects

1. In Design view, select control objects.
2. Click Form Design Tools Arrange tab.
3. Click Align button.
4. Click option at drop-down list.
5. Deselect control objects.

The options in the Align button drop-down list in the Sizing & Ordering group on the Form Design Tools Arrange tab are shown in Figure 4.10. Use these options to align multiple selected control objects at the same horizontal or vertical position and avoid having to adjust each control object individually.

Figure 4.10 Options in the Align Button Drop-Down List

Use one of these options to align a selected control at the left- or right-most position.

Use one of these options to align a selected control at the top- or bottom-most position.

Adjusting the Sizing and Spacing between Control Objects

Size/Space

Quick Steps

Adjust the Spacing between Control Objects
1. In Design view, select control objects.
2. Click Form Design Tools Arrange tab.
3. Click Size/Space button.
4. Click option in *Spacing* section.
5. Deselect controls.

The options provided by the Size/Space button in the Sizing & Ordering group on the Form Design Tools Arrange tab are shown in Figure 4.11. Use these options to assist with the consistent sizing of and spacing between control objects. Use options in the *Size* section of the drop-down list to adjust the height or width to the tallest, shortest, widest, or narrowest of the selected control objects. Use options in the *Spacing* section to adjust the horizontal and vertical spacing between control objects, increase or decrease the space, or provide equal spaces between all the selected control objects.

Using these tools is helpful when creating a new form by adding control objects manually to the grid or after editing an existing form because the space between control objects can be changed easily after objects are added or deleted. To adjust the spacing by moving individual control objects would be too time consuming.

Figure 4.11 Size and Spacing Options in the Size/Space Button Drop-Down List

Use these options to adjust the height or width of multiple control objects.

Use these options to adjust the space between multiple control objects.

Project 2b Sizing, Aligning, and Spacing Multiple Control Objects

Part 2 of 5

1. With **4-RSRCompServ.accdb** open and the WorkOrders form open in Design view, change the title in the *Form Header* section to *Work Orders with Calculations* and then widen the control object to fit the title on one line.
2. With the title control object still selected, position the mouse pointer on the orange border until the pointer changes to the four-headed arrow move icon and then drag the control object to the approximate center of the *Form Header* section.

3. Point to the bottom gray border in the *Form Footer* section bar until the pointer displays as an up-and-down-pointing arrow with a horizontal line in the middle and then drag down approximately 0.5 inch to create space in the *Form Footer* section. Create a label control object with your name in the center of the *Form Footer* section.

4. Click to select the *Descr* text box control object and then drag the right middle sizing handle left until the control object is resized to approximately the 4.5-inch position on the horizontal ruler.
5. Press and hold down the Shift key, use the left mouse button to click the six text box control objects for the fields above the two calculated control objects, and then release the Shift key. Click the Form Design Tools Arrange tab, click the Size/Space button in the Sizing & Ordering group, and then click *To Widest* at the drop-down list. The six text box control objects are now all the same width. (The width is set to fit the widest selected control object).

6. Click in a blank area to deselect the control objects.
7. Use the Align button to align multiple control objects by completing the following steps:
   a. Draw a selection rectangle around all the label control objects at the left side of the form. This selects all eight label control objects.
   b. Click the Align button in the Sizing & Ordering group and then click *Left* at the drop-down list. All the label control objects align at the left edge of the left-most control object.
   c. Deselect the control objects.
   d. Draw a selection rectangle around all the text box control objects at the right of the form to select all eight text box control objects.
   e. Click the Align button in the Sizing & Ordering group and then click *Right* at the drop-down list. All the control objects align at the right edge of the right-most control object.
   f. Deselect the control objects.

8. Adjust the vertical spaces between control objects to make all the control objects in the *Detail* section equally spaced by completing the following steps:

a. Draw a selection rectangle around all the control objects in the *Detail* section.

b. Click the Size/Space button and then click *Equal Vertical* in the *Spacing* section of the drop-down list. All the control objects are now separated by the same amount of vertical space.

c. Deselect the control objects.

9. Save the form.

10. Display the form in Form view and then scroll through a few records to view the revised alignment and spacing. The numeric fields will be formatted in Project 2e to align the numbers correctly.

11. Switch to Design view.

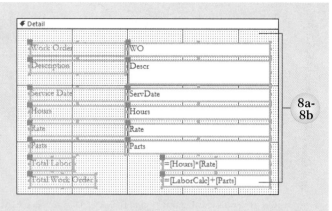

8a-8b

Check Your Work

Tutorial

Adding Graphics to a Form

Adding and Anchoring Graphics to a Form

 Logo

 Insert Image

 Line

Quick Steps

Add an Image to a Form
1. Open form in Design view.
2. Click Insert Image button.
3. Click *Browse* and navigate to folder.
4. Double-click image.
5. Click and drag crosshairs.
6. Move and resize.
7. If necessary, display Property Sheet task pane and change Size Mode property.

A picture that is saved in a graphic file format can be added to a form using the Logo button or Insert Image button in the Controls group on the Form Design Tools Design tab. Click the Logo button and the Insert Picture dialog box opens. Navigate to the drive and/or folder in which the graphic file is stored and then double-click the image file name. Access automatically adds the image to the left side of the *Form Header* section. Move and/or resize the image as needed. Access supports the BMP, GIF, JPEG, JPG, and PNG graphic file formats for a logo control object.

Use the Insert Image button to place the picture in another section or draw a larger control object to hold the picture. Click the Insert Image button and then click *Browse* at the drop-down list to open the Insert Picture dialog box. Navigate to the drive and/or folder in which the graphic file is stored and then double-click the image file name. Position the crosshairs with the image icon attached at the location in the form where the image is to be placed and then drag the crosshairs to draw a control object of the approximate height and width desired. Access supports the GIF, JPEG, JPG, and PNG file formats for an image control object.

Use the Line button in the Controls group to draw horizontal or vertical lines in a form. Press and hold down the Shift key while dragging to draw a straight line. Once the line has been drawn, use the Shape Outline button in the Control Formatting group on the Form Design Tools Format tab to modify the line thickness, type, and color.

Online images can be added to a form. Access does not provide an online pictures button in the Controls group. However, an online picture can be inserted in a Microsoft Word document and then saved to a folder using standard Windows commands. Use the Insert Image button to insert the saved image.

1. With **4-RSRCompServ.accdb** open and the WorkOrders form open in Design view, start Microsoft Word and open a new blank document.
2. Locate and insert an online image in the document and then insert the image into the form in Microsoft Access by completing the following steps:
   a. At a blank Word document, click the Insert tab and then click the Online Pictures button in the Illustrations group.
   b. At the Insert Pictures window, type computer repairs in the text box right of *Bing Image Search* and then press the Enter key.
   c. If necessary, scroll down the results list box, click the image shown to the above right, and then click the Insert button to insert it in the current document. If the image shown is not available, select a similar image or access the computer repair image (**CRStudentFile.png**) from the student data files.

2c

   d. Right-click the image in the Word document and then click *Save as Picture* at the shortcut menu.
   e. Navigate to your AL2C4 folder, type CompRepair in the *File Name* text box, and then click the Save button.

2e

   f. Click the Microsoft Access button on the taskbar.
   g. Click the Insert Image button in the Controls group, click the *Browse* option, navigate to your AL2C4 folder, and then double click *CompRepair*.
   h. Position the crosshairs with the picture icon attached to the right of the text box control objects, drag to create an object of the approximate height and width shown, and then release the mouse button. Access inserts the image and displays the orange border with selection handles.

2h

   i. Right-click the Microsoft Word button on the taskbar and then click *Close Window*. Click Don't Save when prompted to save the document. Click No if prompted to make the Clipboard contents available for other applications.
3. Right-click the image at the right side of the *Detail* section in the form and then click *Properties* at the shortcut menu. If necessary, make Format the active tab in the Property Sheet task pane. Click in the *Size Mode* property box (displays *Zoom*), click the down arrow that appears, and then click *Stretch* at the drop-down list. Close the Property Sheet task pane. Changing the *Size Mode* property box to display *Stretch* instructs Access to resize the image to fit the height and width of the control object. Note that using *Stretch* may skew the appearance of the image.

3

4. Deselect the control object containing the image and then display the form in Form view. Add a line below the title to improve the appearance of the form. Draw and modify the line by completing the following steps:
   a. Switch to Design view and then click the Line button in the Controls group.
   b. Position the crosshairs with the line icon attached below the title in the *Form Header* section beginning a few rows of grid dots below the first letter in the title. Press and hold down the Shift key, drag to the right, release the mouse button below the last letter in the title, and then release the Shift key.
   c. Click the Form Design Tools Format tab, click the Shape Outline button in the Control Formatting group, point to *Line Thickness* at the drop-down list, and then click *3 pt* (fourth option from the top).

   d. With the line control object still selected, click the Shape Outline button and then click the *Dark Red* color (first option in last row of *Standard Colors* section).
   e. Deselect the line control object.
5. Display the form in Form view to see the line under the title.
6. Switch to Design view. If desired, adjust the length and/or position of the line.
7. Save the form.

Check Your Work

Quick Steps

Anchor a Control to a Form

1. Open form in Design view.
2. Select control object(s) to be anchored.
3. Click Form Design Tools Arrange tab.
4. Click Anchoring button.
5. Click anchor position.
6. Deselect control object.
7. Save form.

Anchoring Controls to a Form

A control object in a form can be anchored to a section or another control object using the Anchoring button in the Position group on the Form Design Tools Arrange tab. When a control object is anchored, its position is maintained when the form is resized. For example, if an image is anchored to the top right of the *Detail* section, when the form is resized in Form view, the image automatically moves so that the relative distance between the image and the top right of the *Detail* section is maintained. If the image is not anchored and the form is resized, the position of the image relative to the edges of the form can change.

Anchoring

By default, *Top Left* is selected as the anchor position for each control object in a form. To change the anchor position, select the object(s), click the Form Design Tools Arrange tab, click the Anchoring button, and then click one of these options: *Stretch Down, Bottom Left, Stretch Across Top, Stretch Down and Across, Stretch Across Bottom, Top Right, Stretch Down and Right,* or *Bottom Right*. Click the option that represents how the control object is to move as the form is resized. Note that some options will cause a control object to resize as well as move when the form is changed.

Project 2d Anchoring an Image to a Position within a Section   **Part 4 of 5**

1. With **4-RSRCompServ.accdb** open and the WorkOrders form open in Design view, anchor the image to the top of the *Detail* section of the form by completing the following steps:
   a. Click to select the image.
   b. Click the Form Design Tools Arrange tab.
   c. Click the Anchoring button in the Position group and then click *Top Right* at the drop-down list.

   d. Take note of the distance between the top border of the selected image and the top of the *Detail* section. **Note: If you have a wide monitor, you may want to change the anchoring back to Top Left**.
2. Display the form in Form view. Notice that the image has shifted to the right of the *Detail* section. However, it has maintained the distance between the top of the control object boundary and the top of the *Detail* section.

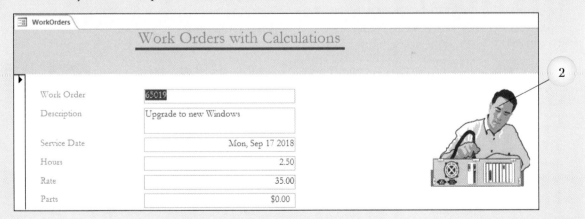

3. Save the form and then switch to Design view.

Check Your Work

1. With **4-RSRCompServ.accdb** open and the WorkOrders form open in Design view, adjust the alignment and formatting of numeric fields by completing the following steps:
   a. Press and hold down the Shift key; click the left mouse button to select the *Rate* and *Parts* text box control objects and both calculated text box control objects; and then release the mouse button.
   b. Click the Form Design Tools Format tab, click the Align Right button in the Font group, and then click the Currency button in the Number group.
   c. Deselect the control objects.
2. Switch to Form view. Notice that the decimal point in the data in the *Hours* text box control object does not align with decimal points in the other numbers in the form. Switch back to Design view. To align the decimal point, complete the following steps:
   a. Right click the *Hours* text box control object and then click *Properties* at the shortcut menu.
   b. Click the Format tab, scroll down if necessary, and then change the Right Margin property from *0* to *0.07*.
   c. Close the Property Sheet task pane.
3. Click to select the title control object box in the *Form Header* section and then drag the bottom middle sizing handle up to decrease the height of the control object to approximately 0.4 inch on the vertical ruler. If necessary, drag down the bottom border of the *Form Header* section in order to select the sizing handle
4. Position the pointer on the top of the gray *Detail* section bar until the pointer displays as an up-and-down-pointing arrow with a horizontal line in the middle and then drag up to decrease the height of the *Form Header* section to approximately 0.5 inch on the vertical ruler.

5. Save the form.
6. Display the form in Form view and compare it with the one shown in Figure 4.12.
7. Print only the selected record with the left and right margins both set to 0.5 inch.
8. Close the form.

Check Your Work

Figure 4.12 Completed WorkOrders Form

Project 3 Create a Restricted-Use Form   1 Part

You will create a datasheet form for use in entering information into a table and set the form's properties to prevent records from being deleted.

Preview Finished Project

Tutorial

Creating a Datasheet Form and Restricing Actions

Creating a Datasheet Form and Restricting Actions

A form can be created that looks just like the datasheet of a table. With the appropriate table selected in the Navigation pane, click the Create tab, click the More Forms button in the Forms group, and then click *Datasheet* at the drop-down list. Access creates a form including all the fields from the selected table presented in a datasheet layout. The datasheet form is similar in appearance and purpose of a table datasheet, and providing the form to users instead of the underlying table prevents them from accessing and modifying the structure of the table.

To restrict what actions users can perform, display the form in Form view and use options on the Data tab of the form's Property Sheet, as shown in Figure 4.13. For example, prevent new records from being added and/or existing records from being deleted, edited, and/or filtered. Setting the *Data Entry* property to *Yes* means the user will see only a blank form when the form is opened. A data entry form is intended to be used only to add new records. The user is prevented from scrolling through existing records in the form.

Quick Steps

Create a Datasheet Form
1. Select table in Navigation pane.
2. Click Create tab.
3. Click More Forms button.
4. Click *Datasheet*.
5. Save form.

Restrict Actions in a Form
1. Open form in Design view.
2. Double-click Form Selector button.
3. Click Data tab.
4. Change *Allow Additions*, *Allow Deletions*, *Allow Edits*, or *Allow Filters* to *No*.
5. Close Property Sheet task pane.
6. Save form.

Figure 4.13 Form Property Sheet Task Pane with the Data Tab Selected

Project 3 Creating a Datasheet Form and Preventing Record Deletions

Part 1 of 1

1. With **4-RSRCompServ.accdb** open, click *Technicians* in the Tables group in the Navigation pane and then click the Create tab.
2. Click the More Forms button in the Forms group and then click *Datasheet* at the drop-down list.
3. Review the Technicians form in the work area. Notice that the form resembles a table datasheet.
4. Switch to Design view.
5. Modify the properties of the Technicians form to prevent users from deleting records by completing the following steps:
    a. Click in a blank area to deselect the control objects.
    b. Double-click the Form Selector button at the top of the vertical ruler and to the left of the horizontal ruler to open the form's Property Sheet task pane.
    c. Click the Data tab.
    d. Double-click in the *Allow Deletions* property box to change *Yes* to *No*.
    e. Close the Property Sheet task pane.
6. Click the Save button and then click OK to accept *Technicians* as the form name.
7. Click the View button arrow in the Views group on the Form Design Tools Design tab. Notice that *Datasheet View* and *Design View* are the only views available. The *Form View* option is not available at the drop-down list or in the View buttons at the right side of the Status bar.
8. Click in a blank area to close the drop-down list.
9. Close the form.

10. Double-click *Technicians* in the Forms group in the Navigation pane. (Be careful to open the form object and not the table object.)

11. Click the record selector bar next to the first row in the datasheet (for technician ID 01) to select the record.

12. Click the Home tab and then look at the Delete button in the Records group. Notice that the Delete button is dimmed. This feature is unavailable because the *Allow Deletions* property box is set to *No*.

13. Best fit the width of each column, print the first page of the Technicians form in landscape orientation, and then close the form.

14. Right-click *Technicians* in the Forms group in the Navigation pane and then click *Layout View* at the shortcut menu. Notice that the datasheet form displays in a columnar layout in Layout view. The Technicians form includes a field named *Attachments*. In this field in the first record, a picture of the technician has been attached to the record. In Layout view, Access automatically opens the image file and displays the contents.

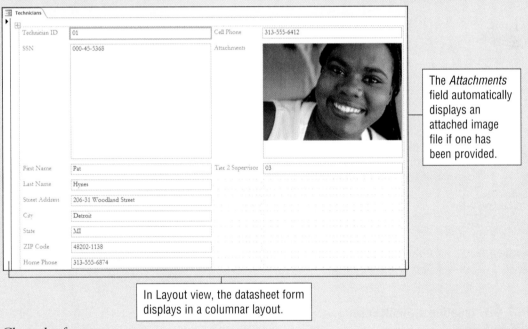

The *Attachments* field automatically displays an attached image file if one has been provided.

In Layout view, the datasheet form displays in a columnar layout.

15. Close the form.

Check Your Work

Project 4 Create a Blank Form with Lists   3 Parts

You will use the Blank Form tool to create a new form for maintaining the FeesSCPlans table, which is used to track service plan fees. In the form, you will create list boxes to provide an easy way to enter data for new service contract plans.

Preview Finished Project

Creating a Blank Form

To quickly build a form that contains a small number of fields, use the Blank Form tool. A blank form begins with no controls or formatting and displays as a blank white page in Layout view.

 Blank Form

Tutorial

Adding a List Box

 List Box

To begin a new form, click the Create tab and then click the Blank Form button in the Forms group. Access opens the Field List task pane at the right side of the work area. Expand the list for the appropriate table and then add fields to the form as needed. If the Field List task pane displays with no table names, click the Show all tables hyperlink at the top of the pane.

Adding a List Box to a Form

A list box displays a list of values for a field within the control object. In Form view, the user can easily see the entire list for the field. Create the list of values when the control object is created or instruct Access to populate the list using values from a table or query. When a list box control object is added to the form, the List Box Wizard begins (as long as the Use Control Wizards button is toggled on). Within the List Box Wizard, specify the values to be shown in the list box.

Quick Steps

Add a List Box
1. Open form in Layout or Design view.
2. Click List Box button in Controls group.
3. Click within form.
4. Create values within List Box Wizard.
5. Save form.

Adding a Combo Box to a Form

A combo box is similar to a list box but it includes a text box within the control object. The user can either type the value for the field or click the arrow to display field values in a drop-down list and then click the desired value. As happens when adding a list box, when a combo box control object is added to the form, the Combo Box Wizard begins (as long as the Use Control Wizards button is toggled on). Within the Combo Box Wizard, specify the values to be shown in the drop-down list.

Tutorial

Adding a Combo
Box

Combo Box

Quick Steps

Add a Combo Box
1. Open form in Layout or Design view.
2. Click Combo Box button in Controls group.
3. Click within form.
4. Create values within Combo Box Wizard.
5. Save form.

Project 4a Creating a Blank Form   Part 1 of 3

1. With **4-RSRCompServ.accdb** open, click the Create tab and then click the Blank Form button in the Forms group.
2. If the Field List task pane at the right side of the work area does not display the table names, click the Show all tables hyperlink. Otherwise, proceed to Step 3.
3. Add fields from the FeesSCPlans table to the form by completing the following steps:
   a. Click the plus symbol (+) next to the FeesSCPlans table to expand the field list.
   b. Click the first field (named *ID*) in the Field List task pane and then drag the field to the top left of the form.
   c. Click the second field (named *Term*) in the Field List task pane, press and hold down the Shift key, click the last field, (named *Rate*) in the Field List task pane to select the remaining fields in the FeesSCPlans table, and then release the Shift key.

d. Position the mouse pointer within the selected field names and then drag the group of fields to the form below the *ID* field. Release the mouse when the pink bar displays below *ID*.

e. With the four fields added to the table still selected, press and hold down the Shift key, click the *ID* field, and then release the Shift key.

f. Position the mouse pointer on the orange border at the right of any of the selected label control objects until the pointer changes to a left-and-right-pointing arrow and then drag the right edge of the label control objects to the right until all the label text is visible, as shown below.

4. Close the Field List task pane.
5. Save the form with the name *SCPlans*.

Check Your Work

Project 4b Creating a List Box

Part 2 of 3

1. With **4-RSRCompServ.accdb** open and the SCPlans form open in Layout view, add a list box control object to show the plan letters in a list by completing the following steps:

a. Click the List Box button in the Controls group on the Form Layout Tools Design tab.

b. Position the pointer with the list box icon attached below the *Plan* field text box control object in the form. Click the mouse when the pink bar displays between *A* and *1* in the right column. The List Box Wizard starts when the mouse is released. ***Note: If the Wizard does not start and the Use Control Wizard button is active, change to Design view and then back to Layout view.***

c. At the first List Box Wizard dialog box, click *I will type in the values that I want* and then click the Next button.

d. At the second List Box Wizard dialog box, click in the first cell below *Col1*, type A, and then press the Tab key.

e. Type B, press the Tab key, type C, press the Tab key, type D, and then click the Next button.

f. At the third List Box Wizard dialog box, click *Store that value in this field* option, click the option box arrow, and then click *Plan* at the drop-down list.

g. Click the Next button.

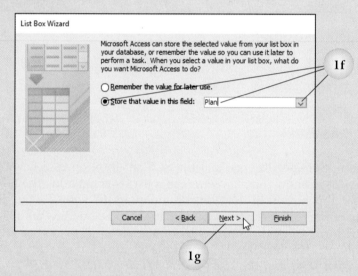

h. At the last List Box Wizard dialog box with the current text already selected in the *What label would you like for your list box?* text box, type PlanList and then click the Finish button. Access adds the list box to the form, displaying all the values entered in the list.

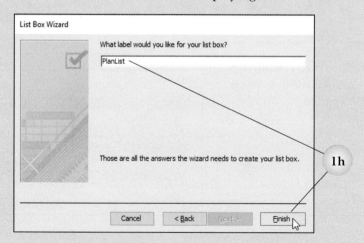

2. Save the form.

Check Your Work

1. With **4-RSRCompServ.accdb** open and the SCPlans form open in Layout view, add a combo box control object to enter the maximum number of computers in a plan by completing the following steps:

   a. Click the Combo Box button in the Controls group on the Form Layout Tools Design tab.

   b. Position the pointer with the combo box icon attached below the *Max No. of Computers* text box control object in the form. Click the mouse when the pink bar displays between *1* and *$60.32* in the right column. The Combo Box Wizard starts when the mouse button is released. ***Note: If the Wizard does not start and the Use Control Wizard button is active, change to Design view and then back to Layout view.***

   c. At the first Combo Box Wizard dialog box, click *I will type in the values that I want* and then click the Next button.

   d. At the second Combo Box Wizard dialog box, click in the first cell below *Col1*, type 1, and then press the Tab key.

   e. Type 2, press the Tab key, type 3, press the Tab key, type 4, press the Tab key, type 5, and then click the Next button.

   f. At the third Combo Box Wizard dialog box, click *Store that value in this field* option, click the option box arrow, click *MaxCptr* at the drop-down list, and then click the Next button.

   g. At the last Combo Box Wizard dialog box with the current text already selected in the *What label would you like for your combo box?* text box, type CptrList and then click the Finish button. Access adds the combo box to the form, displaying a value and an option box arrow at the right side of the text box.

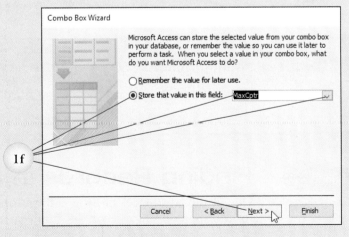

2. Double-click the label for the combo box added in Step 1g (which currently reads *CptrList*), select the text if it is not already selected, and then type Maximum Computers. Edit the label for the list box added in Project 4b (which currently reads *PlanList*) to add a space between *Plan* and *List*.

3. Right-click the label control object above the combo box (which displays the text *Max No. of Computers*) and then click *Select Entire Row* at the shortcut menu. Press the Delete key to remove the selected row from the form.

4. Click the Title button in the Header/Footer group on the Form Layout Tools Design tab and then type the text Service Contract Plans.

5. Switch to Form view and then scroll through the records in the form.

6. Add a new record to the table by completing the following steps:
   a. Click the New button in the Records group on the Home tab.
   b. Press the Tab key to move past the *ID* field since this field is an AutoNumber data type field.
   c. Click the *Term* option box arrow and then click *2 years* at the drop-down list.
   d. Click *B* in the *Plan List* list box. Notice that *B* is entered in the *Plan* field text box control object when the letter *B* is clicked in the list box.
   e. Click the *Maximum Computers* option box arrow and then click *3* at the drop-down list.
   f. Click in the *Rate* text box and then type 360.50.

7. Print the selected record, save, and then close the form.

Check Your Work

Project 5 Finding Records within a Form   1 Part

You will open a custom-built form and use it to find records by using a wildcard character.

Tutorial

Finding Records in a Form

Finding Records in a Form

One of the advantages of using a form for data entry and maintenance is that the form displays a single record at a time within the work area. Seeing one record at a time reduces the likelihood of editing the wrong record; the user can focus on the current record and not be distracted by other records. In a table with many records, quickly finding the specific record to be maintained or viewed is important. Use the Find feature to move to records quickly.

Quick Steps

Find Records Using a Wildcard
1. Open form in Form view.
2. Click in field by which to search.
3. Click Find button or Ctrl + F.
4. Type search string, including asterisk for any variable text.
5. Click Find Next.
6. Continue clicking Find Next until search is finished.
7. Click OK.
8. Close Find and Replace dialog box.

 Find

The Find feature allows searching for records without specifying the entire field value. To do this, substitute wildcard characters in the positions for which the exact text is not specified. Two commonly used wildcard characters are the asterisk (*) and the question mark (?).

For example, suppose that a search is needed for a record by a person's last name but the correct spelling is not known. Use the asterisk wildcard character in a position for which one or more characters vary. Use the question mark wildcard character in a fixed-width word for which the records with the same number of characters in the field are to be viewed. In this case, substitute one question mark for each character not specified. Table 4.1 provides examples of how to use the asterisk and question mark wildcard characters. In Project 5, the asterisk wildcard character will be used to locate customer records for a specified street.

Table 4.1 Examples of Using Wildcard Characters with the Find Feature

Find What Entry	In This Field	Will Find
104?	*Customer ID*	customer records with customer IDs that begin with *104* and have one more character, such as *1041, 1042, 1043,* and so on up to *1049*
4820?	*ZIP Code*	customer records with zip codes that begin with *4820* and have one more character, such as *48201, 48202,* and so on
650??	*Work Order*	work order records with work order numbers that begin with *650* and have two more characters, such as *65023, 65035, 65055,* and so on
313*	*Home Phone*	customer records with telephone numbers that begin with the *313* area code
Peter*	*Last Name*	customer records with last names that begin with *Peter* and have any number of characters following, such as *Peters, Peterson, Petersen, Peterovski,* and so on
4820*	*ZIP Code*	customer records with zip codes that begin with *4820* and have any number of characters following, such as *48201* and *48203-4841*
oak	*Street Address*	customer records with street addresses that have *oak* within them, such as *1755 Oak Drive, 12-234 Oak Street,* and *9 Oak Boulevard*

  Chapter 4 | Creating and Using Custom Forms **121**

1. With **4-RSRCompServ.accdb** open, open the CustMaintenance form in Form view.
2. To locate the name of the customer who resides on Roselawn Street when neither the house number nor the customer's name is known, complete the following steps to find the record using a wildcard character in the criterion:
   a. Click in the *Street Address* field.
   b. Click the Find button in the Find group.
   c. With the insertion point positioned in the *Find What* text box, type *roselawn* and then click the Find Next button.
   The entry **roselawn** means "Find any record in which any number of characters before *roselawn* and any number of characters after *roselawn* exist in the active field." Access displays the first record in the form in which a match was found.

   d. Click the Find Next button to see if any other records exist for customers on Roselawn Street.
   e. At the Microsoft Access message box indicating that Access has finished searching the records, click OK.
   f. Close the Find and Replace dialog box.
3. Close the CustMaintenance form.
4. Close **4-RSRCompServ.accdb**

In this chapter, you have learned techniques for building a custom form using Design view. As you learned in Project 2, you can create a form using one of the form tools, such as the Form Wizard, and then make changes to the form in Design view. As you become more experienced with Access, you will likely use a combination of three methods to build custom forms: a form tool to build the basic table and field structure of the form; Layout view to apply formatting options, add a title and logo, and make other appearance changes; and Design view to add advanced control objects, such as tab controls, subforms, and calculations.

Chapter Summary

- In Design view initially, a new form displays the *Detail* section, which is used to display records from the table associated with the form.

- A *Form Header* section and *Form Footer* section can be added to a form. Control objects placed in the *Form Header* section display at the top of the form or print at the beginning of a printout of records from Form view. Control objects placed in the *Form Footer* section display at the bottom of the form or print at the end of a printout of records from Form view.

- A form can contain three types of control objects: bound, unbound, and calculated.

- Click the Title button to display the *Form Header* and *Form Footer* sections and add a label control object in the *Form Header* section that contains the form name.

- Click the Label button in the Controls group to add a label control object within any section of the form.

- To specify the table to be connected to the form, use the *Record Source* property box on the Data tab of the form's Property Sheet task pane. Open this task pane by double-clicking the Form Selector button.

- Once a table has been connected to a form, click the Add Existing Fields button to open the Field List task pane.

- To add fields to a form, drag selected field names individually or in groups from the Field List task pane to the *Detail* section of the form.

- Use the move handle (the large dark-gray square at the top left of the selected control object) to move a selected control object independently of its connected label control or text box control object.

- Use the buttons in the Font group on the Form Design Tools Format tab to apply various types of formatting to selected control objects.

- Format multiple control objects at the same time by drawing a selection rectangle around a group of adjacent control objects or pressing and holding down the Shift key while clicking individual control objects.

- Open the Tab Order dialog box to change the order that fields are selected in when using the Tab key to move from field to field in Form view.

- Add a tab control object to a form to organize groups of related fields or insert subforms that display on separate pages.

- Click the Subform/Subreport button in the Controls group to add a subform to a page.

- Add a calculated control object to a form using the Text Box button in the Controls group.

- Type a formula in a text box control object (which displays *Unbound*) beginning with an equals sign. Enclose field names within the formula in square brackets.

- Use the Size/Space button and Align button in the Sizing & Ordering group on the Form Design Tools Arrange tab to position, align, size, or adjust spacing between multiple selected control objects.

- Add graphics to a form using the Logo button in the Header/Footer group or the Insert Image button in the Controls group.

- Draw a horizontal or vertical line in a form using the Line button in the Controls group. To draw a straight line, press and hold down the Shift key while dragging. Use the Shape Outline button on the Form Design Tools Format tab to adjust a line's thickness, type, or color.
- Online images can be added to a form after being inserted in a Microsoft Word document and then saved to a folder using standard Windows commands. Insert the saved image in the form using the Insert Image button.
- Change a control object's Size Mode property to resize an image within a control object while maintaining the original proportions of height and width.
- Use the Anchoring button in the Position group to anchor a control object to a section or another control object so that its position relative to the edges of the form is maintained when the form is resized.
- A datasheet form looks like a table datasheet.
- Use options on the Data tab of the form's Property Sheet task pane to restrict what actions a user can perform when viewing records in Form view.
- Use the Blank Form tool in the Forms group on the Create tab to create a new form with no controls or formatting applied. The form displays as a blank white page in Layout view with the Field List task pane open at the right of the work area.
- A list box displays a list of values for a field within the control object. The values to be shown in the list box can be specified within the List Box Wizard.
- A combo box includes a text box within the control object so the user can type the field value into the text box or click the option box arrow to pick the field value from a drop-down list. The values to be shown in the drop-down list can be specified within the Combo Box Wizard.
- Find specific records quickly using the Find feature.
- The Find feature allows the use of wildcard characters, such as the asterisk and question mark, to search records without specifying the entire field value.
- To find a record in a form, click in a field, click the Find button, and then enter the search criterion in the *Find What* text box.

Commands Review

FEATURE	RIBBON TAB, GROUP	BUTTON	KEYBOARD SHORTCUT
add existing fields	Form Design Tools Design, Tools		
adjust size of multiple controls	Form Design Tools Arrange, Sizing & Ordering		
align multiple controls at same position	Form Design Tools Arrange, Sizing & Ordering		
anchor controls to form	Form Design Tools Arrange, Position		
blank form	Create, Forms		
change tab order of fields	Form Design Tools Design, Tools		
combo box	Form Layout Tools Design, Controls		

FEATURE	RIBBON TAB, GROUP	BUTTON	KEYBOARD SHORTCUT
datasheet form	Create, Forms		
Design view	Home, Views OR Form Design Tools Design, Views		
equal spacing between control objects	Form Design Tools Arrange, Sizing & Ordering		
Find	Home, Find		Ctrl + F
Form view	Home, Views OR Form Design Tools Design, Views		
insert image	Form Design Tools Design, Controls		
label control object	Form Design Tools Design, Controls	Aa	
line	Form Design Tools Design, Controls		
list box	Form Design Tools Design, Controls		
Property Sheet task pane	Form Design Tools Design, Tools		F4
subform	Form Design Tools Design, Controls		
tab control object	Form Design Tools Design, Controls		
text box control object	Form Design Tools Design, Controls	ab|	
title control object	Form Design Tools Design, Header/Footer		

Workbook

Chapter study tools and assessment activities are available in the *Workbook* ebook. These resources are designed to help you further develop and demonstrate mastery of the skills learned in this chapter.

Unit assessment activities are also available in the *Workbook*. These activities are designed to help you demonstrate mastery of the skills learned in this unit.

Microsoft® Access® Level 2

Unit 2

Advanced Reports, Access Tools, and Customizing Access

Microsoft®

Access®
Creating and Using Custom Reports

Performance Objectives

Precheck

Check your current skills to help focus your study.

Upon successful completion of Chapter 5, you will be able to:

1 Create a custom report in Design view using all five report sections

2 Connect a table or query to a report and add fields

3 Move, size, format, and align control objects

4 Insert a subreport into a report

5 Add page numbers and date and time control objects to a report

6 Add graphics to a report

7 Group records and add functions and totals

8 Add a calculated field to a report

9 Modify section or group properties to control print options

10 Insert and edit a chart in a report

11 Create a blank report

12 Add tabs control objects, list boxes, combo boxes, and hyperlinks to a report

13 Change the shape of a control object

14 Change the tab order of fields

15 Insert a subform into a report

Reports are used to generate printouts from the tables in a database. Although the Print feature can be used to print data from a table datasheet, query results datasheet, or form, the formatting of the data in this printout cannot be changed or customized. The Report feature provides tools and options that can be used to control the content and formatting to produce professional-quality reports that serve particular purposes. In this chapter, you will learn how to build custom reports.

SNAP

If you are a SNAP user, launch the Precheck and Tutorials from your Assignments page.

Data Files

Before beginning chapter work, copy the AL2C5 folder to your storage medium and then make AL2C5 the active folder.

Project 1 **Design and Create a Custom Report**   **5 Parts**

You will create a custom report in Design view with fields from two tables and insert a subreport.

Preview Finished Project

Report
Design

Quick Steps

Start a New Report in Design View
1. Click Create tab.
2. Click Report Design button.

Add a Report Title
1. Open report in Design view.
2. Click Title button.
3. Type title text.
4. Press Enter.

Add a Label Control Object
1. Open report in Design view.
2. Click Label button.
3. Drag to create control object of approriate size.
4. Type label text.
5. Press Enter.

Creating Custom Reports Using Design View

Access provides the Report tool and Report Wizard to help quickly create reports that can be modified later. Customize the content, format, and layout of a report in Layout view or Design view. In most cases, use one of the report tools to generate the report structure and then customize the report using a different view. However, if a report requires several custom options, begin in Design view and build the report from scratch. Click the Create tab and then click the Report Design button in the Reports group to create a new report using Design view, as shown in Figure 5.1.

Creating a custom report in Design view involves using the same techniques taught in Chapter 4 for designing and building a custom form. Adding a title; connecting a table or query to the report; adding fields; and aligning, moving, resizing, and formatting control objects is done the same way as customizing a form.

A report can contain up to five sections, each of which is described in Table 5.1. *Group Header* and *Group Footer* sections can be added to group records that contain repeating values in a field, such as a department or city. How to use these additional sections will be demonstrated in Project 3. A report that is grouped by more than one field can have multiple *Group Header* and *Group Footer* sections.

Figure 5.1 Report Design View

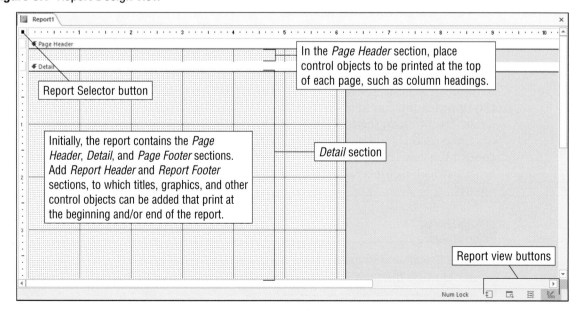

Table 5.1 Report Sections

Report Section	Description
Report Header	Content prints at the beginning of the report. Add control objects to this section for the report title and company logo or another image.
Page Header	Content prints at the top of each page in the report. Add control objects to this section for column headings in a tabular report format.
Detail	Add control objects to this section for the fields from the table or query that make up the body of the report.
Page Footer	Content prints at the bottom of each page in the report. Add a control object to this section to print a page number at the bottom of each page.
Report Footer	Content prints at the end of the report. Add a control object in this section to print a grand total or perform another function, such as calculating the average, maximum, minimum, or count.

Project 1a Starting a New Report Using Design View and Adding a Title and Label Control Object

Part 1 of 5

1. Open **5-RSRCompServ.accdb** and enable the content.
2. Click the Create tab and then click the Report Design button in the Reports group.
3. Add a title in the *Report Header* section of the report by completing the following steps:
   a. With the Report Design Tools Design tab active, click the Title button in the Header / Footer group. Access adds the *Report Header* section above the *Page Header* section and places a title object containing the selected text *Report1*.
   b. Type RSR Computer Service Work Orders and then press the Enter key.

4. With the title control object still selected, click the Report Design Tools Format tab and then click the Center button in the Font group.
5. Drag the right edge of the report grid until it is aligned at the 8-inch position on the horizontal ruler.
6. Scroll down the report until the *Page Footer* and *Report Footer* sections are visible. The *Report Footer* section was added to the design grid at the same time the *Report Header* section was added when the title was created in Step 3.

7. Drag down the bottom edge of the *Report Footer* section until the bottom of the report is aligned at the 0.5-inch position on the vertical ruler.
8. Click the Report Design Tools Design tab and then click the Label button in the Controls group. Add a label control object containing your first and last names at the left side of the *Report Footer* section.
9. Click in a blank area of the report to deselect the label control object.
10. Save the report and name it *WorkOrders*.

Check Your Work

Tutorial

Connecting a
Table to a Report
and Adding Fields

Quick Steps

**Connect a Table or
Query to a Report**
1. Open report in Design view.
2. Double-click Report Selector button.
3. Click Data tab in Property Sheet task pane.
4. Click arrow in *Record Source* property box.
5. Click table or query.
6. Close Property Sheet task pane.

**Add Fields
to a Report**
1. Click Add Existing Fields button.
2. Drag field name(s) from Field List task pane to *Detail* section.

**Add a Field from
a Related Table**
1. Open Field List task pane.
2. Click Show all tables hyperlink.
3. Click expand button next to table name in *Fields available in related tables* section.
4. Drag field name from related table list to *Detail* section.

 Report
Selector

 Add Existing
Fields

Connecting a Table or Query to a Report and Adding Fields

A new report that is started in Design view does not have a table or query associated with it. To display data in the report, Access needs to know what source to draw the data from. Connect a table or query to the report using the Record Source property in the report's Property Sheet task pane. Make sure to complete this step before adding fields to the *Detail* section.

The steps for connecting a table or query to a report are the same as the steps for connecting a table to a form. Double-click the Report Selector button above the vertical ruler and left of the horizontal ruler to open the report's Property Sheet task pane. Click the Data tab and then select the table or query name in the drop-down list at the *Record Source* property box. Display the Field List task pane and then drag individual fields or a group of fields from the table or query to the *Detail* section. After adding the fields, move and resize the control objects as needed.

The Field List task pane displays in one of two ways: showing one section only, with the fields from the table or query associated with the report, or showing two additional sections, with fields from other tables in the database. If the Field List task pane contains only the fields from the associated table or query, add fields from other tables by displaying other table names in the database within the Field List task pane.

At the top of the Field List task pane, Access displays a Show all tables hyperlink. Click the hyperlink to display the *Fields available in related tables* and *Fields available in other tables* sections. Next to each table name is an expand button, which displays as a plus symbol. Click the expand button next to the table name to display the fields stored within the table and then drag the field name(s) to the *Detail* section of the report. You will perform these steps in Project 1b.

1. With **5-RSRCompServ.accdb** open and the WorkOrders report open in Design view, scroll to the top of the report in the work area.
2. Connect the WorkOrders table to the report so that Access knows which fields to display in the Field List task pane by completing the following steps:
   a. Double-click the Report Selector button at the top of the vertical ruler and left of the horizontal ruler to open the report's Property Sheet task pane.
   b. Click the Data tab in the Property Sheet task pane, click the *Record Source* property option box arrow, and then click *WorkOrders* at the drop-down list.
   c. Close the Property Sheet task pane.

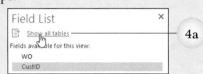

3. Click the Add Existing Fields button in the Tools group on the Report Design Tools Design tab to open the Field List task pane.
4. Add fields from the WorkOrders table and related fields from the Customers table by completing the following steps:
   a. Click the <u>Show all tables</u> hyperlink at the top of the Field List task pane. Access adds two sections to the pane: one containing related tables and the other containing tables in the database that do not have established relationships with the report's table. Next to each table name is an expand button (plus symbol), which is used to display field names for the table. ***Note: Skip this step if the <u>Show only fields in the current record source</u> hyperlink displays at the top of the Field List task pane. This means that the other sections have already been added to the pane.***

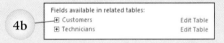

   b. Click the expand button next to *Customers* in the *Fields available in related tables* section of the Field List task pane. Access expands the list to display the field names in the Customers table.

   c. Drag the *WO*, *CustID*, *WODate*, and *Descr* fields from the WorkOrders table to the design grid, as shown below.
   d. Drag the *FName* and *LName* fields from the Customers table to the design grid, as shown at the right. Notice that the Customers table and field names move to the *Fields available for this view* section in the Field List task pane after the first field has been added from the Customers table to the *Detail* section.

5. Close the Field List task pane.
6. Save the report.

Check Your Work

Moving Control Objects to Another Section

Quick Steps

**Move Control Objects
to Another Section**
1. Open report in
   Design view.
2. Select control
   objects to be moved.
3. Click Home tab.
4. Click Cut button.
5. Click bar of section
   to move control
   objects to.
6. Click Paste button.
7. Deselect controls.

When a field is added to the *Detail* section of a report, a label control object containing the caption or field name is placed to the left of a text box control object that displays the field value from the record when the report is viewed or printed. Recall from Chapter 4 that the same thing happens when a form is customized.

In the WorkOrders report, the label control object for each field needs to be moved to the *Page Header* section so that the field names or captions print at the top of each page as column headings. In Project 1c, the control objects will be cut from the *Detail* section and pasted into the *Page Header* section.

Project 1c Moving Control Objects to Another Section

Part 3 of 5

1. With **5-RSRCompServ.accdb** open and the WorkOrders report open in Design view, move the label control objects from the *Detail* section to the *Page Header* section by completing the following steps:
   a. Click to select the *Work Order* label control object.
   b. Press and hold down the Shift key, click to select each of the other label control objects, and then release the Shift key.
   c. Click the Home tab and then click the Cut button in the Clipboard group.
   d. Click the *Page Header* section bar.
   e. Click the Paste button in the Clipboard group. (Do not click the button arrow.) Access pastes the label control objects and expands the *Page Header* section.
   f. Deselect the control objects.
2. Click to select the *Customer ID* label control object and then move the control object to the top of the *Page Header* section next to the *Work Order* label control object by hovering the mouse pointer over the *Customer ID* label control object until the four-headed arrow move icon displays and then dragging the control object to the location shown below.

3. Move the remaining four label control objects to the top of the *Page Header* section in the order shown in the image below by completing a step similar to Step 2.
4. Drag the top of the *Detail* section bar up until the top of the bar is aligned at the bottom edge of the label control objects in the *Page Header* section, as shown below.

5. Save the report.

Check Your Work

Tutorial

Formatting a
Report

 Themes

Applying a Theme

Apply a theme to a report using the Themes button on the Report Design Tools Design tab. The theme sets the default colors and fonts for the report. The themes available in Access align with the themes available in Word, Excel, and PowerPoint. This allows having the same look in Access reports as in other documents, worksheets, and presentations. Note that changing a theme for one report in a database automatically changes the theme for all the reports and forms in the database.

Project 1d **Moving Controls, Resizing Controls, and Applying a Theme**   Part 4 of 5

1. With **5-RSRCompServ.accdb** open and the WorkOrders report open in Design view, move each text box control object in the *Detail* section below its associated label control object in the *Page Header* section so that the field values align below the correct column headings in the report, as shown below.

2. Click the Report Design Tools Design tab, click the View button arrow in the Views group, and then click *Print Preview* at the drop-down list. (Note that there is also a Print Preview button in the view area at the right side of the Status bar.) Notice that the field value in the *WO Date* column displays pound symbols (#); this indicates that the field's text box control object needs to be widened. ***Note: If you receive an error message with the text*** The section width is greater than the page width, ***click OK.***

3. Return to Design view by clicking the Design View button in the view area at the bottom right side of the Status bar, next to the Zoom slider.

4. Resize the *WODate* text box control object in the *Detail* section so that the right edge of the control meets the left edge of the *Descr* text box control object.
5. Resize the *Descr* text box control in the *Detail* section so that the right edge of the control object is aligned at approximately the 7.5-inch position on the horizontal ruler.
6. Deselect the *Descr* control object.
7. Click the Themes button in the Themes group on the Report Design Tools Design tab and then click *Organic* at the drop-down gallery (third column, second row in the *Office* section).

8. Save the report.
9. Display the report in Print Preview to review the changes made in this project. Switch back to Design view when finished.

Check Your Work

Tutorial

Inserting a Subreport

Inserting a Subreport

A report that is inserted inside another report is called a *subreport*. Similar to a nested query, a subreport allows for reusing a group of fields, formats, and calculations in more than one report without having to recreate the setup each time.

Subform/ Subreport

Use the Subform/Subreport button in the Controls group on the Report Design Tools Design tab to insert a subreport into a report. The report into which the subreport is inserted is called the *main report*. Adding a related table or query as a subreport creates a control object within the main report that can be moved, formatted, and resized independently of the other control objects. Make sure the Use Control Wizards button is toggled on in the expanded Controls group before clicking the Subform/Subreport button. This will enable the subreport to be added using the SubReport Wizard, shown in Figure 5.2.

Quick Steps

Insert a Subreport
1. Open report in Design view.
2. Make sure *Use Control Wizards* is active.
3. Click Subform/ Subreport button.
4. Drag crosshairs to appropriate height and width in *Detail* section.
5. Click Next.
6. Choose table or query and fields.
7. Click Next.
8. Choose field by which to link main report with subreport.
9. Click Next.
10. Click Finish.

A subreport is stored as a separate object outside the main report. An additional report name will display in the Navigation pane with *subreport* at the end. Do not delete a subreport object in the Navigation pane. If the subreport object is deleted, the main report will no longer display the fields from the related table or query in the report.

Figure 5.2 First Dialog Box in the SubReport Wizard

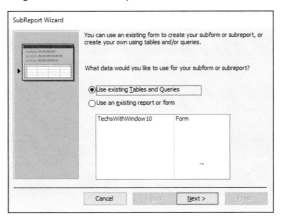

Project 1e   Inserting a Subreport

Part 5 of 5

1. With **5-RSRCompServ.accdb** open and the WorkOrders report open in Design view, insert a subreport into the WorkOrders report with fields from a query for the service date, labor, and parts for each work order by completing the following steps:
   a. By default, the Use Control Wizards button is toggled on in the Controls group. Click the More button in the Controls group to expand the Controls group and view two rows of buttons and the Controls drop-down list. View the current status of the Use Control Wizards button; if it displays with a pink or gray background, the feature is active. Recall from Chapter 4 that the active Control Wizard button is pink with the initial release of Access. If a later Access 2016 Service Pack has been installed on your computer the active Control Wizard button will be gray. If the button is pink or gray, click in a blank area to close the expanded Controls list. If the feature is not active (displays with a white background), click the Use Control Wizards button to turn on the feature.

   b. Click the More button in the Controls group and then click the Subform/Subreport button.

   A pink or gray background means the Use Control Wizards button is toggled on. Check the status and click the button to turn on the feature if necessary in Step 1a.

   c. Move the crosshairs with the subreport icon attached to the *Detail* section below the *WO* text box control object and then drag down and to the right to create a subreport object of the approximate height and width shown below. Release the mouse and the SubReport Wizard begins.

d. With *Use existing Tables and Queries* already selected at the first SubReport Wizard dialog box, click the Next button.

e. At the second SubReport Wizard dialog box, select the query fields to be displayed in the subreport by completing the following steps:

   1) Click the *Tables/Queries* option box arrow and then click *Query: TotalWorkOrders* at the drop-down list.

   2) Move all the fields from the *Available Fields* list box to the *Selected Fields* list box.

   3) Click the Next button.

f. At the third SubReport Wizard dialog box, choose the field by which to link the main report with the subreport by completing the following steps:

   1) With *Choose from a list* and the first option in the list box selected, read the description of the linked field that displays below the list box. The text indicates that the main report will be linked to the subreport using the *CustID* field. This is not the correct field; your report is to show the service date, labor, and parts based on the work order number.

   2) Click the second option in the list box and then read the text below the list box.

   3) Since the second option indicates that the two reports will be linked using the *WO* field, click the Next button.

g. Click the Finish button at the last SubReport Wizard dialog box to accept the default subreport name *TotalWorkOrders subreport*.

2. Access inserts the subreport with a label control object above it that contains the name of the subreport. Click the label control displaying the text *TotalWorkOrders subreport* to select the object and then press the Delete key.

3. Click the Report View button in the Views group on the Report Design Tools Design tab. (Note that a Report View button is also included in the View group, the first button on the right side of the Status bar.) Report view is not the same as Print Preview. Report view displays the report with data in the fields and is useful for viewing reports within the database. However, this view does not show how the report will look when printed. For printing purposes, always use Print Preview to resize and adjust control objects.

4. Notice that the work order number in the subreport is the same work order number that is displayed in the first record in the main report.

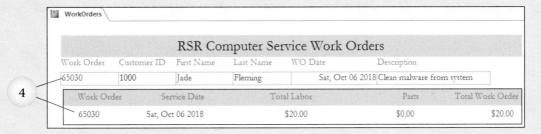

5. Switch back to Design view.

6. Now that you know the subreport is linked correctly to the main report, the work order number does not need to be displayed in the subreport. Delete the work order number control objects in the subreport by completing the following steps:

   a. Click to select the subreport control object and then drag down the bottom middle sizing handle to increase the height of the subreport until all the controls are visible in the *Report Header* and *Detail* sections.

   b. Click to select the *Work Order* label control object in the *Report Header* section, press and hold down the Shift key, click the *WO* text box control object in the *Detail* section in the subreport, and then release the Shift key.

   c. Press the Delete key.

   d. Select all the label control objects in the *Report Header* section and all the text box control objects in the *Detail* section. Move the control objects to the left so the left edge of the *Service Date* control objects are at the left margin. Click outside the subreport to deselect the control objects.

7. Click to select the subreport control object and then drag up the bottom middle sizing handle of the control until the height of the subreport is approximately 0.5 inch.

8. Scroll down the report until the *Page Footer* section bar is visible.

9. Drag up the top of the *Page Footer* section bar until the section bar is just below the subreport control object at the 1-inch mark in the *Detail* section, as shown below.

10. Save the report and then switch to Report view to view the revised report. Resizing the *Detail* section in Step 9 to reduce the spaces between sections allows more records and related subreport records to display on the page.

Reducing the height of the *Detail* section allows Access to display more records on the page.

11. Close the report.

Check Your Work

Project 2 Add Features and Enhance a Report   2 Parts

You will modify the WorkOrders report to add page numbers, date and time control objects, and graphics.

Preview Finished Project

Tutorial

Adding Page Numbers and the Date and Time Control Objects to a Report

Adding Page Numbers and the Date and Time Control Objects to a Report

When creating a report using the Report tool, page numbers and the current date and time are automatically added to the top right of the report. The Report Wizard automatically inserts the current date at the bottom left and page numbers at the bottom right of the report.

In Design view, add page numbers to a report using the Page Numbers button in the Header / Footer group on the Report Design Tools Design tab. Click the button to open the Page Numbers dialog box, shown in Figure 5.3. Choose the appropriate format, position, and alignment for the page number and then click OK. Access inserts a control object in the *Page Header* or *Page Footer* section, depending on the *Position* option selected in the dialog box. Including page numbers in a report allows referring to specific pages and putting pages back in order if they get rearranged.

Quick Steps
Add Page Numbers
1. Open Report in Design view.
2. Click Page Numbers button.
3. Select format, position, and alignment options.
4. Click OK.

 Page Numbers

Add the current date and/or time in the *Report Header* section by clicking the Date and Time button in the Header / Footer group to open the Date and Time dialog box, shown in Figure 5.4. By default, both the *Include Date* and *Include Time* check boxes contain check marks. Access creates one control object for the date format and another for the time format. Access places the date control object above the time control object and aligns both at the right edge of the *Report Header* section. Once the control objects have been inserted, they can be moved to another section in the report. Adding a date and/or time control object means that the current date and/or time the report is printed will be included on the printout. At a minimum, always include a date control. Depending on users' needs, the time control may or may not be necessary.

Figure 5.3 Page Numbers Dialog Box

Figure 5.4 Date and Time Dialog Box

Project 2a Adding Page Numbers and the Date and Time to a Report   Part 1 of 2

1. With **5-RSRCompServ.accdb** open, right-click *WorkOrders* in the Report group in the Navigation pane and then click *Design View* at the shortcut menu.
2. When the subreport was inserted in Project 1e, the width of the report may have been automatically extended beyond the page width. Look at the Report Selector button. If a green diagonal triangle displays in the upper left corner, correct the page width by completing the following steps. (Skip this step if the Report Selector button does not display with a green diagonal triangle.)
   a. Click the subreport control object to display the orange border and sizing handles. Point to the orange border and then drag the subreport left until the left edge is at the left edge of the *Detail* section.
   b. Drag the right middle sizing handle left to decrease the subreport width until the right edge of the subreport is aligned with the right edge of the *Descr* text box control object above it.

c. Click the green triangle to display the error-checking options button and then click the button to display the drop-down list of options.

d. Click *Remove Extra Report Space* at the drop-down list to automatically decrease the width of the report. Notice that the green diagonal triangle is removed from the Report Selector button once the report width has been corrected.

3. Add a page number at the bottom center of each page by completing the following steps:

a. Click the Page Numbers button in the Header / Footer group on the Report Design Tools Design tab.

b. Click *Page N of M* in the *Format* section of the Page Numbers dialog box.

c. Click *Bottom of Page [Footer]* in the *Position* section.

d. With the *Alignment* option box set to *Center* and a check mark in the *Show Number on First Page* check box, click OK. Access adds a control object in the center of the *Page Footer* section that contains the codes required to print the page numbers centered at the bottom of all pages, including the first page.

4. Add the current date and time to the end of the report along with a label control object that contains the text *Date and Time Printed:* by completing the following steps:

a. Click the Date and Time button in the Header / Footer group on the Report Design Tools Design tab.

b. Click the second option in the *Include Date* section in the Date and Time dialog box, which displays the date in the format *dd-mmm-yy*—for example, *17-Dec-18*.

c. Click the second option in the *Include Time* section, which displays the time in the format *hh:mm AM/PM*—for example, *3:07 PM*.

d. Click OK. Access adds two control objects, one above the other, at the right side of the *Report Header* section with the date code *=Date()* and time code *=Time()*.

e. Select the date and time control objects added to the *Report Header* section. Click the Home tab and then click the Cut button in the Clipboard group.

f. Click the *Report Footer* section bar and then click the Paste button in the Clipboard group. Access pastes the two control objects at the left side of the *Report Footer* section. With the date and time control objects still selected, position the mouse pointer on the orange border until the pointer displays with the four-headed arrow move icon and then drag the control objects to the right side of the *Report Footer* section, aligning the right edge of the control objects near the right edge of the report grid.

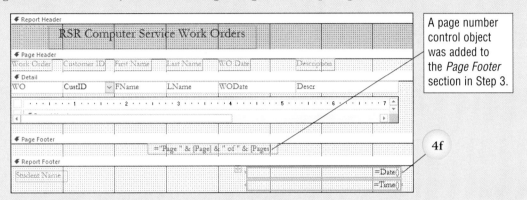

A page number control object was added to the *Page Footer* section in Step 3.

4f

g. Resize the date and time controls to be approximatively 0.75-inch wide as shown at the right.
h. Create the two label control objects, type the text Date Printed: and Time Printed:, and then position the label control objects left of the date control object and time control object, as shown at the right.

4g-4h

5. Save the report and then display it in Print Preview.
6. Scroll to the bottom of the first page to view the page number.
7. Click the Last Page button in the Page Navigation bar to scroll to the last page in the report and view the date and time.
8. Notice that in Print Preview, the subreport data is cut off at the right edge of the report, which means the total work order value is not visible. Exit Print Preview to switch back to Design view.
9. Adjust the size and placement of the subreport control objects by completing the following steps:
   a. Since the subreport control objects are not visible within the WorkOrders report, it is easier to work within the separate TotalWorkOrders subreport to make changes to its content. Close the WorkOrders report.
   b. Right-click the *TotalWorkOrders* subreport in the Navigation pane and then click *Design View* at the shortcut menu.
   c. Using the diagram below as a guide, adjust the widths of the Total Labor and/or Parts label control objects and text box control objects. Remove any space between the control objects.
   d. Drag the right edge of the grid left to approximately the 7-inch position on the horizontal ruler.

9c

9d

10. Save and close the TotalWorkOrders subreport.
11. Open the WorkOrders report. Notice that the data on the right side of the subreport data is no longer cut off.
12. Display the report in Design view.

Check Your Work

Tutorial

Adding a Graphic to a Report

Adding a Graphic
to a Report

 Insert Image

The same techniques learned in Chapter 4 for adding online images or drawing lines in a form in Design view can be applied to a report. An image in a standard picture file format (such as .gif, .jpg, or .png) can be inserted in an image control object. Click the Insert Image button in the Controls group on the Report Design Tools Design tab, browse to the drive and folder containing the image, double-click the image file name, and then drag to create an image control object of the required height and width within the report. Recall from Chapter 4 that when a control object containing an image is resized, parts of the image can be cut off. Display the Property Sheet task pane for the control object and then change the Size Mode property to *Zoom* or *Stretch* to resize the image to the height and width of the control object.

Project 2b Adding Graphics and Formatting Control Objects   Part 2 of 2

1. With **5-RSRCompServ.accdb** open and the WorkOrders report open in Design view, insert a company logo in the report by completing the following steps:
   a. Position the mouse pointer on the top of the *Page Header* section bar until the pointer displays as an up-and-down-pointing arrow with a horizontal line in the middle and then drag down approximately 0.5 inch to increase the height of the *Report Header* section.
   b. Click the Insert Image button in the Controls group on the Report Design Tools Design tab and then click *Browse* at the drop-down list.
   c. At the Insert Picture dialog box, navigate to the drive and/or folder for the AL2C5 data files on your storage medium and then double-click the file named *RSRlogo.png*.
   d. Position the crosshairs with the image icon attached at the top of the *Report Header* section near the 6-inch position on the horizontal ruler and then drag to create an image control object of the approximate height and width shown.

2. Select the title control object in the *Report Header* section and then click the Bold button in the Font group on the Report Design Tools Format tab.

3. Draw and format a horizontal line below the title by completing the following steps:
   a. Click the More button in the Controls group on the Report Design Tools Design tab and then click the Line button in the expanded Controls group.
   b. Position the crosshairs with the line icon attached below the first letter in the title in the *Report Header* section, press and hold down the Shift key, click the left mouse button and drag to the right, release the mouse button below the last letter in the title, and then release the Shift key.
   c. Click the Report Design Tools Format tab and then click the Shape Outline button in the Control Formatting group.
   d. Point to *Line Thickness* and then click *3 pt* (fourth option).
   e. With the line still selected, click the Shape Outline button, click *Blue-Gray, Accent 3* (seventh column, first row in the *Theme Colors* section), and then deselect the line.

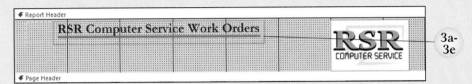

4. Draw and format a horizontal line below the column headings by completing the following steps:
   a. Drag down the top of the *Detail* section bar approximately 0.25 inch to add grid space in the *Page Header* section.
   b. Click the Report Design Tools Design tab, click the More button in the Controls group, and then click the Line button in the expanded Controls group.
   c. Draw a straight horizontal line that extends the width of the report along the bottom of the label control objects in the *Page Header* section.
   d. Click the Shape Outline button on the Report Design Tools Format tab, point to *Line Thickness*, and then click *2 pt*. Change the line color to the same Blue-Gray applied to the line below the report title.
   e. Deselect the line.

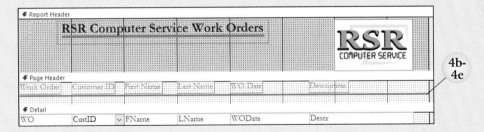

5. Format, move, and resize the control objects as follows:
   a. Select all the label control objects in the *Page Header* section, apply bold formatting, change the font size to 12 points, and then apply the Blue-Gray, Accent 3, Darker 50% font color (seventh column, last row in the *Theme Colors* section).
   b. Resize the control objects as needed to show all the label text after increasing the font size.
   c. Move the *WO Date* label control object in the *Page Header* section until the left edge of the control object is aligned at the 4.5-inch position on the horizontal ruler.
   d. Click the *Report Header* section bar, click the Shape Fill button in the Control Formatting group on the Report Design Tools Format tab, and then click *White, Background 1* (first column, first row in the *Theme Colors* section).

e. Select all the text box control objects in the *Detail* section. Open the Property Sheet task pane, click the Format tab, click in the *Border Style* property box, click the arrow that appears, and then click *Transparent* at the drop-down list. This removes the borders around the data in the fields.

f. With all the text box control objects still selected, click the *Fore Color* property box on the Format tab of the Property Sheet task pane. Click the Build button to open the color palette and then click *Black, Text 1* (second column, first row in the *Theme Colors* section).

g. Deselect the text box control objects and then select the *WODate* text box control object. Click in the *Width* property box in the Property Sheet task pane, change *1.5* to *1.4*.

h. Select the *Desc* text box control object, change the number in the *Width* property box to *2.25*, and then close the Property Sheet task pane.

6. Display the report in Report view.

7. Compare the report with the partial report shown in Figure 5.5. If necessary, return to Design view; adjust the formats, alignments, or positions of the control objects; and then redisplay the report in Report view.

8. Save the report.

9. Print the report. ***Note: This report is four pages long. Check with your instructor before printing it.***

10. Close the WorkOrders report.

Check Your Work

Figure 5.5 Partial View of the Completed WorkOrders Report

Project 3 Group Records and Add Functions to Count and Sum   3 Parts

You will create a new report using the Report Wizard and then modify the report in Design view to add count and sum functions.

Preview Finished Project

Tutorial

Creating a Report
Using the Report
Wizard

Grouping Records and Adding Functions and a Calculated Field in a Report

A field that contains repeated values—such as a department, city, or name—is an appropriate field to group records on in a report. For example, organize a report to show all the records for the same department or city. By summarizing the records by a common field value, totals can be produced using functions to calculate the sum, average, maximum, minimum, or count for each group. For example, a report similar to the partial report shown in Figure 5.6, which organizes work orders by customer, allows the owners of RSR Computer Service to see which customer has provided the most revenue to their service business. In this report, the *CustID* field (column heading *Customer ID*) is used to group the records and a Sum function has been added to each group.

Group & Sort

Recall from Level 1, Chapter 6 that either the Group & Sort button or the Report Wizard can be used to group records in a report. At the Report Wizard dialog box, shown in Figure 5.7, double-click a field name in the list box to add a grouping level. The preview window updates to display the grouped field in blue.

Figure 5.6 Example Report with the Work Order Records Grouped by Customer

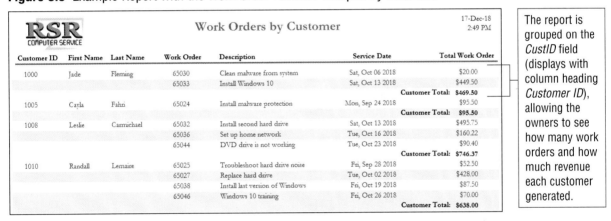

The report is grouped on the *CustID* field (displays with column heading *Customer ID*), allowing the owners to see how many work orders and how much revenue each customer generated.

Figure 5.7 Grouping by a Field Using the Report Wizard

In this list box, double-click the field by which to group records.

Click this button to open the Grouping Intervals dialog box to change the default grouping interval. For example, group dates by quarter instead of month.

A grouped field is displayed in blue at the top of the report and the remaining fields are indented below.

Double-click a second field name to add a second grouping level. For example, group records by state and then by city.

More than one grouping level can be added to a report. To remove a grouping level, use the Remove Field button (the button with the left-pointing arrow) to remove the grouped level. Use the Priority buttons (the buttons with up-pointing and down-pointing arrows) to change the grouping order when there are multiple grouped fields.

If a report was not grouped when using the Report Wizard, group records can be added after the report has been generated using Layout view or Design view. In Layout view, click the Group & Sort button in the Grouping & Totals group on the Report Layout Tools Design tab. In Design view, click the Group & Sort button in the Grouping & Totals group on the Report Design Tools Design tab. Clicking the button in either view opens the Group, Sort, and Total pane, shown in Figure 5.8, at the bottom of the work area. Click the Add a group button and then click the field name by which to group records in the pop-up list.

Figure 5.8 Group, Sort, and Total Pane

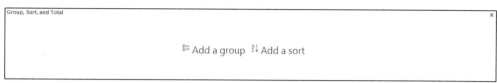

Project 3a Creating a Report with a Grouping Level Using the Report Wizard   Part 1 of 3

1. With **5-RSRCompServ.accdb** open, modify the TotalWorkOrders query to add two fields to include in a report by completing the following steps:
   a. Open the TotalWorkOrders query in Design view.
   b. Drag the *CustID* field from the *WorkOrders* table field list box to the *Field* row in the second column in the query design grid. *ServDate* and other fields will shift right to accommodate the new field.
   c. Drag the *Descr* field from the *WorkOrders* table field list box to the *Field* row in the third column in the query design grid.
   d. Save the revised query.
   e. Run the query.

   In Step 1e, the revised query is run with the new fields added.

   f. Close the query.
2. Create a report based on the TotalWorkOrders query that is grouped by service date by month using the Report Wizard by completing the following steps:
   a. Click the Create tab and then click the Report Wizard button in the Reports group.

b. At the first Report Wizard dialog box with *Query: TotalWorkOrders* already selected in the *Tables/Queries* option box, move all the fields from the *Available Fields* list box to the *Selected Fields* list box and then click the Next button.

c. At the second Report Wizard dialog box, specify that the report is to be grouped by the *ServDate* field by completing the following steps:

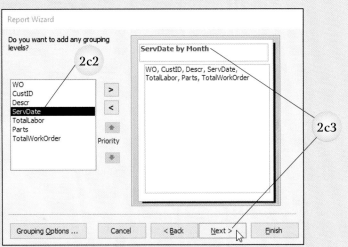

1) With *CustID* displayed in blue in the preview section, indicating that the report will be grouped by customer number, click the Remove field button (the left-pointing arrow) to remove the grouping level.

2) Double-click *ServDate* in the field list box to add a grouping level by the service date field. By default, Access groups a date field by month.

3) With the preview section now displaying that the report will be grouped by *ServDate by Month*, click the Next button.

d. At the third Report Wizard dialog box, click the arrow at the right of the first sort option box, click *WO* at the drop-down list to sort each group by work order number in ascending order, and then click the Next button.

e. At the fourth Report Wizard dialog box, click *Landscape* in the *Orientation* section and then click the Next button.

f. At the last Report Wizard dialog box, select the existing text in the *What title do you want for your report?* text box, type WorkOrdersbyMonth, and then click the Finish button.

3. Minimize the Navigation pane.

4. Preview the report and then switch to Layout view or Design view. Edit the text in the report title and column heading labels, adjust column widths and the *Report Header* section height as necessary until the report looks similar to the one shown below. The Organic theme was applied in Project 1d. Modify the colors for the *Report Header* and *Page Header* sections to most closely match the theme colors shown below.

Work Orders by Month							
ServDate by Month	Work Order	CustID	Descr	Service Date	Total Labor	Parts	Total Work Order
September 2018							
	65019	1025	Upgrade to new Windows	Mon, Sep 17 2018	$87.50	$0.00	$87.50
	65020	1030	Troubleshoot noisy fan	Mon, Sep 17 2018	$37.50	$62.77	$100.27
	65021	1035	Customer has blue screen upon boot	Tue, Sep 18 2018	$113.75	$0.00	$113.75
	65022	1040	Customer reports screen is fuzzy	Sat, Sep 22 2018	$52.50	$55.47	$107.97
	65023	1045	Upgrade RAM	Sun, Sep 23 2018	$43.75	$62.50	$106.25
	65024	1005	Install malware protection	Mon, Sep 24 2018	$20.00	$75.50	$95.50
	65025	1010	Troubleshoot hard drive noise	Fri, Sep 28 2018	$52.50	$0.00	$52.50
	65026	1025	Upgrade memory	Sat, Sep 29 2018	$26.25	$75.75	$102.00

5. Save the report.

Check Your Work

Adding Functions to a Group

When a report is grouped, the Group, Sort, and Total pane can be used to add a calculation below a numeric field at the end of each group. Functions can also be added to more than one field within the group. For example, calculate a Sum function on a sales field and a Count function on an invoice field. The following functions are available for numeric fields: Sum, Average, Count Records, Count Values, Maximum, Minimum, Standard Deviation, and Variance. A non-numeric field can have a Count Records or Count Values function added.

Quick Steps

Add Functions to a Group

1. Open report in Design view or Layout view.
2. Click Group & Sort button.
3. Click More Options button.
4. Click arrow next to *with no totals*.
5. Choose field in *Total On* list box.
6. Choose function in *Type* list box.
7. If desired, click *Show Grand Total* check box.
8. If required, click *Show group subtotal as % of Grand Total* check box.
9. Click *Show subtotal in group header* or *Show subtotal in group footer* check box.
10. Repeat Steps 5–9 as needed for other fields.
11. Click outside *Totals* option box.
12. Close Group, Sort, and Total pane.

The Group, Sort, and Total pane for a report with an existing grouping level looks similar to the one shown in Figure 5.9. Click the More Options button next to the group level to which a total is to be added to expand the available group options.

Click the option box arrow next to *with no totals* to open a *Totals* option box, similar to the one shown in Figure 5.10. Use the option boxes within this box to select the field a function should be added to and the type of aggregate function to calculate. Use the check boxes to choose to add a grand total to the end of the report, calculate group subtotals as percentages of the grand total, and decide whether to add the subtotal function to the *Group Header* or *Group Footer* section. Continue adding functions to other fields as needed and then click outside the *Totals* option box to close it.

Figure 5.9 Group, Sort, and Total Pane with a Grouping Level Added

Click the More Options button to expand the pane to show group interval options, the *Totals* option, and other group options.

Hint Apply formatting options such as bold, color, and borders (in the Property Sheet task pane) to totals to make them stand out in a report. For totals without a border style, use the Line tool to underline them. For example, draw two lines below a grand total to create a double underline.

Figure 5.10 *Totals* Option Box in the Group, Sort, and Total Pane

Click here in the expanded options list to open the *Totals* option box, in which the field(s) and function(s) to add to the report are specified. Also add functions to calculate a grand total at the end of the report and group totals as percentages of the grand total.

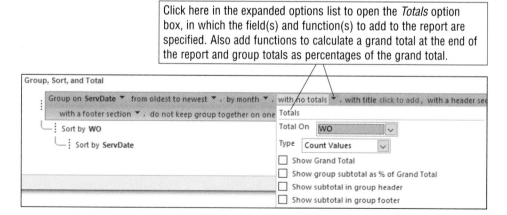

Project 3b Adding Functions to a Report

1. With **5-RSRCompServ.accdb** open, display the WorkOrdersbyMonth report in Design view.
2. Add two functions at the end of each month to show the number of work orders and the total value of the work orders by completing the following steps:

   a. In the Grouping & Totals group on the Report Design Tools Design tab, click the Group & Sort button.

   b. At the Group, Sort, and Total pane at the bottom of the work area, click the More Options button next to *from oldest to newest* in the *Group on ServDate* group options.

   c. Click the option box arrow next to *with no totals* in the expanded group options.

   d. At the *Totals* option box with *WO* selected in the *Total On* option box, specify the type of function and the placement of the result by completing the following steps:

      1) Click the *Type* option box arrow and then click *Count Records* at the drop-down list.

      2) Click the *Show Grand Total* check box to insert a check mark. Access adds a Count function in a control object in the *Report Footer* section below the *WO* column.

      3) Click the *Show subtotal in group footer* check box to insert a check mark. Access displays a new section with the title *ServDate Footer* in the section bar below the *Detail* section and inserts a Count function in a control object below the *WO* column.

A *Group Footer* (*ServDate Footer*) section is created and a Count function control object is added in Step 2d3.

A Count function control object is added to the *Report Footer* section in Step 2d2.

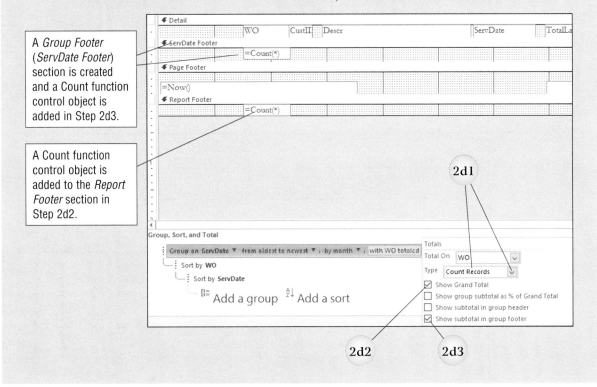

e. With the *Totals* option box still open, click the *Total On* option box arrow and then click *TotalWorkOrder* at the drop-down list. The *Type* option defaults to *Sum* for a numeric field.

f. Click the *Show Grand Total* check box to insert a check mark. Access adds a Sum function in a control object in the *Report Footer* section.

g. Click the *Show subtotal in group footer* check box to insert a check mark. Access adds a Sum function in a control object in the *ServDate Footer* section.

h. Click outside the *Totals* option box to close it.

3. Click the Group & Sort button to close the Group, Sort, and Total pane.

4. Review the two Count functions and two Sum functions added to the report in Design view.

5. Display the report in Print Preview to view the calculated results. Notice that the printout requires two pages and that the report's grand totals print on page 2. If any totals display with pound signs (#) switch to Design view, adjust the width of the control object, and then switch back to Print Preview. Also notice that Access added the Sum function below the Count function rather than at the bottom of the *Total Work Order* column.

6. Close Print Preview to switch back to Design view.

7. Click to select the Sum function control object in the *ServDate Footer* section, press and hold down the Shift key, click to select the Sum function control object in the *Report Footer* section, and then release the Shift key. Position the mouse pointer on the orange border of one of the selected control objects and then drag to move the two control objects simultaneously to the right below the TotalWorkOrder control object in the *Detail* section.

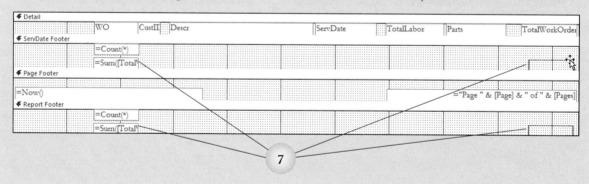

8. Add a label control object left of the Count function in the *ServDate Footer* section that displays the text *Work Order Count:* and another label control object left of the Sum function that displays the text *Month Total:*. Apply bold formatting and the red font color and right-align the text in the two label control objects. Resize and align the two label control objects as necessary. ***Note: Access displays an error flag on the two label control objects, indicating that these control objects are not associated with another control object. Ignore these error flags because the label control objects have been added for descriptive text only.***

9. Move up the Sum function control object and *Month Total:* label control object until they are at the same horizontal position as the Count function and then decrease the height of the *ServDate Footer* section as shown below.

8-9

10. Display the report in Print Preview to view the labels. If necessary, return to Design view to further adjust the size and alignment.

10

ServDate by Month	Work Order	CustID	Descr	Service Date	Total Labor	Parts	Total Work Order
September 2018							
	65019	1025	Upgrade to new Windows	Mon, Sep 17 2018	$87.50	$0.00	$87.50
	65020	1030	Troubleshoot noisy fan	Mon, Sep 17 2018	$37.50	$62.77	$100.27
	65021	1035	Customer has blue screen upon boot	Tue, Sep 18 2018	$113.75	$0.00	$113.75
	65022	1040	Customer reports screen is fuzzy	Sat, Sep 22 2018	$52.50	$55.47	$107.97
	65023	1045	Upgrade RAM	Sun, Sep 23 2018	$43.75	$62.50	$106.25
	65024	1005	Install malware protection	Mon, Sep 24 2018	$20.00	$75.50	$95.50
	65025	1010	Troubleshoot hard drive noise	Fri, Sep 28 2018	$52.50	$0.00	$52.50
	65026	1025	Upgrade memory	Sat, Sep 29 2018	$26.25	$75.75	$102.00
Work Order Count:	8					Month Total:	$765.74

11. With the report displayed in Design view, select the Sum function control object in the *Report Footer* section and move up the control until it is positioned at the same horizontal position as the Count function below the *WO* column.

12. Click to select the *Work Order Count:* label control object, press and hold down the Shift key, click to select the *Month Total:* label control object, release the Shift key, click the Home tab, and then click the Copy button in the Clipboard group. Click the *Report Footer* section bar and then click the Paste button in the Clipboard group. Move and align the copied labels as shown below. Edit the *Month Total:* label control object to *Grand Total:* as shown.

12

13. Display the report in Report view. Scroll to the bottom of the page to view the labels next to the grand totals. If necessary, return to Design view to further adjust the size and alignment and then save and close the report.

Check Your Work

Adding a Calculated Field to a Report

Several options are available for adding a calculated field to a report. Either create a query that includes a calculated column and then create a new report based on the query or create a calculated control object in an existing report using Design view. A calculated value can be placed in any section of the report. To create a calculated control object in a report, follow the same steps learned in Chapter 4 for adding a calculated control object to a form. Remember that field names in a formula are enclosed in square brackets.

A calculated control object can be used as a field in another formula. To do this, reference the calculated control object in the formula by its Name property (found on the Other tab of the Property Sheet task pane). If necessary, change the name of the calculated control object to a more descriptive or succinct name.

Project 3c Adding a Calculated Field to a Report   Part 3 of 3

1. With **5-RSRCompServ.accdb** open, display the WorkOrdersbyMonth report in Design view. In the following steps you will create a calculated control object to project the value of November's work orders. Assume that the value for November will be a 10% increase over the value for October.
2. Change the name of the text box control object that contains the summed value of October's work orders to a shortened name by completing the following steps:
   a. Click the control object that contains the summed monthly value (displays part of the formula =*Sum([TotalWorkOrder])*) in the *ServDate Footer* section.
   b. Click the Property Sheet button in the Tools group on the Report Design Tools Design tab.
   c. Click the Other tab in the Property Sheet task pane.
   d. Select and delete the existing text (displays *AccessTotalsTotal Work Order1*) in the *Name* property box, type MonthlyTotal, and then close the Property Sheet task pane.
3. Add a calculated text box control object to the *Report Footer* section by completing the following steps:
   a. Click the Text Box button in the Controls group.
   b. Position the crosshairs with the text box icon attached at the 6-inch mark on the horizontal ruler in the *Report Footer* section. Drag to create a control object that is approximately 2 inches wide by 0.25 inch tall at the same vertical position as the other control objects in the *Report Footer* section and then release the mouse.
   c. Click in the text box control object (displays *Unbound*), type =[MonthlyTotal]*1.1, and then press the Enter key.

3b-
3c

   d. Format the calculated control object using the Currency format.

e. Select the entry in the label control object (displays *Textxx,* where *xx* is the text box control object number) and then type November's Projected Total:. The two control objects will be resized and moved in steps below.

f. Apply bold formatting and the red font color to the text in both control objects.

g. Resize the text box control that contains the new formula until the left edge of the control object is aligned at approximately the 7-inch position on the horizontal ruler.

h. Resize the label control object that contains the text *November's Projected Total:* until the right edge of the control object meets the left edge of the text box control object, as shown below. Right-align the text in the label control object.

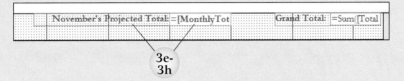

4. Display the report in Report view. Scroll to the bottom of the page to view the calculated field. If necessary, return to Design view to further adjust the size and alignment and then save and close the report. Further changes to the report will be made in Project 4.

5. Redisplay the Navigation pane.

Check Your Work

Project 4 Modify Section and Group Properties   **1 Part**

You will change a report's page setup and then modify section and group properties to control print options.

Preview Finished Project

Tutorial

Modifying Section Properties

Modifying Section Properties

Quick Steps

Modify Section Properties
1. Open report in Design view.
2. Double-click white section bar.
3. Change properties.
4. Close Property Sheet task pane.

A report has a Property Sheet, each control object within a report has a Property Sheet, and each section within a report has a Property Sheet. Section properties control whether the section is visible when printed, along with the section's height, background color, special effects, and so on.

Figure 5.11 displays the Format tab in the Property Sheet task pane for the *Report Header* section. Some of the options can be changed without opening the Property Sheet task pane. For example, increase or decrease the height of a section by dragging the top or bottom of a white section bar in Design view. The background color can also be set using the Fill/Back Color button in the Font group on the Report Design Tools Format tab.

Use the Keep Together property to ensure that a section does not split over two pages because of a page break. If necessary, Access prints the section at the top of the next page. However, if the section is longer than can fit on one page, Access continues printing the section on the following page. In that case, decrease the margins and/or apply a smaller font size to fit all the text for the section on one page.

Use the Force New Page property to insert a page break before a section begins *(Before Section)*, after a section ends *(After Section)*, or before and after a section *(Before & After)*.

Keeping a Group Together on the Same Page

Open the Group, Sort, and Total pane and click the More Options button for a group to specify whether to keep a group together on the same page. By default, Access does not keep a group together. Click the option box arrow next to *do not keep group together on one page* and then click a print option, as shown in Figure 5.12.

Figure 5.12 Group, Sort, and Total Pane with Keep Group Together Print Options

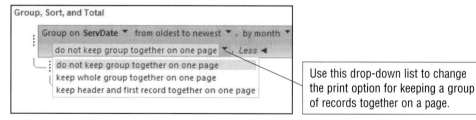

Use this drop-down list to change the print option for keeping a group of records together on a page.

1. With **5-RSRCompServ.accdb** open, display the WorkOrdersbyMonth report in Print Preview and then click the Zoom button (not the button arrow) in the Zoom group to change the zoom to view an entire page within the window.
2. Click the Next Page button in the Page Navigation bar to view page 2 of the report, which shows the grand totals.
3. Switch to Design view and then minimize the Navigation pane.
4. Change the section properties for the *ServDate Footer* and *Report Footer* sections displaying the Count and Sum functions and control objects by completing the following steps:

   a. Double-click the *ServDate Footer* section bar to open the section's Property Sheet task pane.
   b. Click in the *Back Color* property box and then click the Build button to open the color palette.
   c. Click *Blue-Gray, Accent 3, Lighter 80%* (seventh column, second row in the *Theme Colors* section).
   d. Close the Property Sheet task pane.
   e. Select the Count function control object and Sum function control object in the *ServDate Footer* section and then change the font color to red and apply bold formatting.
   f. With the Count and Sum function control objects still selected, right-click one of the selected control objects, point to *Fill/Back Color* at the shortcut menu, and then click *Transparent*. The background color applied in Step 4c will now display behind the calculations.
   g. Double-click the *Report Footer* section bar, change the Back Color property to the same color as the *ServDate Footer* section (see Steps 4b and 4c), and then close the Property Sheet task pane.
   h. Apply the formatting in Steps 4e and 4f to the Count and Sum function control objects in the *Report Footer* section.
   i. Right-click the text box control object containing the formula *=[MonthlyTotal]*1.1* and then click *Properties* at the shortcut menu. Change the Back Style property to *Transparent* and the Border Style property to *Transparent*. Close the Property Sheet task pane.
5. Print each month's work orders on a separate page by completing the following steps:
   a. Click the Group & Sort button on the Report Design Tools Design tab.
   b. Click the More Options button in the Group, Sort, and Total pane.

   c. Click the option box arrow next to *do not keep group together on one page* and then click *keep whole group together on one page* at the drop-down list.
   d. Close the Group, Sort, and Total pane.
6. Create a label control object at the top right of the *Report Header* section with your first and last names. Apply bold formatting to the label control object and click the *Blue-Gray, Accent 3, Darker 50%* font color (seventh column, last row in the *Theme Colors* section).
7. Display the report in Print Preview and then change the zoom to view an entire page within the window. Compare the report with the one shown in Figure 5.13. Scroll to page 2 to view all of work orders for October on the same page.
8. Save, print, and then close the report.
9. Redisplay the Navigation pane.

Figure 5.13 Page 1 of the Completed Report in Project 4

Work Orders by Month							Student Name
ServDate by Month	Work Order	CustID	Descr	Service Date	Total Labor	Parts	Total Work Order
September 2018							
	65019	1025	Upgrade to new Windows	Mon, Sep 17 2018	$87.50	$0.00	$87.50
	65020	1030	Troubleshoot noisy fan	Mon, Sep 17 2018	$37.50	$62.77	$100.27
	65021	1035	Customer has blue screen upon boot	Tue, Sep 18 2018	$113.75	$0.00	$113.75
	65022	1040	Customer reports screen is fuzzy	Sat, Sep 22 2018	$52.50	$55.47	$107.97
	65023	1045	Upgrade RAM	Sun, Sep 23 2018	$43.75	$62.50	$106.25
	65024	1005	Install malware protection	Mon, Sep 24 2018	$20.00	$75.50	$95.50
	65025	1010	Troubleshoot hard drive noise	Fri, Sep 28 2018	$52.50	$0.00	$52.50
	65026	1025	Upgrade memory	Sat, Sep 29 2018	$26.25	$75.75	$102.00
Work Order Count:	8					Month Total:	$765.74

Monday, December 17, 2018

Page 1 of 2

Project 5 Create and Format a Chart   2 Parts

You will create and format a chart in a customer report to show the total parts and labor on work orders by month.

Preview Finished Project

Inserting, Editing, and Formatting a Chart in a Report

A chart can be added to a report to graphically display the numerical data from another table or query. The chart is linked to a field in the report that is common to both objects. Access summarizes and graphs the data from the charted table or query based on the fields selected for each record in the report.

Tutorial

Inserting a Chart

 Insert Chart

Inserting a Chart

With a report open in Design view, increase the height or width of the *Detail* section to make room for the chart, click the Insert Chart button in the Controls group on the Report Design Tools Design tab, and then drag the crosshairs with the chart icon attached to create the approximate height and width of the chart. Release the mouse and Access launches the Chart Wizard, which has six dialog boxes that guide the user through the steps of creating a chart. The first Chart Wizard dialog box is shown in Figure 5.14.

Quick Steps

**Insert a Chart
in a Report**

1. Open report in
   Design view.
2. Click Insert Chart
   button.
3. Drag to create
   control object of
   required height
   and width.
4. Select table or
   query for chart
   data.
5. Click Next.
6. Add fields to use
   in chart.
7. Click Next.
8. Click chart type.
9. Click Next.
10. Add fields as
    needed to chart
    layout.
11. Click Preview
    Chart.
12. Close Sample
    Preview window.
13. Click Next.
14. Select field to link
    report with chart.
15. Click Next.
16. Type chart name.
17. Click Finish.

Figure 5.14 First Chart Wizard Dialog Box

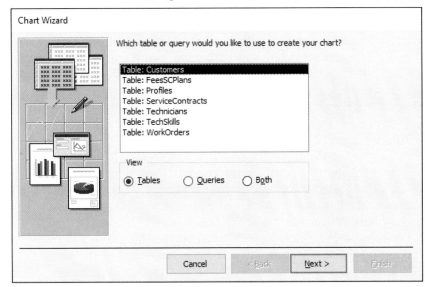

Project 5 uses the Chart Wizard to insert a chart in a customer report that depicts the total value of work orders for each customer by month. The data for the chart will be drawn from a related query. A chart can also be inserted into a form and formatted by completing steps similar to those in Projects 5a and 5b.

Project 5a Creating a Report and Inserting a Chart   Part 1 of 2

1. With **5-RSRCompServ.accdb** open, create a new report using the Report Wizard by completing the following steps:
   a. Click *Customers* in the Tables group in the Navigation pane, click the Create tab, and then click the Report Wizard button.
   b. At the first Report Wizard dialog box with *Table: Customers* selected in the *Tables/Queries* option box, move the *CustID*, *FName*, *LName*, and *ServCont* fields from the *Available Fields* list box to the *Selected Fields* list box and then click the Next button.
   c. At the second Report Wizard dialog box, with no group field selected, click the Next button.
   d. Click the Next button at the third Report Wizard dialog to choose not to sort the report.
   e. Click *Columnar* at the fourth Report Wizard dialog box and then click the Next button.
   f. Click at the end of the current text in the *What title do you want for your report?* text box, type WOChart so that the report title is *CustomersWOChart*, and then click the Finish button.
2. Minimize the Navigation pane and display the report in Design view.
3. To minimize the number of pages printed, change the page layout of the report to two columns by completing the following steps:
   a. Delete the date and page number control objects in the *Page Footer* section.
   b. Drag the right side of the grid to the left to meet the right edge of the *LName* text box control object. The grid will be approximately 3.8 inches wide.
   c. Click the Columns button in the Page Layout group on the Report Design Tools Page Setup tab, change *1* to *2* in the *Number of Columns* text box, and then click OK.
   d. Switch to Print Preview and review the report.

4. There is not enough room to place a chart showing the value of the work orders for each customer. Switch the report back to one column by completing the following steps:
   a. Close Print Preview and press the keys Ctrl + Z three times or until the two text box control objects are deleted and the change in the grid size is undone.
   b. Click the Columns button in the Page Layout group on the Report Design Tools Page Setup tab, change *2* to *1* in the *Number of Columns* text box, and then click OK.
5. Select the text in the report title and then type Customers with Work Orders by Month.
6. Drag down the top of the *Page Footer* section bar until the bottom of the *Detail* section is positioned at the 2-inch mark on the vertical ruler.
7. Insert a chart at the right side of the report to show the value of the work orders for each customer by month by completing the following steps:
   a. Click the More button in the Controls group on the Report Design Tools Design tab and then click the Chart button in the second row. (Depending on the size of your screen, the Chart button may be in the first row).
   b. Position the crosshairs with the chart icon attached in the *Detail* section at the 5-inch mark on the horizontal ruler aligned near the top of the *CustID* control object and then drag down and to the right to create a chart control object of the approximate height and width shown below.

c. At the first Chart Wizard dialog box, click *Queries* in the *View* section, click *Query: TotalWorkOrders* in the list box, and then click the Next button.

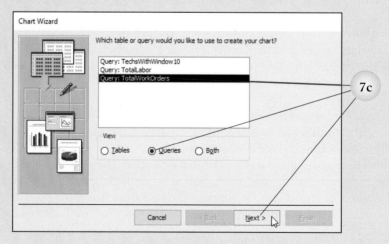

d. At the second Chart Wizard dialog box, double-click *ServDate* and *TotalWorkOrder* in the *Available Fields* list box to move the fields to the *Fields for Chart* list box and then click the Next button.

e. At the third Chart Wizard dialog box, click the second chart type in the first row (*3-D Column Chart*) and then click the Next button.
f. At the fourth Chart Wizard dialog box, look at the fields that Access has already placed to lay out the chart. Since only two fields were added, Access automatically used the numeric field with a Sum function as the data series for the chart and the date field as the *x*-axis category. Click the Next button.
g. At the fifth Chart Wizard dialog box, notice that Access has correctly detected *CustID* as the field to link records to in the Customers report with the chart (based on the TotalWorkOrders query). Click the Next button.
h. At the last Chart Wizard dialog box, click the Finish button. Access inserts a chart within the height and width of the chart control. The chart displayed in the control object in Design view is not the actual chart based on the query data; it is only a sample to show the chart elements.
8. Display the report in Print Preview and scroll through the four pages. Customers for which an empty chart displays have no work order data to be graphed.

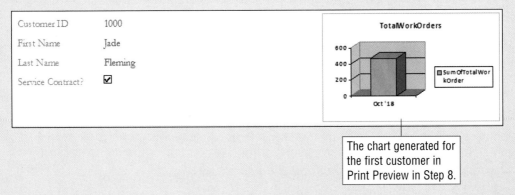

The chart generated for the first customer in Print Preview in Step 8.

9. Save and close the report and then redisplay the Navigation pane.

Check Your Work

Editing and Formatting a Chart

The Chart feature within Access is not the same Chart tool available in Word, Excel, and PowerPoint. Access uses the Microsoft Graph application for charts, which means the editing and formatting processes are different than in other Office applications.

Open a report in Design view and then double-click a chart object to edit the chart. In chart-editing mode, a Menu bar and a toolbar display at the top of the Access window, as well as a datasheet for the chart in the work area. Use these tools to change the chart type; add, remove, or change chart options; and format chart elements.

Click Chart on the Menu bar and then click *Chart Options* at the drop-down menu to add, delete, or edit text in chart titles and add or remove chart axes, gridlines, the legend, data labels, or a data table at the Chart Options dialog box. Click *Chart Type* at the Chart drop-down menu to open the Chart Type dialog box and choose a different type of chart, such as a bar chart or pie chart.

Right-click an object within a chart—such as the chart title, legend, chart area, or data series—and a format option displays in the shortcut menu for the selected chart element. Click the format option to open a Format dialog box for the selected element. Make the required changes and then click OK.

After editing the chart, click outside the chart object to exit chart-editing mode. Sometimes, Access displays a sample chart within the control object in chart-editing mode instead of the actual chart, which can make editing specific chart elements difficult if the chart does not match the sample. If this occurs, exit chart-editing mode, close and reopen the report in Design view, or switch views to cause Access to update the chart displayed in the control object.

Project 5b Changing the Chart Type and Chart Options and Formatting the Chart   Part 2 of 2

1. With **5-RSRCompServ.accdb** open, display the CustomersWOChart report in Design view.
2. Change the chart type, edit the chart title, and remove the chart legend by completing the following steps:
   a. Double-click within the chart to open the chart in chart-editing mode. Access displays a datasheet with the chart and opens the Microsoft Graph application, in which charts are edited. ***Note: If the chart shown is not the actual chart but a sample chart showing multiple data bars, you may still make the following edits.***
   b. Click Chart on the Menu bar and then click *Chart Type.*

2b

c. At the Chart Type dialog box with the Standard Types tab selected, click *Bar* in the *Chart type* list box and then click the first chart in the second row in the *Chart sub-type* section.

d. Click OK.

e. Click Chart on the Menu bar and then click *Chart Options*.

f. At the Chart Options dialog box with the Titles tab selected, edit the text in the *Chart title* text box by inserting spaces between the words so the title text reads *Total Work Orders*.

g. Click the Legend tab.

h. Click the *Show legend* check box to remove the check mark. Since there is only one data series, the chart title sufficiently describes the data and the legend is not necessary.

i. Click OK.

3. Format the bars in the chart to change the shape and colors by completing the following steps. *Note: If the chart shown is not the actual chart but a sample chart showing multiple data bars, click outside the chart object to exit chart-editing mode and then save and close the report. Reopen the report in Report view, switch to Design view, and then double-click the chart to open Microsoft Graph.*

a. Right-click the bar in the chart and then click *Format Data Series* at the shortcut menu.

b. At the Format Data Series dialog box, click the Shape tab.

c. Click *4* in the *Bar shape* section (cylinder shape).

d. Click the Patterns tab.

e. Click the bright blue color square (last column, last row).

f. Click OK.

4. Right-click the chart title, click *Format Chart Title* at the shortcut menu, click the Font tab, apply the Red color (first column, third row of the drop-down list), and then click OK.

5. Click outside the chart object to exit Microsoft Graph.

6. Create a label control object with your first and last names in the *Report Header* section with the right edge of the control aligned with the right edge of the chart.

7. Display the report in Print Preview. *Note: Your x-axis values may be in different increments.*

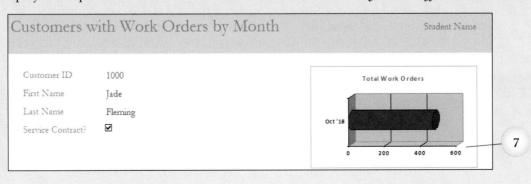

8. Save and then print only the first page of the report. Keep the report open in Print Preview.
9. Open the Customers table, modify the data source by inserting a check mark in the *Service Contract?* check box for Kirk Cobb (Customer ID 1020), and then close the Customers table.
10. Go to page 2 of the report. Notice that the information for Kirk Cobb has not been updated. To refresh the data, either switch to another view and then go back to Print Preview or close the report and open it again. Go to page 2, verify that the data has been updated, and then close the report.

Check Your Work

Project 6 **Create a Blank Report with Hyperlinks, a List Box,** **1 Part**
and a Subform

You will use the Blank Report tool to create a new report for viewing technician certifications. In the report, you will reorder the tab fields, create a list box inside a tab control object, change the shape of the tab control object, and add hyperlinks and a subform.

Preview Finished Project

Tutorial

Creating a Report
Using the Blank
Report Tool

Blank Report

Quick Steps
Create a Blank Report
1. Click Create tab.
2. Click Blank Report button.
3. Expand field list for table.
4. Drag fields to report as needed.
5. Add title, control objects, or format, or make other design changes as needed.
6. Save report.

Tab Control

Tutorial

Adding a List Box
to a Report

List Box

Creating a Report Using the Blank Report Tool

A blank report created with the Blank Report tool begins with no control objects or formatting and displays as a blank white page in Layout view, similar to a form created with the Blank Form tool, as learned in Chapter 4. Click the Create tab and then click the Blank Report button in the Reports group to begin a new report. Access opens the Field List task pane at the right side of the work area. Expand the list for the appropriate table and then add fields to the report as needed. If the Field List task pane displays with no table names, click the Show all tables hyperlink at the top of the task pane.

Adding a Tab Control Object to a Report

Recall from Chapter 4 that a tab control object can be added to a form to display fields from different tables on separate pages. In Form view, a page is displayed by clicking the page tab. Similarly, a tab control object can be used in a report to display fields from the same table or a different table in pages. To create a tab control object in a report, follow the steps from Chapter 4 for adding a tab control object to a form.

Adding a List Box or Combo Box to a Report

Like a list box in a form, a list box in a report displays a list of values for a field within the control object. In Report view, the entire list for the field can easily be seen. If a list is too long for the size of the list box control object, scroll bars display that can be used to scroll up or down the list when viewing the report.

Although the data cannot be edited in a report, a list box can be used to view all the field values and see which values have been selected for the current record.

A combo box added to a report does not display as a list. However, the field value that was entered into the field from the associated table, query, or form is shown in the combo box. Since the data cannot be edited in a report, the combo box field is not shown as a drop-down list. A combo box can be changed to display as a list box within the report. In this case, the list box displays all the field values and the value stored in the current record shown is selected within the list. A list box or combo box can be added to a report by following the steps from Chapter 4 for adding a list box or combo box to a form.

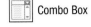 Combo Box

Adding Hyperlinks to a Report

Use the the Hyperlink button in the Controls group on the Report Layout Tools Design tab to create a link in a report to a web page, graphic, email address, or program. Click the Hyperlink button and then click within the report to open the Insert Hyperlink dialog box, in which the user provides the text to display in the control object and the address to which the object should be linked. Use the Places bar left of the Insert Hyperlink dialog box to choose to link to an existing file or web page, another object within the database, or an email address.

Changing the Shape of a Control Object

The Change Shape button in the Control Formatting group on the Report Layout Tools Format tab contains a drop-down list with eight shape options. Use the shape options to modify the appearance of a command button, toggle button, navigation button, or tab control object. Select the control object to be modified, click the Change Shape button, and then click a shape at the drop-down list.

Changing the Tab Order of Fields

Recall from Chapter 4 how to open the Tab Order dialog box and change the order in which the Tab key moves from field to field. In a report, the order in which the Tab key moves from field to field in Report view can also be changed. Although data is not added, deleted, or edited in Report view, use the Tab key to move within a report. Display the report in Design view, click the Tab Order button in the Tools group on the Report Design Tools Design tab, and then drag the fields up or down the *Custom Order* list.

Adding a Subform to a Report

A subform can be added to a report using the Subform/Subreport button in the Control group on the Report Design Tools Design tab. (This method was used in Project 1e.) With the report open in Design view, a subform can also be created by dragging the form from the Navigation pane to the appropriate location in the report. After the form has been placed in the report, check the Link Master Fields and Link Child Fields properties in the Property Sheet to ensure that the record sources are related using the fields to be linked.

Quick Steps

Add a Hyperlink to a Report
1. Open report in Layout view or Design view.
2. Click Hyperlink button in Controls group.
3. Click in location within report.
4. Type text to display in control object in *Text to display* text box.
5. Type URL in *Address* text box.
6. Click OK.

Change the Shape of a Control Object
1. Open report in Layout view.
2. Click to select control object.
3. Click Report Layout Tools Format tab.
4. Click Change Shape button.
5. Click shape.

 Hyperlink

 Change Shape

 Tab Order

1. With **5-RSRCompServ.accdb** open, click the Create tab and then click the Blank Report button in the Reports group.
2. If the Field List task pane at the right side of the work area does not display the table names, click the <u>Show all tables</u> hyperlink. If the table names display, proceed to Step 3.
3. Add fields from the Technicians table and a tab control object to the report by completing the following steps:
   a. Click the plus symbol next to the *Technicians* table name to expand the field list.
   b. Click *TechID* in the Field List task pane and then drag the field to the top left of the report.
   c. Right-click in the *Technician ID* column, point to *Layout* at the shortcut menu, and then click *Stacked*. A stacked layout is better suited to this report because it shows each technician's certifications next to his or her name in a tab control object.
   d. Drag the *FName* field from the Field List task pane below the first *Technician ID* text box control object. Release the mouse when the pink bar is below the *01* text box control object next to *Technician ID*.

3d

   e. Drag the *LName* field from the Field List task pane below the first *First Name* text box control object. Release the mouse when the pink bar displays below *Pat*.
   f. Click the Tab Control button in the Controls group on the Report Layout Tools Design tab.

3f

   g. Position the mouse pointer with the tab control icon attached right of the first *Technician ID* text box control object in the report. Click the mouse when the pink bar displays right of the *01* text box control object.
   h. Right-click the selected tab control object, point to *Layout*, and then click *Remove Layout* at the shortcut menu.

3g

   i. Select the *HPhone* and *CPhone* fields in the Field List task pane and then drag the two fields below the *Last Name* text box control object. Release the mouse when the pink bar displays below *Hynes*.
   j. Double-click the first *Pagexx* tab (where *xx* is the page number) in the tab control object right of the report to select the tab control object. Point to the bottom orange border of the selected tab control object until the pointer displays as an up-and-down-pointing arrow and then drag down the bottom of the object until it aligns with the bottom of the *Cell Phone* control object.

Your page numbers may vary.

3i

3j

4. Add a field from the TechSkills table to the tab control object and change the control to a list box by completing the following steps:
   a. Click the plus symbol next to the *TechSkills* table name in the *Fields available in related tables* section of the Field List task pane to expand the list.
   b. Click to select the *Certifications* field name and then drag the field to the first page in the tab control object, next to *Technician ID 01*.
   c. Access inserts the field in the page with both the label control object and text box control object selected. To change the field to display as a list box, click to select only the text box control object (displays *CCNA Cloud, CCNA Wireless,* and *Microsoft MCT* in the first record).
   d. Right-click the selected text box control object, point to *Change To*, and then click *List Box* at the shortcut menu.

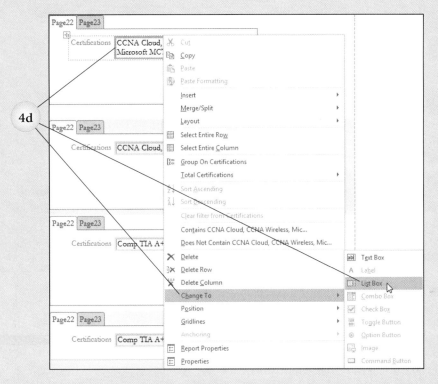

5. Add a hyperlink to the bottom of the tab control object by completing the following steps:
   a. Click the Hyperlink button in the Controls group on the Report Layout Tools Design tab.
   b. Position the mouse pointer with the hyperlink icon attached below *Certifications* in the tab control object. Click the mouse when the pink bar displays.
   c. At the Insert Hyperlink dialog box, click in the *Text to display* text box and then type Cisco Certifications.
   d. Click in the *Address* text box, type http://www.cisco.com/c/en/us/training -events/training-certifications /overview.html, and then click OK.
   e. Drag the right orange border of the hyperlink control object to the right until all the text displays within the control object.

6. Click the second page in the tab control to select it, right-click, and then click *Delete Page* at the shortcut menu. Do not be concerned if Access displays the first page with an empty list box. The screen will refresh at the next step.

6

7. Double-click over *Pagexx* (where *xx* is the page number) in the tab control object to select the entire tab control object. Click the Report Layout Tools Format tab, click the Change Shape button in the Control Formatting group, and then click *Snip Single Corner Rectangle* at the drop-down list (third column, second row).

7

8. Click to select *Pagexx* (where *xx* is the page number), click the Report Layout Tools Design tab, and then click the Property Sheet button to open the Property Sheet task pane. With *Selection type: Page* displayed at the top of the Property Sheet task pane, click in the *Caption* property box, type Technician's Certifications, and then close the Property Sheet task pane.

9. Right-click the *Technician ID* text box control object (displays *01*) and then click *Select Entire Column* at the shortcut menu. Click the Report Layout Tools Format tab, click the Shape Outline button, and then click *Transparent* at the drop-down list.

10. Save the report and name it *TechCertifications*.

11. Switch to Report view. Click in the first *Technician ID* text box and press the Tab key four times to see how active field moves through the report in order starting at the left side of the report.

12. Switch to Design view. You want the Tab key to move to the technician's last name first and then to the first name. The *TechID* field will be moved to the last field in the order. Change the tab order of the fields by completing the following steps:

12b

12c

12d

   a. Click the Tab Order button in the Tools group on the Report Design Tools Design tab.
   b. At the Tab Order dialog box, click in the bar next to *LName* in the *Custom Order* section to select the *LName* field and then drag the field to the top of the list until the black line displays above *TechID*.
   c. Drag *TechID* to the bottom of the list.
   d. Click OK.

13. Save the revised report and then switch to Report view. Press the Tab key. Notice that the first field selected is the *Last Name* field. Press the Tab key a second time. Notice that the selected field moves to *First Name*. Press the Tab key two more times to watch the selected fields move to the *Home Phone* and *Cell Phone* fields below the *Last Name* field.

14. Click the <u>Cisco Certifications</u> hyperlink to open a Microsoft Edge window and display the Cisco Training & Certifications web page.
15. Close the browser window and then display the report in Design view.
16. Add a subform to the report by completing the following steps:
    a. Click the TechsWithWindows10 form in the Navigation pane, drag it to the right of the tab control object as shown below, and then release the mouse.

    b. Access inserts the subform with a label control object above it that contains the name of the subform. Click the label control object displaying the text *TechsWithWindows10* to select it and then press the Delete key.
17. Link the fields to relate a field in the subform to a field in the report by completing the following steps:
    a. Click the subform to select it and then press the F4 function key to display the Property Sheet task pane.
    b. Click the Data tab. Notice that the *Link Master Fields* and *Link Child Fields* property boxes are blank because no fields are linked.
    c. Click in the *Link Master Fields* property box and then click the ellipsis to open the Subreport Field Linker.

    d. Click OK to accept the linking of the *TechID* field and then close the Property Sheet task pane.
18. Save the revised report and display it in Print Preview.
19. Switch the report to landscape orientation, print only the first page, and then close Print Preview.
20. Save and close the TechCertifications report and then close **5-RSRCompServ.accdb**.

Check Your Work

    In this chapter, you have learned how to build a custom report from scratch using Design view. You have also created reports using the Report Wizard and Blank Report tool and used options in Design view and Layout view to customize the reports. As you become more comfortable with reports, explore other tools available in Layout View and Design view using the Design, Arrange, Format, and Page Setup tabs. More features are available to assist you with creating professional-quality reports.

Chapter Summary

- Click the Create tab and then click the Report Design button to create a custom report using Design view.

- A report can contain up to five sections: *Report Header, Page Header, Detail, Page Footer,* and *Report Footer.*

- *Group Header* and *Group Footer* sections can be added to group records that contain repeating values in a field, such as a department or city.

- Connect a table or query to a report using the *Record Source* property box in the Data tab of the report's Property Sheet task pane.

- Display the Field List task pane and then drag individual fields or a group of fields from the table or query to the *Detail* section of the report, which represents the body of the report.

- Place label control objects to be used as column headings in a tabular report within the *Page Header* section.

- Apply a theme to a report to maintain a consistent look to all reports.

- A related table or query can be inserted as a subreport within a main report. A subreport is stored as a separate object outside the main report.

- Click the Page Numbers button in the Header / Footer group to open the Page Numbers dialog box, where the format, position, and alignment of page numbers in a report are specified.

- The current date and/or time can be added as a control object within the *Report Header* section using the Date and Time button in the Header / Footer group.

- Add online graphics and draw lines in a report using the same techniques for adding graphics and drawing lines in a form.

- A report can be grouped by a field at the Report Wizard or by opening the Group, Sort, and Total pane.

- Functions such as Sum, Average, and Count can be added to each group within a report and grand totals can be added to the end of a report by expanding the group options in the Group, Sort, and Total pane.

- Create a calculated control object in a report using the Text Box button in the Controls group.

- Each section within a report has a set of properties that can be viewed or changed by opening the section's Property Sheet task pane.

- Use the Keep Together property to prevent a section from splitting across two pages.

- Use the Force New Page property to automatically insert a page break before a section begins, after a section ends, or before and after a section.

- At the Group, Sort, and Total pane, specify whether to keep an entire group together on the same page.

- A chart can be added to a report to graphically display numerical data from another table or query.

- A report can be formatted into multiple columns using the Columns button in the Report Design Tools Page Setup tab.

- To create a chart in a report, open the report in Design view, click the Chart button in the Controls group, and then use the Chart Wizard to generate the chart.

- Open a report in Design view and then double-click a chart control object to edit the chart using Microsoft Graph by changing the chart type; adding, removing, or changing chart options; and formatting chart elements.
- Use the Blank Report tool in the Reports group on the Create tab to create a new report with no control objects or formatting applied. The report opens as a blank white page in Layout view; the Field List task pane opens right of the work area.
- A tab control object, list box, and combo box can be added to a blank report using the same techniques for adding these control objects to a form.
- Use the Hyperlink button to create a link in a report to a web page, graphic, email address, or program.
- Modify the shape of a command button, toggle button, navigation button, or tab control object using the Change Shape button in the Control Formatting group on the Report Layout Tools Format tab.
- Change the order in which the Tab key moves from field to field within a report at the Tab Order dialog box. Display a report in Design view and click the Tab Order button in the Tools group on the Report Design Tools Design tab.
- To add a subform to a report in Design view, drag the subform from the Navigation pane to the specified location in the report.
- After a subform has been placed in a report, check the Link Master Fields and Link Child Fields properties in the Property Sheet to ensure that the record sources are related.

Commands Review

FEATURE	RIBBON TAB, GROUP	BUTTON	KEYBOARD SHORTCUT
add existing fields	Report Design Tools Design, Tools		
blank report	Create, Reports		
change shape of selected control	Report Layout Tools Format, Control Formatting		
date and time	Report Design Tools Design, Header / Footer		
Design view	Report Design Tools Design, Views		
group and sort	Report Design Tools Design, Grouping & Totals		
insert chart	Report Design Tools Design, Controls		
insert hyperlink	Report Layout Tools Design, Controls		
insert image	Report Design Tools Design, Controls		
page numbers	Report Design Tools Design, Header / Footer		
Property Sheet task pane	Report Design Tools Design, Tools		F4
report design	Create, Reports		

FEATURE	RIBBON TAB, GROUP	BUTTON	KEYBOARD SHORTCUT
Report view	Report Design Tools Design, Views		
Report Wizard	Create, Reports		
subreport	Report Design Tools Design, Controls		
tab control object	Report Layout Tools Design, Controls		
tab order	Report Design Tools Design, Tools		
theme	Report Design Tools Design, Themes		
title control object	Report Design Tools Design, Header / Footer		

Workbook

Chapter study tools and assessment activities are available in the *Workbook* ebook. These resources are designed to help you further develop and demonstrate mastery of the skills learned in this chapter.

Microsoft®

Access®

Using Access Tools and Managing Objects

Performance Objectives

Upon successful completion of Chapter 6, you will be able to:

1. Create a new database using a template

2. Save a database as a template

3. Add prebuilt objects to a database using an Application Parts template

4. Create a new form using an Application Parts Blank Form

5. Create a form to be used as a template in a database

6. Create a table by copying the structure of another table

7. Evaluate a table using the Table Analyzer Wizard

8. Evaluate a database using the Performance Analyzer

9. Split a database

10. Print documentation about a database using the Database Documenter

11. Rename and delete objects within a database file

12. Create a database using templates, Application Parts, Quick Start, and wizards

Precheck

Check your current skills to help focus your study.

Access provides tools to assist with creating and managing databases. Use a template to create a new database or a new table and/or a related group of objects. A blank form template provides a predefined layout and may include a form title and command buttons. If none of the predefined templates is suitable, create a custom template. Access provides wizards to assist with analyzing tables and databases to improve performance. A database can be split into two files to store the tables separately from the queries, forms, and reports. Use the Database Documenter to print a report that provides details about objects and their properties. In this chapter, you will learn how to use these Access tools and how to rename and delete objects in the Navigation pane.

SNAP

If you are a SNAP user, launch the Precheck and Tutorials from your Assignments page.

Data Files

Before beginning chapter work, copy the AL2C6 folder to your storage medium and then make AL2C6 the active folder.

Project 1 **Create a New Contact Database Using a Template** **3 Parts**

You will create a new database using one of the database templates supplied with Access and create your own template.

Preview Finished Project

Tutorial →

Creating a New Database Using a Template

Ö̈uick Steps

Create a Database from a Template
1. Start Access.
2. Click template.
3. Click Browse button.
4. Navigate to drive and/or folder.
5. Edit file name as required.
6. Click OK.
7. Click Create button.

Creating a New Database Using a Template

At the Open or New backstage area, create a new database using one of the professionally designed templates provided by Microsoft. The database templates provide a complete series of objects, including predefined tables, forms, reports, queries, and relationships. Use a template as provided and immediately start entering data or base a new database on a template and modify the objects as needed. If a template exists for a database application that is needed, save time by basing the database on one of the template designs.

Along with desktop templates, Access 2016 contains templates for creating web apps. These apps require having Microsoft SharePoint to share data with other users. (SharePoint is a server application that allows for collaborating on and sharing of documents.) Some advanced database features such as crosstab or action queries cannot be performed in an Access app database. The Table Analyzer wizard, the Performance Analyzer, and the Database Documenter—all discussed later in this chapter—are additional unsupported tools. Figure 6.1 shows the difference between a desktop template icon and a web app template icon. When looking for a desktop template, look for one that does not have a globe icon.

Figure 6.1 Desktop Contacts and Contacts (SharePoint Web App) Icons

Contacts (SharePoint web app)

The globe indicates that this template is an Access app template.

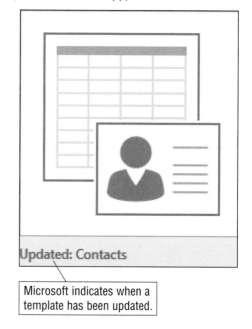

Updated: Contacts

Microsoft indicates when a template has been updated.

To create a new database using a template, start Access and then click one of the available templates in the Open backstage area. If Access is already open, click one of the available templates at the New backstage area. The templates are constantly being updated so they may vary. When the template is clicked, a preview appears, similar to what is shown in Figure 6.2. The name of the template provider, a description of the template, and the download size are displayed in the preview. Use the directional arrows on either side of the preview to move through the other available templates. Once a template has been chosen, click the Browse button to navigate to the drive and/or folder where the database is to be stored and then type a file name at the *File Name* text box. Access opens the previous screen and displays the new database file name entered below the *File Name* text box. Click the Create button to create the database.

If none of the sample templates is suitable for the type of database to be created, close the preview and search for templates online by clicking one of the hyperlinked suggested searches (such as <u>Database</u>, <u>Business</u>, or <u>Small Business</u>). Another option is to type search words in the search text box. Templates are downloaded from Office.com.

Figure 6.2 Available Templates in the New Backstage Area

1. Start Microsoft Access 2016.
2. At the Open backstage area, click the *Updated: contacts* template. ***Note: The templates are constantly being updated, so the objects and steps may vary.***
3. Click the Browse button (which displays as a file folder icon) next to the *File Name* text box in the template preview.
4. At the File New Database dialog box, navigate to the AL2C6 folder on your storage medium, select the current entry in the *File name* text box, and then type 6-Contacts.
5. Click OK.

File name: 6-Contacts

Save as type: Microsoft Access 2007 - 2016 Databases (*.accdb)

⌃ Hide Folders   Tools ▾   OK   Cancel

6. Click the Create button.
7. The database is created with all the objects from the template loaded into the current window and the Contact List form open. A Welcome to the Contacts Database form appears that provides information on using this database. Click the *Show Welcome when this database is opened* check box to remove the check mark. If the box is left checked, this form will open every time the database is opened.
8. Close the Welcome form.
9. Click the Enable Content button in the message bar. Notice that the Title bar contains the text *Contact Management Database* rather than the name of the database, *6-Contacts.accdb*. (How to change the Title bar to display a more descriptive database title will be discussed in Chapter 7.)
10. Review the list of objects that Access has created in the Navigation pane.
11. Double-click to open the Contacts table.
12. Scroll right to view all the fields in the Contacts table and then close the table.
13. Review the Contact List form that is open in the work area and then close it.

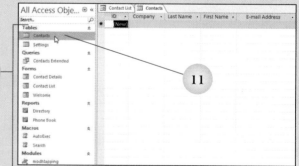

1. With **6-Contacts.accdb** open, open the Contact Details form in Form view, and then add the following record to modify the data source file using the form:

First Name	Ariel
Last Name	Grayson
Company	Grayson Accounting Services
Job Title	Accountant
E-mail	ariel@emcp.net
Web Page	www.emcp.net/grayson **Note: Press the Tab key three times after this field to move to the Street field.**
Street	17399 Windsor Avenue
City	Detroit
State/Province	MI
Zip/Postal Code	48214-3274
Country/Region	USA
Business Phone	800-555-4988
Home Phone	313-555-9684
Mobile Phone	313-555-6811
Fax Number	800-555-3472
Notes	Ariel recommended to RSR by Pat Hynes.

2. Add a picture of the contact using the *Attachments* field by completing the following steps:
   a. Click the Edit Picture button at the top left part of the form.

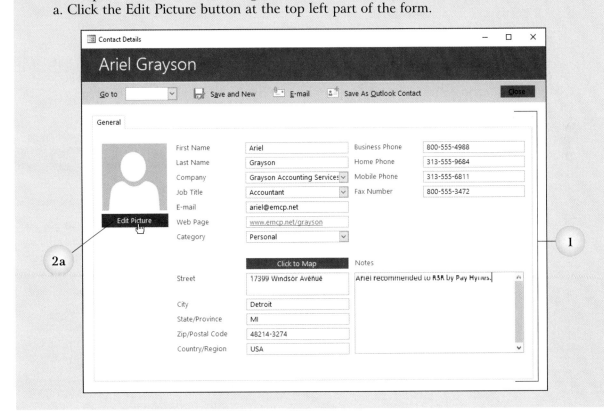

b. At the Attachments dialog box, click the Add button.
c. At the Choose File dialog box, navigate to the AL2C6 folder on your storage medium.
d. Double-click **ArielGrayson.jpg** to add the file to the Attachments dialog box and then click OK.

e. Notice that the picture now displays in the form. If a Word document had been selected in the Attachments dialog box, a Word icon would display.

3. Click the Close button in the upper right corner of the form to close the form. ***Note: Do not use the purple Close button right of*** **Save as Outlook Contact,** ***as macro errors may occur.***
4. Double-click *Directory* in the Reports group in the Navigation pane. Review the report.
5. Display the report in Print Preview and then print the report.
6. Close Print Preview and then close the Directory report.

Check Your Work

Saving a Database as a Template

Q̃uick Steps
**Save a Database
as a Template**
1. Open database.
2. Make changes.
3. Click File tab.
4. Click *Save As.*
5. Click Browse button.
6. Change *Save as type*
   to *Template (*.accdt).*
7. Type information
   in Contact
   Management dialog
   box.
8. Click OK.
9. Click OK.

If none of the existing templates is suitable and the same database structure is being developed often, then create a custom template. As with using templates in other Microsoft applications, using templates in Access can save time and effort. To create a database template, either create an entirely new database or modify an existing database based on a template and then save it as a new template.

To save a database as a template, click the File tab and then click the *Save As* option. With *Save Database As* selected in the *File Types* section, click *Template (*.accdt)* in the *Database File Types* section and then click the Save As button. Fill in the Create New Template from This Database dialog box, shown in Figure 6.3, and then click OK. Click OK at the Contact Management Database dialog box that states that the template has been saved as [c:]\Users*username*\AppData\Roaming\ Microsoft\Templates\Access\TemplateName.accdt. Note the default location in which the templates are stored.

Figure 6.3 Create New Template from This Database Dialog Box

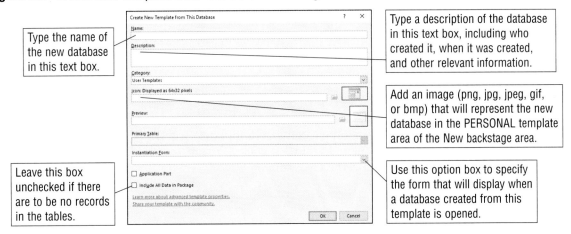

Type the name of the new database in this text box.

Type a description of the database in this text box, including who created it, when it was created, and other relevant information.

Add an image (png, jpg, jpeg, gif, or bmp) that will represent the new database in the PERSONAL template area of the New backstage area.

Leave this box unchecked if there are to be no records in the tables.

Use this option box to specify the form that will display when a database created from this template is opened.

Project 1c Saving a Database as a Template

Part 3 of 3

1. With **6-Contacts.accdb** open, open the Contact Details form in Design view, click the Close button that contains a close command macro, and then press the Delete key. (Macros will be discussed in Chapter 7.) Save and close the form.
2. Save the revised database as a template by completing the following steps:
   a. Click the File tab.
   b. Click *Save As*.
   c. Click *Template (*.accdt)* in the *Database File Types* section.
   d. Click the Save As button.
   e. At the Create New Template from This Database dialog box, enter data as follows:

Name	CustomContacts
Description	Created by [Student Name] on [current date]. (Substitute your name for *[Student Name]* and today's date for *[current date]*.)
Preview	Click the Browse button, navigate to the AL2C6 data folder, and then double-click ***CustomizedContacts.png***.

3. Click OK.
4. Click OK.
5. Close **6-Contacts.accdt**.
6. To view the new template, click the File tab and then click PERSONAL. The CustomContacts template created is shown with **CustomizedContacts.png** as the image. Click the Back button.

Using a Custom Template

To start a user-created template, click the File tab and then click *New*. At the New backstage area, click PERSONAL. This opens the PERSONAL template area. Double-click the name of a template to open it.

Deleting a Custom Template

To delete a custom template, use the Open dialog box to navigate to [c:]\Users\ *username*\AppData\Roaming\Microsoft\Templates\Access\. Right-click the name of the template to be deleted and then click *Delete* at the shortcut menu. Click the Cancel button to close the Open dialog box.

Project 2 Create Objects Using a Template   3 Parts

You will use Application Parts templates to create a series of objects in an existing database. You will also define a form as a template for all the new forms in a database.

Preview Finished Project

Creating Objects Using an Application Parts Template

Application Parts

Access 2016 provides templates for prebuilt objects that can be inserted into an existing database using the Application Parts button in the Templates group on the Create tab. The *Quick Start* section of the Application Parts button drop-down list includes the options *Comments*, which creates a table; *Contacts*, which creates a table, a query, forms, and reports; and *Issues*, *Tasks*, and *Users*, each of which creates a table and two forms.

Creating Objects Using Quick Start

Tutorial

Creating Objects Using Quick Start

Quick Steps

Create Objects Using an Application Parts Template
1. Open database.
2. Click Create tab.
3. Click Application Parts button.
4. Click template.
5. Choose relationship options.
6. Add data or modify objects as required.

If any of these kinds of tables need to be created in an existing database, consider creating it using the Application Parts template because related objects, such as forms and reports, will be generated automatically. Once the application part is added, any part of an object's design can be modified as needed. To create a group of objects based on a template, click the Create tab and then click the Application Parts button in the Templates group. Click a template in the *Quick Start* section of the drop-down list, as shown in Figure 6.4.

Access opens the Create Relationship Wizard to guide the user through creating the relationship for the new table. Decide in advance of creating the new table what relationship, if any, will exist between the new table and an existing table in the database. At the first Create Relationship dialog box, shown in Figure 6.5, click the first option if the new table will be the "many" table in a one-to-many relationship. Use the drop-down list to choose the "one" table and then click the Next button. If the new table will be the "one" table in a one-to-many relationship, click the second option, use the drop-down list to choose the "many" table, and then click the Next button.

At the second Create Relationship dialog box, enter the settings for the lookup column between the two tables. Choose the field to use to join the tables, choose a sort order if needed, assign the name of the lookup column, and then click the Create button. If the new table will not be related to any of the existing tables in the database, choose the *There is no relationship* option at the first Create Relationship dialog box and then click the Create button.

Figure 6.4 Application Parts Button Drop-Down List

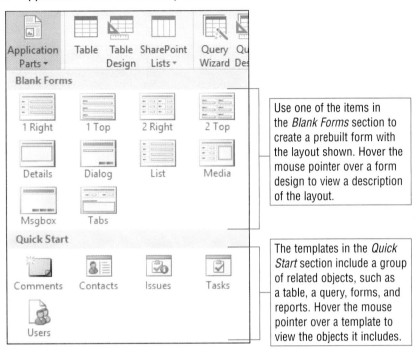

Use one of the items in the *Blank Forms* section to create a prebuilt form with the layout shown. Hover the mouse pointer over a form design to view a description of the layout.

The templates in the *Quick Start* section include a group of related objects, such as a table, a query, forms, and reports. Hover the mouse pointer over a template to view the objects it includes.

Figure 6.5 First Dialog Box in the Create Relationship Wizard

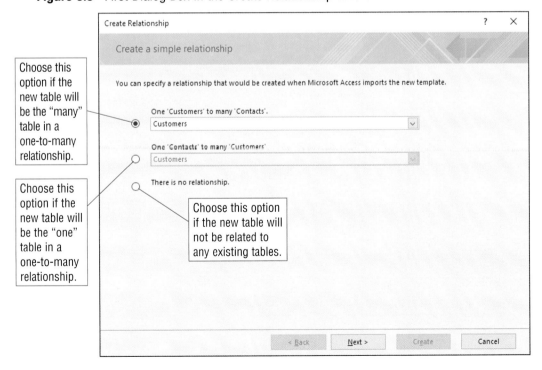

Choose this option if the new table will be the "many" table in a one-to-many relationship.

Choose this option if the new table will be the "one" table in a one-to-many relationship.

Choose this option if the new table will not be related to any existing tables.

1. Open **6-RSRCompServ.accdb** and enable the content.
2. Use a template to create a new table, a query, forms, and reports related to contacts by completing the following steps:
   a. Click the Create tab.
   b. Click the Application Parts button in the Templates group and then click *Contacts* in the *Quick Start* section of the drop-down list.

   c. The Create Relationship Wizard starts. At the first Create Relationship dialog box, click the *There is no relationship* option and then click the Create button. Access imports a Contacts table; a ContactsExtended query; ContactDetails, ContactDS, and ContactList forms; and ContactAddressBook, ContactList, and ContactPhoneBook reports into the database.

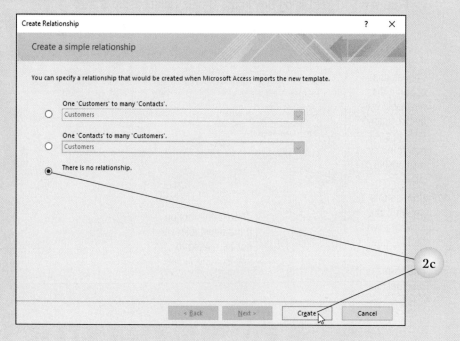

3. Double-click *Contacts* in the Tables group in the Navigation pane. Scroll right to view all the fields in the new table and then close the table.
4. Double-click *ContactDetails* in the Forms group in the Navigation pane.
5. Enter the following record using the ContactDetails form:

First Name	Terry
Last Name	Silver
Job Title	Sales Manager
Company	Cityscape Electronics **Note: Press the Tab key two times after this field to move to the E-mail field.**
E-mail	terry_s@emcp.net
Web Page	www.emcp.net/cityscape
Business Phone	800-555-4968
Fax	800-555-6941
Home Phone	(leave blank)
Mobile Phone	313-555-3442
Address	3700 Woodward Avenue
City	Detroit
State/Province	MI
ZIP/Postal Code	48201-2006
Country/Region	(leave blank)
Notes	(leave blank)

6. Click the Save & Close button at the top right of the form.

7. Open the ContactList report.
8. Display the report in Print Preview and then print it.
9. Close Print Preview and then close the ContactList report.

Check Your Work

Creating a New Form Using an Application Parts Blank Form

The Application Parts button drop-down list also includes various blank form layouts. Using one of them makes the task of creating a new form easier because the layout has already been defined. The *Blank Forms* section of the Application Parts button drop-down list contains 10 prebuilt blank forms. Most of the forms contain command buttons that perform actions such as saving changes or saving and closing the form. Hover the mouse pointer over a blank form option at the Application Parts button drop-down list to display a description of the form's layout in a ScreenTip. When a blank form option is clicked, Access creates the form object using a predefined form name. For example, if the *1 Right* is clicked, Access creates a form named *SingleOneColumnRightLabels*. Locate the form name in the Navigation pane and then open the form in Layout view or Design view to customize it as needed.

Each Application Parts form has a control layout applied, which means all the form's control objects move and resize together. Remove the control layout to make individual size adjustments. To do this in Design view, select all the control objects and then click the Remove Layout button in the Table group on the Form Design Tools Arrange tab.

Quick Steps

Create a Form Using a Blank Application Parts Form
1. Click Create tab.
2. Click Application Parts button.
3. Click blank form layout.
4. Add fields to form.
5. Customize form as needed.
6. Save form.

Project 2b Creating a New Form Using an Application Parts Blank Form   Part 2 of 3

1. With **6-RSRCompServ.accdb** open, use an Application Parts blank form to create a new form for maintaining records in the Parts table by completing the following steps:
   a. If necessary, click the Create tab.
   b. Click the Applications Parts button in the Templates group and then click *1 Right* in the *Blank Forms* section of the drop-down list. Access creates a form named *SingleOneColumnRightLabels*.
   c. If necessary, position the mouse pointer on the right border of the Navigation pane until the pointer changes to a left-and-right-pointing arrow and then drag right to widen the Navigation pane until all the object names are visible.
   d. Double-click *SingleOneColumnRightLabels* in the Forms group in the Navigation pane.
2. Switch to Layout view.
3. Click to select the *Field1* label control object. Press and hold down the Shift key; click to select the *Field2*, *Field3*, and *Field4* label control objects, release the Shift key, and then press the Delete key.
4. Associate the Parts table with the form and add fields from the Parts table by completing the following steps:
   a. If the Field List task pane is not open, click the Add Existing Fields button in the Tools group on the Form Layout Tools Design tab.
   b. Click the Show all tables hyperlink at the top of the task pane. Skip this step if the Field List task pane already displays all the table names in the database.

---

c. Click the plus symbol next to the *Parts* option in the Field List task pane to expand the list and show all the fields in the Parts table.

d. Drag the *PartNo* field to the second column in the row, as shown at the right.

e. Drag the remaining fields (*PartName*, *Supplier*, and *Cost*) below *PartNo*, as shown at the right.

f. Close the Field List task pane.

5. With the *Cost* field selected, drag up the bottom orange border of the control to decrease the height of the control object so the bottom border is approximately 0.5 inch below the label text.

6. Select the four label control objects and drag the right orange border of the selected control objects right to widen the labels until all the label text is visible.

7. With the four label control objects still selected, click the Form Layout Tools Arrange tab, click the Control Padding button in the Position group, and then click *Wide* at the drop-down list.

8. Double-click the form title to place the insertion point inside the title text, delete *Form Title*, type Repair Parts, and then press the Enter key.

9. Make formatting changes to the form as follows:

a. Click the Save button at the top right of the form. Press and hold down the Ctrl key, click the Save & Close button, and then release the Ctrl key. Click the Form Layout Tools Format tab, click the Quick Styles button, and then click *Intense Effect - Blue-Gray, Accent 3* (fourth column, last row).

b. Select the *Repair Parts* title control object and apply the Blue-Gray, Accent 3 font color (seventh column, first row in the *Theme Colors* section).

c. Apply the Blue-Gray, Accent 3 font color to the four label control objects.

d. Apply the Blue-Gray, Accent 3 Lighter 80% background color (seventh column, second row in the *Theme Colors* section) to the four text box control objects adjacent to the labels.

e. Click the label control object that displays the text *Supplier*. Use the bottom sizing handle to increase the height of the object so all the text displays.

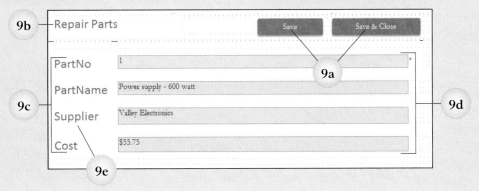

f. Click in a blank area of the form to deselect the label control object.

10. Click the File tab, click the *Save As* option, click *Save Object As*, and then click the Save As button. Type Parts in the *Save 'SingleOneColumnRightLabels' to* text box at the Save As dialog box and then click OK.

11. Click the Home tab and then switch to Form view.

12. Scroll through a few records in the Parts form and then click the Save & Close button at the top right. Your record may look different than the one shown below.

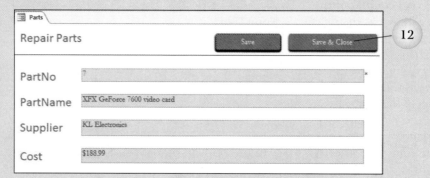

13. The SingleOneColumnRightLabels form is no longer needed. Click *SingleOneColumnRightLabels* in the Forms group in the Navigation pane and then press the Delete key. Answer Yes to the question *Do you want to permanently delete the form 'SingleOneColumnRightLabels'?*

Check Your Work

Tutorial

Creating a User-Defined Form Template

Setting Form Control Defaults and Creating a User-Defined Form Template

Quick Steps

Create a User-Defined Form Template
1. Create new form in Design view.
2. Add control object to form.
3. Format control object.
4. Click More button in Control group.
5. Click *Set Control Defaults.*
6. Repeat Steps 2–5 for each type of control object to be used.
7. Save form, naming it *Normal.*

Hint Delete the Normal form if you want to go back to using the standard default options for control objects in forms.

Using a standard design for all the forms in a database is an effective way of ensuring consistency and portraying a professional image—for example, formatting all the label control objects as 14-point blue text on a gray background. However, changing these options manually in each form is time consuming and may lead to inconsistencies. To save time and ensure consistency, customize the default settings instead.

The *Set Control Defaults* option at the Controls drop-down list allows the user to change the default properties for all the new labels in a form. To do this, open the form in Design view, format one label control object, click the More button in the Controls group, and then click *Set Control Defaults* at the drop-down list. All the new label control objects added to the form will now be formatted with the options that have been defined.

To further customize the database, create a form template that will set the default for each type of control object placed in a form. To do this, open a new form in Design view and create one control object of each type for which a default setting is to be specified. For example, add a label control object, text box control object, command button, and list box, making sure to format each with colors and backgrounds. When each control object is finished, use the *Set Control Defaults* option to change the default settings. Another option is to select all the control objects after the form is finished and then perform one *Set Control Defaults* command. Save the form using the name *Normal*. The Normal form becomes the template for all the new forms in the database. Existing forms retain their initial formatting, unless they are changed manually.

Project 2c Creating and Using a User-Defined Form Template

Part 3 of 3

1. With **6-RSRCompServ.accdb** open, create a form template for the database by completing the following steps:
   a. Click the Create tab and then click the Form Design button in the Forms group.
   b. Click the Themes button in the Themes group. Notice that the database uses the Organic theme for any new forms. Click in a blank area of the form to close the Themes list.
   c. Click the Label button in the Controls group on the Form Design Tools Design tab, draw a label in the *Detail* section, type Sample Label Text, and then press the Enter key. Do not be concerned with the position and size of the label control object at this time, since this control object will be used only to set new default formatting options.
   d. Click the Form Design Tools Format tab. Apply bold formatting and change the font color to Blue-Gray, Accent 3 (seventh column, first row in the *Theme Colors* section) and the background color to Blue-Gray, Accent 3, Lighter 80% (seventh column, second row in the *Theme Colors* section).

   1c-1d

   e. Click the Form Design Tools Design tab, click the Text Box button in the Controls group, and then draw a text box control object in the *Detail* section. Format the text box control object and its associated label control object as follows:
      1) To the label control object, apply bold formatting and the same font and background colors that were applied to the label control object in Step 1d.
      2) Select the text box control object (displays *Unbound*) and apply the same background color applied to the label control object in Step 1d.

   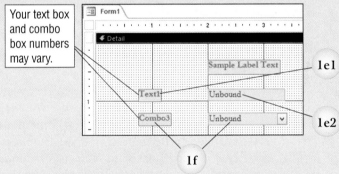
   1e1
   1e2
   1f

   f. Click the Form Design Tools Design tab, click the Combo Box button in the Controls group, and then draw a combo box in the *Detail* section. If the Combo Box Wizard begins, click Cancel. Format the combo box control object using the same options applied to the text box control object in Steps 1e1 and 1e2.
   g. Press Ctrl + A to select all the control objects in the form.
   h. Click the Form Design Tools Design tab, click the More button in the Controls group, and then click *Set Control Defaults*.

   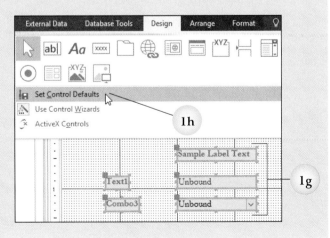
   1h
   1g

2. Save the form with the name *Normal*.
3. Close the Normal form. Normal becomes the form template for **6-RSRCompServ.accdb**. Any new form created will have labels, text boxes, and combo boxes formatted as specified in Step 1.

4. Click *WorkOrders* in the Tables group in the Navigation pane, click the Create tab, and then click the Form button in the Forms group. The new WorkOrders form uses the formatting applied to the labels, text boxes, and combo boxes in the Normal form template.
5. With the first record displayed in the WorkOrders form in Form view, click the File tab, click *Print*, and then click *Print Preview*. Click the Columns button in the Page Layout group. Select the current value in the *Width* text box in the *Column Size* section, type 7.5, and then click OK. Close Print Preview.
6. Close the WorkOrders form. Click Yes when prompted to save changes to the design of the form and then click OK to accept the default form name *WorkOrders*.

> **Check Your Work**

Project 3 Copy Table Structure   1 Part

You will create a new table to store contact information for manufacturer sales representatives by copying an existing table's field names and field properties.

> **Preview Finished Project**

Tutorial

Copying a Table
Structure to a
New Table

Ǫuick Steps

**Copy a Table
Structure**
1. Select table.
2. Click Copy button.
3. Click Paste button.
4. Type new table name.
5. Click *Structure Only.*
6. Click OK.

Copying a Table Structure to a New Table

Use the copy and paste commands to create a new table that uses the same or similar fields as an existing table. For example, in Project 3, the structure of the Contacts table will be copied to create a new table for manufacturer contacts that need to be maintained separately from other contact records. Since the fields needed for the manufacturer contact records are the same as those for the existing contact records, base the new table on the existing table.

To copy a table structure, click the existing table name in the Navigation pane, click the Copy button in the Clipboard group on the Home tab, and then click the Paste button in the Clipboard group. When a table has been copied to the Clipboard, clicking the Paste button causes the Paste Table As dialog box to appear, as shown in Figure 6.6. Type the name for the new table in the *Table Name* text box, click *Structure Only* in the *Paste Options* section, and then click OK. Once the table has been created, fields can be added, deleted, and modified as needed.

Figure 6.6 Paste Table As Dialog Box

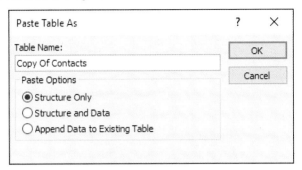

Project 3 Copying a Table Structure to Create a New Table

Part 1 of 1

1. With **6-RSRCompServ.accdb** open, copy the structure of the Contacts table by completing the following steps:
   a. Click *Contacts* in the Tables group in the Navigation pane.
   b. Click the Home tab and then click the Copy button in the Clipboard group.
   c. Click the Paste button in the Clipboard group. (Do not click the Paste button arrow.)
   d. At the Paste Table As dialog box, type MfrContacts in the *Table Name* text box and then click *Structure Only* in the *Paste Options* section.
   e. Click OK.

2. Open the MfrContacts table. Note that the table structure contains the same fields as the Contacts table.
3. Enter the following data in a new record using Datasheet view. Press the Tab key to move past the remaining fields after *ZIP/Postal Code*.

ID	(AutoNumber)
Company	Dell Inc.
Last Name	Haldstadt
First Name	Cari
Email Address	haldstadt@emcp.net
Job Title	Northeast Sales Manager
Business Phone	800-555-9522
Home Phone	(leave blank)
Mobile Phone	800-555-4662
Fax Number	800-555-7781
Address	One Dell Way
City	Round Rock
State/Province	TX
ZIP/Postal Code	78682

4. Close the table.
5. With *MfrContacts* selected in the Tables group in the Navigation pane, click the Create tab and then click the Form button in the Forms group. The form should appear similar to the one shown below.

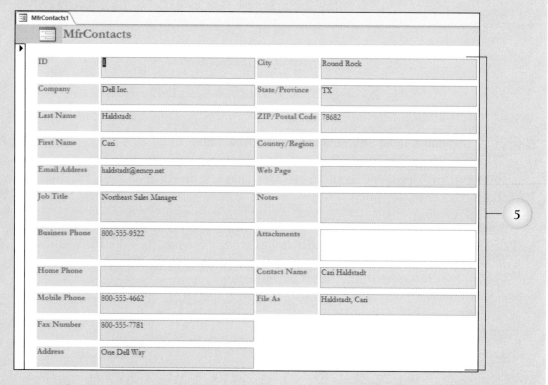

6. Select the label control object and text box control object for the *Attachments* field. Press the Delete key.
7. To move the *Contact Name* field and *File As* field up one spot, select the label and text box control objects for both of these fields and then click the Move Up button in the Move group on the Form Layout Tools Arrange tab.
8. Click the File tab, click the *Print* option, and then click *Print Preview* to display the form in Print Preview. Change to landscape orientation, change the left and right margins to 1 inch, and then close Print Preview.
9. Save the form using the default name *MfrContacts*.
10. Print the selected record and then close the form.

Check Your Work

Project 4 Use Access Tools to Optimize and Document a Database   5 Parts

You will use the Table Analyzer Wizard to improve a table's design and the Performance Analyzer to optimize database design and you will split a database by separating tables from queries, forms, and reports. Finally, you will use the Database Documenter to print a report that documents the table structure.

Preview Finished Project

Evaluating a Table Using the Table Analyzer Wizard

Repeating information within a table can result in inconsistencies and wasted storage space. Use the Table Analyzer Wizard to examine a table and determine if duplicate information can be split into smaller related tables to improve the table design. The wizard suggests fields that can be separated into a new table and remain related to the original table with a lookup field. The user can either accept the proposed solutions or modify the suggestions.

Project 4a uses the Table Analyzer Wizard in a new Parts table. The table was created to store information about the parts commonly used by technicians at RSR Computer Services. Access will examine the table and propose moving the *Supplier* field to a separate table. Making this change will improve the design because several parts records can be associated with the same supplier. In the current table design, the supplier name is typed into a field in each record. Since several parts are associated with each supplier name, the field contains many duplicate entries that take up more storage space than necessary. Furthermore, entering the same data more than once increases the potential for introducing errors in records, which could result in a query that produces incorrect results.

To begin the Table Analyzer Wizard, click the Database Tools tab and then click the Analyze Table button in the Analyze group. This opens the first Table Analyzer Wizard dialog box, shown in Figure 6.7. At the first two dialog boxes, review the information about what the Table Analyzer can do to improve the table design. At the third dialog box in the wizard, select the table to be analyzed. At the fourth dialog box, either choose to let the wizard decide which fields to group in the smaller tables or split the tables manually by dragging and dropping fields.

The wizard looks for fields with repetitive data and then suggests a solution. Confirm the grouping of fields and primary key fields in the new tables. At the final step in the wizard, elect to have Access create a query so the fields in the split tables are presented together in a datasheet that resembles the original table.

Quick Steps

Evaluate a Table with the Table Analyzer Wizard

1. Click Database Tools tab.
2. Click Analyze Table button.
3. Click Next.
4. Click Next.
5. Click table name.
6. Click Next.
7. If necessary, click *Yes, let wizard decide*.
8. Click Next.
9. Confirm grouping of fields in proposed tables.
10. Rename each table.
11. Click Next.
12. Confirm and/or set primary key field in each table.
13. Click Next.
14. If necessary, click *Yes, create the query*.
15. Click Finish.
16. Close Help window.
17. Close query.

 Analyze Table

Hint Use the Table Analyzer Wizard to help normalize a table.

Figure 6.7 First Table Analyzer Wizard Dialog Box

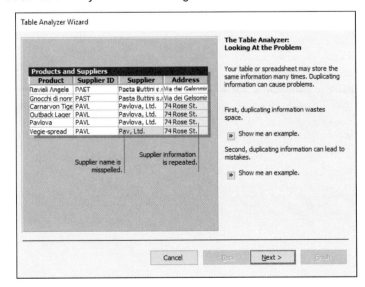

1. With **6-RSRCompServ.accdb** open, open the Parts table in Datasheet view and review the table structure and data. Notice that the table includes four fields: *PartNo*, *PartName*, *Supplier*, and *Cost*. Also notice that the supplier names are repeated in the *Supplier* field.
2. Close the Parts table.
3. Use the Table Analyzer Wizard to evaluate the Parts table design by completing the following steps:
   a. Click the Database Tools tab.
   b. Click the Analyze Table button in the Analyze group.
   c. Read the information at the first Table Analyzer Wizard dialog box and then click the Next button.
   d. Read the information at the second Table Analyzer Wizard dialog box and then click the Next button.
   e. At the third Table Analyzer Wizard dialog box with *Parts* selected in the *Tables* list box, click the Next button.
   f. At the fourth Table Analyzer Wizard dialog box with *Yes, let the wizard decide* selected for *Do you want the wizard to decide what fields go in what tables?*, click the Next button.
   g. At the fifth Table Analyzer Wizard dialog box, look at the two tables the wizard is proposing. Notice that the *Supplier* field has been moved to a new table and that a one-to-many relationship has been created between the tables. Access names the new tables *Table1* and *Table2* and asks two questions: *Is the wizard grouping information correctly?* and *What name do you want for each table?* **Note: If necessary, resize the table field list boxes to see all the proposed fields.**
   h. The proposed tables have the fields grouped correctly. Double-click the *Table1* Title bar to give the table a new name.

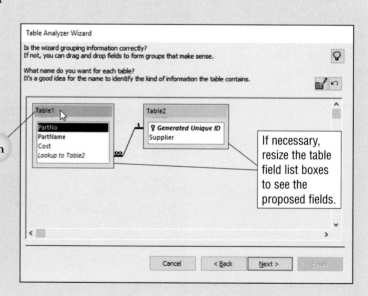

If necessary, resize the table field list boxes to see the proposed fields.

i. Type PartsAndCosts in the *Table Name* text box and then click OK.

j. Click the *Table2* Title bar and then click the Rename Table button near the top right of the dialog box, above the table field list boxes. Type PartsSuppliers in the *Table Name* text box and then press the Enter key.

k. Click the Next button.

l. At the sixth Table Analyzer Wizard dialog box, the unique identifier, or primary key field, for each table is set and/or confirmed. The primary key field is displayed in bold in each table field list box. Notice that the PartsAndCosts table does not have a primary key field defined. Click the *PartNo* field in the PartsAndCosts table field list box and then click the Primary Key button near the top right of the dialog box. Access sets the *PartNo* field as the primary key field, displays a key icon, and applies bold formatting to the field name.

m. Click the Next button.

n. At the last Table Analyzer Wizard dialog box, you can choose to have Access create a query with the original table name that includes the fields from the new tables. Creating the query means that existing forms or reports that were based on the original table will still operate. With *Yes, create the query* selected, click the Finish button. Access renames the original table *Parts_OLD*, creates the query with the name *Parts*, and opens the Parts query results datasheet with the Access Help window in the foreground.

o. Close the Help window.

4. Examine the Parts query datasheet and the object names added in the Navigation pane, including the new tables, PartsAndCosts and PartsSuppliers, along with the original table, Parts_OLD. The Parts query looks just like the original table opened in Step 1, with the exception of the additional field named *Lookup to PartsSuppliers*. The lookup field displays the supplier name, which is also displayed in the original *Supplier* field. The second *Supplier* field can be deleted from the query.

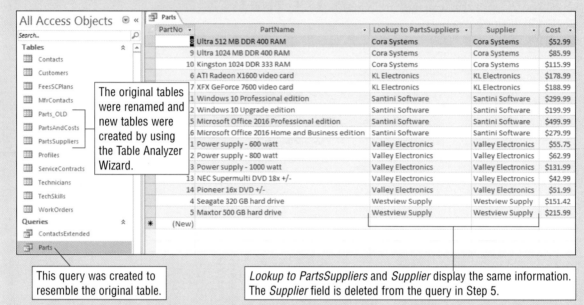

The original tables were renamed and new tables were created by using the Table Analyzer Wizard.

This query was created to resemble the original table.

Lookup to PartsSuppliers and *Supplier* display the same information. The *Supplier* field is deleted from the query in Step 5.

5. Switch to Design view and then delete the *Supplier* field.
6. Save the revised query. Switch to Datasheet view, adjust all the column widths to best fit, and then print the query results datasheet in landscape orientation.
7. Close the query, saving changes to the layout.

Check Your Work

Tutorial

Using the Performance Analyzer

Using the Performance Analyzer

The Performance Analyzer can evaluate an individual object, a group of objects, or an entire database for ways that objects can be modified to optimize the use of system resources (such as memory) and improve the speed of data access. If a database seems to run slowly, consider running the tables, queries, forms, reports, or entire database through the Performance Analyzer.

 Analyze Performance

To use the Performance Analyzer, click the Database Tools tab and then click the Analyze Performance button in the Analyze group to open the Performance Analyzer dialog box, shown in Figure 6.8. Select an object type tab, click the check box next to an object to have it analyzed, and then click OK. Select multiple objects or click the Select All button to select all the objects on the current tab for analysis. To evaluate the entire database, click the All Object Types tab and then click the Select All button. Click OK to begin the analysis.

Three types of results are presented to optimize the selected objects: recommendation, suggestion, and idea. Click an item in the *Analysis Results* list box to read a description of the proposed optimization method in the *Analysis*

Figure 6.8 Performance Analyzer Dialog Box

Select a tab for the object type to be anaylzed.

Select one or more objects to be analyzed.

Click this button to select all of the objects to be analyzed.

Notes section. Click a recommendation or suggestion in the *Analysis Results* list box and then click the Optimize button to instruct Access to carry out the recommendation or suggestion. Access will modify the object and mark the item as fixed when completed. The Performance Analyzer may provide ideas for improving the design, such as assigning a different data type for a field based on the type of data that has been entered into records or creating relationships between tables that are not already related.

Project 4b Analyzing a Database to Improve Performance   Part 2 of 5

1. With **6-RSRCompServ.accdb** open, use the Performance Analyzer to evaluate the database by completing the following steps:
   a. If necessary, click the Database Tools tab.
   b. Click the Analyze Performance button in the Analyze group.
   c. At the Performance Analyzer dialog box, click the All Object Types tab.
   d. Click the Select All button.
   e. Click OK. The Performance Analyzer displays the name of each object as it is evaluated and then presents a full list of results when the analysis is finished.

2. Review the items in the *Analysis Results* list box and then optimize a relationship by completing the following steps:

   a. Click the first entry in the *Analysis Results* list box (contains the text *Application: Save your application as an MDE file*) and then read the description of the idea in the *Analysis Notes* section. (Saving an application as an MDE file will be discussed in Chapter 7.)

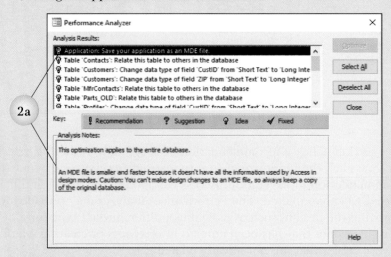

   b. Click the fifth entry in the *Analysis Results* list box (contains the text *Table 'MfrContacts': Relate this table to others in the database*) and then read the description of the idea in the *Analysis Notes* section. The contact information stored in this table is for manufacturer sales representatives and cannot be related to any other tables.

   c. Scroll down the *Analysis Results* list box and then click the item with the green question mark, which identifies a suggestion (contains the text *Table 'WorkOrders': Relate to table 'WorkOrders'*). Read the description of the suggestion in the *Analysis Notes* section. Note that the optimization will benefit the TotalWorkOrders query. This optimization refers to a query that contains a subquery with two levels of calculations. The suggestion is to create a relationship to speed up the query calculations.

   d. Click the Optimize button.

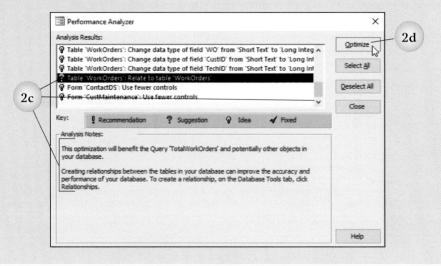

e. Access creates the relationship and changes the question mark next to the item in the *Analysis Results* list box to a check mark (✓). The check mark indicates that the item has been fixed.

f. Click the last item in the *Analysis Results* list box (contains the text *Form 'CustMaintenance': Use fewer controls*) and then read the description of the idea. The idea is to break the form into multiple forms, retaining information that is used often in the existing form. Information viewed less often would be split out into individual forms. To implement this optimization idea would require redesigning the form.

3. Click the Close button to close the Performance Analyzer dialog box.

Splitting a Database

If a database is placed on a network where multiple users can access it simultaneously, the speed with which the data is accessed may decrease. One way to improve performance is to split the database into two files.

The file containing the tables (called the *back-end database*) is stored in the network share folder, while the file containing the queries, forms, and reports (called the *front-end database*) is stored on individual users' computers. The users can create and/or customize their own queries, forms, and reports to serve their individual purposes. The front-end database contains tables linked to the back-end data, so all the users update a single data source file.

To split an existing database into back-end and front-end databases, Access provides the Database Splitter Wizard. Click the Database Tools tab and then click the Access Database button in the Move Data group to open the first Database Splitter Wizard dialog box, shown in Figure 6.9.

Click the Split Database button to open the Create Back-end Database dialog box and navigate to the drive and/or folder where the database file containing the original tables is to be stored. By default, Access uses the original database file name with *_be* added to the end (before the file extension). Change the file name if required and then click the Split button. Access moves the table objects to the back-end file, creates links to the back-end tables in the front-end file, and then displays a message stating that the database was successfully split.

Figure 6.9 First Database Splitter Wizard Dialog Box

Project 4c Splitting a Database

Part 3 of 5

1. With **6-RSRCompServ.accdb** open, split
   the database to create back-end and front-
   end databases by completing the following
   steps:
   a. If necessary, click the Database Tools tab.
   b. Click the Access Database button in the
      Move Data group.
   c. At the first Database Splitter Wizard
      dialog box, click the Split Database
      button.
   d. At the Create Back-end Database dialog
      box, navigate to the same folder as the
      original database (AL2C6). To accept the
      default file name **6-RSRCompServ_be.accdb** in
      the File name text box, click the Split button.

e. Click OK at the Database Splitter message box stating that the database was successfully split.

2. When the database was split, Access moved the tables to the back-end file and created links to the tables in the front-end file. Notice that each table name in the Navigation pane is preceded by a right-pointing arrow. The arrow indicates that the table is a linked object. Opening a linked table causes Access to retrieve the records from the back-end database to display in the table datasheet. Double-click the linked *Contacts* table in the Tables section to open it and review the data.

3. Switch to Design view. Click *Company* in the *Field Name* list, change the field size to 50 characters, and then click the Save button. Access displays a message stating that the operation is not supported for this type of object. Since the table is linked to an external source, Access will not allow making changes to the table design. Click OK and then close the table without saving the changes.

An arrow indicates that a table is linked to an external source.

4. Close **6-RSRCompServ.accdb**.
5. Open **6-RSRCompServ_be.accdb** and enable the content.
6. Notice that the back-end database file contains only the tables. Open the Customers table in Datasheet view and review the data.
7. Switch to Design view. Note that in the back-end database, switching to Design view to make changes does not prompt display of the message box that displayed in Step 3. The message does not display because this database contains the original source table.
8. Close the table.

Another reason to split a database is to overcome the file size restriction in Access 2016. Database specifications for Access 2016 set the maximum file size at 2 gigabytes (GB). This size includes the space needed by Access to open system objects while working with the database, which means the actual maximum file size is even less. However, the size restriction does not include links to external data source files. Splitting a database extends the size beyond the 2-gigabyte limitation.

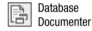

Documenting a Database

Another Access feature, the Database Documenter feature, prepares and prints a report with details about the definition of a database object. This report can be used as hard-copy documentation of the table structure, including field properties and information regarding a query, form, or report. Relationship diagrams can also be included for all the defined relationships for the table. Relationship options are documented below each relationship diagram.

Quick Steps

Print the Object Documentation
1. Click Database Tools tab.
2. Click Database Documenter button.
3. Click Options button.
4. Choose report options.
5. Click OK.
6. Click object name.
7. Click OK.
8. Print report.
9. Close report.

It is a good idea to store the database documentation report in a secure place. That way, if the data gets corrupted or destroyed, the information needed to manually repair, rebuild, or otherwise recreate the database is available.

Click the Database Tools tab and then click the Database Documenter button in the Analyze group to open the Documenter dialog box, shown in Figure 6.10. Insert a check mark in the check box next to the name of the object the report is to be generated for and then click OK.

Database Documenter

Figure 6.10 Documenter Dialog Box

Project 4d Generating a Table Definition Documentation Report   Part 4 of 5

1. With **6-RSRCompServ_be.accdb** open, generate a report providing details of the table structure, field properties, and relationships for an individual table by completing the following steps:
   a. Click the Database Tools tab.
   b. In the Analyze group, click the Database Documenter button.
   c. At the Documenter dialog box, click the Options button.

d. At the Print Table Definition dialog box, click the *Permissions by User and Group* check box in the *Include for Table* section to remove the check mark.

e. Make sure *Names, Data Types, Sizes, and Properties* is selected in the *Include for Fields* section.

f. Click *Nothing* in the *Include for Indexes* section.

g. Click OK.

h. With Tables the active tab in the Documenter dialog box, click the *PartsSuppliers* check box to insert a check mark.

i. Click OK.

2. Access generates the table definition report and displays it in Print Preview. Print the report.

3. Notice that the Save option is dimmed. A report generated by the Database Documenter cannot be saved, but it can be exported as a PDF, XPS, or one of the other file options found in the Data group on the Print Preview tab. Click the Close Print Preview button in the Close Preview group on the Print Preview tab.

Check Your Work

Tutorial

Renaming and Deleting Objects

Renaming and Deleting Objects

Quick Steps

Rename an Object
1. Right-click object in Navigation pane.
2. Click *Rename*.
3. Type new name.
4. Press Enter.

Delete an Object
1. Right-click object in Navigation pane.
2. Click *Delete*.
3. Click Yes.

As part of managing a database, objects may need to be renamed or deleted within the database file. To do this, right-click the object name in the Navigation pane and then click *Rename* or *Delete* at the shortcut menu. An object may also be deleted from a database by selecting the object in the Navigation pane and then pressing the Delete key. Click Yes at the Microsoft Access message box asking you to confirm deletion of the object. Consider making a backup copy of a database before renaming or deleting objects in case the database needs to be restored to its previous state.

Be cautious when deleting objects that have dependencies to other objects. For example, if a table is deleted and a query exists that is dependent on fields within that table, the query will no longer run.

1. With **6-RSRCompServ_be.accdb** open, rename the MfrContacts table by completing the following steps:
   a. Right-click *MfrContacts* in the Tables group in the Navigation pane.
   b. Click *Rename* at the shortcut menu.
   c. Type ManufacturerContacts and then press the Enter key.

2. Delete the original table that was split using the Table Analyzer Wizard in Project 4a by completing the following steps:
   a. Right-click *Parts_OLD* in the Tables group in the Navigation pane.
   b. Click *Delete* at the shortcut menu.
   c. Click Yes at the Microsoft Access message box asking if you want to delete the table *Parts_OLD*.

3. Close **6-RSRCompServ_be.accdb**.
4. Open **6-RSRCompServ.accdb** (the front-end database) and enable the content.
5. Double-click *MfrContacts* in the Tables group in the Navigation pane. Because the table was renamed in Step 1, Access can no longer find the source data. At the Microsoft Access message box stating that the database engine cannot find the input table, click OK. The link will have to be recreated to establish a new connection to the renamed table. (Creating a link to an external table will be discussed in Chapter 8.)

6. Double-click *Parts_OLD* in the Tables group in the Navigation pane. Because this table was deleted in Step 2, the same message appears. Click OK to close the message box.

7. Right-click *Parts_OLD* in the Tables group in the Navigation pane and then click *Delete* at the shortcut menu. Click Yes at the Microsoft Access message box asking if you want to remove the link.

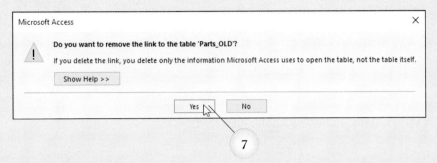

8. Delete the ContactPhoneBook report by completing the following steps:
   a. Click *ContactPhoneBook* in the Reports group in the Navigation pane.
   b. Press the Delete key.
   c. Click Yes at the Microsoft Access message box asking if you want to permanently delete the report.

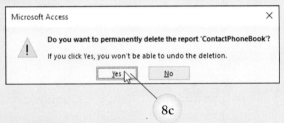

9. Close **6-RSRCompServ.accdb**.

Project 5 Use Access Features to Quickly Create a Database   **1 Part**

You will use Application Parts templates and Quick Start options to quickly create a series of objects in a new database. You will also create a relationship and a report.

Preview Finished Project

Creating Databases Using Templates, Application Parts, Quick Start, and Wizards

In earlier versions of Access, a wizard goes through the steps of creating a customized database. Access 2016 provides many ways to effectively create and customize a database. Start by creating a database from one of the predefined templates, as demonstrated in Project 1, or by using the Blank desktop database template, which was discussed in Chapter 1.

Tables, queries, forms, and reports can be added using one or more of the following wizards or Quick Start options. Project 2 demonstrated that Application Parts templates can be used to add tables, queries, forms, and reports depending on the option chosen in the *Quick Start* section of the Application Parts drop-down list. In Level 1, Chapter 1, the *Quick Start* section of the More Fields drop-down list was used to quickly add a group of related fields to a table in one easy step. For example, when the *Address* option is clicked, Access inserts *Address, City, StateProvince, ZIPPostal,* and *CountryRegion* fields. The short text data type and a caption have been assigned to each field. Once tables are created in the database, use the Query Wizard, Form Wizard, and Report Wizard to efficiently generate queries, forms, and reports. The Query, Form, and Report Wizards have been used throughout Level 1 and Level 2.

Project 5 Creating a Database Using Application Parts, Quick Start, and Wizards

Part 1 of 1

1. Complete the following steps to create a new database and then save it to an external drive. ***Note: If you do not have an external drive or if you already save your work to an external drive, save the database to the AL2C6 folder on your storage medium.***
   a. At the Open backstage area, click the *Blank desktop database* template.
   b. At the Blank desktop database window, click the Browse button and then navigate to the external drive. Select the current text in the *File Name* text box, type 6-ConvTask, and then click OK.
   c. Click the Create button.
2. Close the Table1 blank table datasheet.
3. Use a template to create a new table and two new forms by completing the following steps:
   a. Click the Create tab.
   b. Click the Application Parts button in the Templates group and then click *Tasks* in the *Quick Start* section of the drop-down list.
4. Click the Enable Content button.
5. You want to keep track of the employees responsible for specific tasks. Create an Employees table to hold name and address information by completing the following steps:
   a. Click the Table button in the Tables group to create a new table.
   b. With the Table Tools Fields tab selected, click the More Fields button in the Add & Delete group. Scroll down the list and then click *Name*. *Last Name* and *First Name* fields are added.
   c. Click in the blank row under *Click to Add*, click the More Fields button, scroll down the list, and then click *Address*. Five fields related to the employee's address are added. ***Note: If you do not click in the blank row in the* Click to Add *column, the* First Name *field will appear after the* Country Region *field.***
6. Save the table with the name *Employees*.
7. Switch to Design view and then change the name and data type of the primary key field from *ID* and AutoNumber to *EmpID* and Short Text, respectively. Delete the *Country Region* field. Save the table.

5b

8. Add yourself as an employee. Type E10 for your *EmpID* field value and then close the table.
9. Open the Tasks table and then add the short text field *EmpID* after the *Active* field.
10. Save the changes and then enter the following record in the Tasks table:

Task Title	Review Convention Venues
Priority	(1) High
Status	Not Started
Description	Investigate major convention centers in Miami.
Start Date	(Enter the current date.)
Due Date	(Enter a due date that is approximately one month from the current date.)
Attachments	(leave blank)
Percent Complete	(leave at default value of 0%)
Active	(leave at value of true)
EmpID	E10

Close the table after entering the data.

11. Create the relationship shown at the right. Save and close the Relationships window.

12. Use the Simple Query Wizard to create a query that uses the *ID*, *TaskTitle*, *Priority*, and *Description* fields from the Tasks table and the *LastName* and *FirstName* fields from the Employee table. Use the default name for the query.
13. Adjust the column widths and then save and close the query.
14. Create the Report shown below using the Report Wizard and the query created in Step 12. Use the default settings.

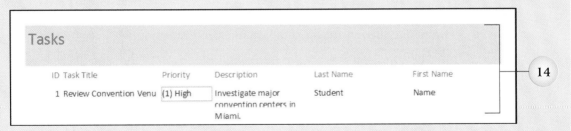

15. Close the report and then close **6-ConvTask.accdb**.

Check Your Work

In this chapter, you have learned to use some of the tools that Access provides to create a new database, create new tables and related objects, improve database and individual object design and performance, and document a database. You have also learned how to rename and delete objects.

Chapter Summary

- Access provides professionally designed database templates that include predefined tables, queries, forms, and reports for use in creating a new database.

- Choose a database template from the sample templates stored on your computer or download a database template from Office.com.

- Predefined table and related object templates for Comments; Contacts; and Issues, Tasks, and Users are available in the *Quick Start* section of the Application Parts button drop-down list in the Templates group on the Create tab.

- The *Blank Forms* section of the Application Parts button drop-down list contains 10 prebuilt blank forms. Most of these forms include command buttons that perform actions such as saving changes and saving and closing the form.

- Define a custom form template by creating a form named *Normal* that includes a sample of each control object with the formatting options required for future forms. Select all the controls and use the *Set Control Defaults* option to save the new settings.

- When a table has been copied to the Clipboard from the Navigation pane, clicking the Paste button causes the Paste Table As dialog box to open. At this dialog box, choose one of the three options: *Structure Only*, *Structure and Data*, or *Append Data to Existing Table*.

- Use the Table Analyzer Wizard to evaluate a table for repeated data and determine if the table can be split into smaller related tables.

- Use the Performance Analyzer to evaluate an individual object, a group of objects, or an entire database for ways to optimize the use of system resources and improve the speed of data access.

- The Performance Analyzer provides three types of results in the *Analysis Results* list box: recommendation, suggestion, and idea.

- Click a recommendation or suggestion in the *Analysis Results* list box and then click the Optimize button to instruct Access to carry out the recommendation or suggestion.

- A database can be split into two individual files—a back-end database and a front-end database—to improve performance for a multiuser database or overcome the maximum database file size restriction.

- To split a database using the Database Splitter Wizard, begin by clicking the Access Database button in the Move Data group on the Database Tools tab.

- Use the Database Documenter feature to print a hard-copy report with details about the definition of a database object, query, form, or report or the structure of a table.

- Rename an object by right-clicking the object name in the Navigation pane, clicking *Rename* at the shortcut menu, typing the new name, and then pressing the Enter key.

- Delete an object by right-clicking the object name in the Navigation pane, clicking *Delete* at the shortcut menu, and then clicking Yes at the message box asking you to confirm deletion of the object.

- Tables, queries, forms, and reports can be added to a database using the Query, Form, and Report Wizards and the Application Parts options.

Commands Review

FEATURE	RIBBON TAB, GROUP	BUTTON	KEYBOARD SHORTCUT
Application Parts template	Create, Templates		
Database Documenter	Database Tools, Analyze		
Paste Table As	Home, Clipboard		Ctrl + V
Performance Analyzer	Database Tools, Analyze		
split database	Database Tools, Move Data		
Table Analyzer Wizard	Database Tools, Analyze		

Workbook

Chapter study tools and assessment activities are available in the *Workbook* ebook. These resources are designed to help you further develop and demonstrate mastery of the skills learned in this chapter.

Microsoft®
Access®

Automating, Customizing, and Securing Access

Performance Objectives

Upon successful completion of Chapter 7, you will be able to:

1 Create, run, edit, and delete a macro

2 Create a command button to run a macro

3 View an embedded macro in the Property Sheet task pane

4 Convert a macro to Visual Basic for Applications

5 Create and edit a Navigation form

6 Customize database startup options

7 Limit access to options in ribbons and menus

8 Customize the Navigation pane

9 Define error-checking options

10 Import and export customized settings

11 Customize the ribbon and the Quick Access Toolbar

Precheck

Check your current skills to help focus your study.

Macros are used to automate repetitive tasks and to store these actions so that they can be executed by clicking a button in a form. A Navigation form is used as a menu to provide an interface between the user and objects within the database file. In this chapter, you will learn how to automate a database using macros and a Navigation form. You will also learn how to customize the Access environment.

Data Files

Before beginning chapter work, copy the AL2C7 folder to your storage medium and then make AL2C7 the active folder.

SNAP

If you are a SNAP user, launch the Precheck and Tutorials from your Assignments page.

Tutorial

Creating and
Running a Macro

💡 **Hint** To create a complex macro, begin by working through the steps to be saved. Write down all the parameters before attempting to record the macro.

Creating and Running a Macro

A macro is a series of instructions stored in sequence that can be recalled and carried out as needed. A macro is generally created for a task that never varies and that is frequently repeated. For example, a macro could be created to open a query, form, or report. The macro object stores a series of instructions (called *actions*) in the sequence in which they are to be performed. Macros appear as objects within the Navigation pane. A macro that opens a query, form, or report can be run by double-clicking the macro name in the Navigation pane.

Not all macros can be run by this method, however. Some need to be assigned to buttons that are clicked in order to run them. For example, a user can create a macro in a form that automates the process of searching through the records for a specific client's last name. The macro will contain two instructions: to move to the field in which the last name is stored and to open the Find and Replace dialog box. In general, a macro that does not include an instruction containing the query, form, or report name must be assigned to a button. Otherwise, an error message will appear stating that the object is not currently selected or is not in the active view.

To create a macro, click the Create tab and then click the Macro button in the Macros & Code group. This opens the Macro Builder window, shown in Figure 7.1. Click the arrow at the right side of the *Add New Action* option box and then click an instruction at the drop-down list. As an alternative, add an action using the Action Catalog task pane, as described in Figure 7.1.

Figure 7.1 Macro Builder Window

Each new action entered into the Macro task pane is associated with a set of arguments that displays once the action has been added. Similar to the field properties displayed in Table Design view, the arguments displayed in the Macro task pane vary depending on the active action that has been expanded. Figure 7.2 displays the action arguments for the OpenForm action.

The OpenForm action is used to open a form. Within the Macro task pane, specify the name of the form to open and the view in which the form is to be presented. Choose to open the form in Form view, Datasheet view, Layout view, Design view, or Print Preview. Use the Filter Name or Where Condition argument to restrict the records displayed in the report.

The Data Mode argument is used to place editing restrictions on records while the form is open. Choose to open the form in Add mode to allow only adding new records (users cannot view existing records); Edit mode to allow adding, editing, and deleting records; or Read Only mode to allow viewing records. The Window Mode argument is used to instruct Access to open the form in Normal mode (the way forms are normally viewed in the work area), Hidden mode (form is hidden), Icon mode (the form opens minimized), or Dialog mode (the form opens in a separate window similar to a dialog box).

To create a macro that performs multiple actions, use the *Add New Action* option box to add the second action below the first action. Access executes the actions in the order they appear in the Macro task pane. Project 1a demonstrates how to create a macro with multiple actions that will instruct Access to open a form, make active a control within the form, and then open the Find and Replace dialog box to search for a record.

The GoToControl action is used to make active a control within a form or report, and the RunMenuCommand action is used to execute an Access command. For each action, a single argument specifies the name of the control to move to and the name of the command to run.

As actions are added to the Macro task pane, expand and collapse them as needed. When several actions have been added to the Macro task pane, collapsing them allows the user to focus on the current action being edited.

Figure 7.2 Macro Task Pane with Action Arguments for the OpenForm Action

1. Open **7-RSRCompServ.accdb** and enable the content. Create a macro to open the
   TechMaintenance form by completing the following steps:
   a. Click the Create tab.
   b. Click the Macro button in the Macros & Code group.
   c. At the Macro task pane, click the *Add New Action*
      option box arrow, scroll down the list, and then click
      OpenForm. Access adds the action and the arguments
      associated with the action. Most actions require at
      least one argument.
   d. Click the *Form Name* option box arrow in
      the *OpenForm* action section and then click
      TechMaintenance at the drop-down list.

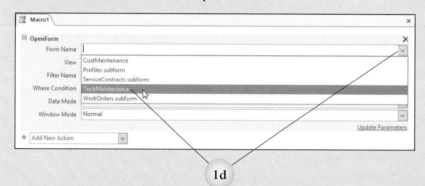

2. Add additional instructions to move to the field for the technician's last name and then
   open the Find and Replace dialog box by completing the following steps:
   a. Click the *Add New Action* option box arrow, scroll down the list, and then click
      GoToControl. Notice that only one action argument is required for the GoToControl
      action.
   b. Click in the *Control Name* text box in the GoToControl action and then type LName.
      (Entering the name of the field that is to be made active in the form is required.)

   c. Click the *Add New Action* option box arrow, scroll down the list, and then click
      RunMenuCommand.

d. Click the *Command* option box arrow, scroll down the list, and then click *Find*.

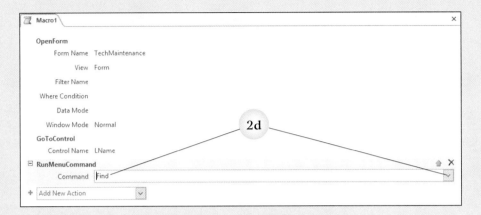

3. Click the Save button on the Quick Access Toolbar, type FormFindTech in the *Macro Name* text box at the Save As dialog box, and then click OK.

4. Click the Run button (which displays as a red exclamation point) in the Tools group on the Macro Tools Design tab. The Run button instructs Access to carry out the instructions in the macro. The TechMaintenance form opens, the *Last Name* field is active, and the Find and Replace dialog box appears with the last name of the first technician entered in the *Find What* text box. Type Sadiku and then click the Find Next button. ***Note: If the Find and Replace dialog box overlaps the Last Name field in the form, drag the dialog box to the bottom or right edge of the work area.***

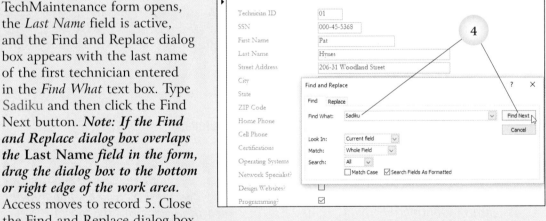

5. Access moves to record 5. Close the Find and Replace dialog box. Notice that the last name text is selected in the form. Read the data displayed in the form for the technician named Madir Sadiku.

6. Close the form.

7. At the Macro Builder window, click the Close button at the top right of the Macro task pane and left of the Action Catalog task pane. This closes the FormFindTech macro. Notice that a Macros group has been added to the Navigation pane and that FormFindTech appears as an object below this new group name.

A macro can also be created by dragging and dropping an object name from the Navigation pane into the *Add New Action* option box in a Macro task pane. By default, Access creates an OpenTable, OpenQuery, OpenForm, or OpenReport action depending on the object that was dragged to the window. The object name is also automatically entered in the Object Name argument list box.

Project 1b Creating a Macro by Dragging and Dropping an Object

Part 2 of 8

1. With **7-RSRCompServ.accdb** open, use the drag and drop method to create a macro to open the CustMaintenance form by completing the following steps:
   a. Click the Create tab.
   b. Click the Macro button in the Macros & Code group.
   c. Position the mouse pointer on the CustMaintenance form name in the Navigation pane, click and hold down the left mouse button, drag the object name into the *Add New Action* option box in the Macro task pane, and then release the mouse button. Access inserts an OpenForm action with *CustMaintenance* entered in the *Form Name* option box.
2. Click the Save button, type FormCustMaint, and then click OK.
3. Click the Run button in the Tools group on the Macro Tools Design tab.
4. Close the form.
5. Close the macro by clicking the Close button at the top right of the Macro task pane and left of the Action Catalog task pane.

Project 1c Creating a Macro Using the Action Catalog Task Pane

Part 3 of 8

1. With **7-RSRCompServ.accdb** open, use the Action Catalog task pane to create a macro to find a record in a form by making active the home telephone field and then opening the Find and Replace dialog box by completing the following steps. *Note: This macro will be assigned to a button in Projects 1e and 1f. An error will occur if you try to run the macro by double-clicking it in the Navigation pane.*
   a. Click the Create tab.
   b. Click the Macro button in the Macros & Code group.
   c. Click the expand button (which displays as a white triangle) next to *Database Objects* in the *Actions* list in the Action Catalog task pane to expand the category and display the actions available for changing controls or objects in the database. *Note: If the Action Catalog task pane was accidentally closed and does not redisplay in the new Macro Builder window, restore the task pane by clicking the Action Catalog button in the Show/Hide group on the Macro Tools Design tab.*

d. Double-click *GoToControl* at the expanded *Database Objects* actions list in the Action Catalog task pane to add the action to the Macro task pane.

e. With the insertion point positioned in the *Control Name* text box in the Macro task pane, type HPhone.

f. Click in the search text box at the top of the Action Catalog task pane and then type Run. As this text is typed, Access displays available actions in the Action Catalog task pane that begin with the same text.

g. Double-click *RunMenuCommand* in the *Macro Commands* list in the Action Catalog task pane.

h. With the insertion point positioned in the *Command* text box in the Macro task pane, type Find.

i. Click the Save button on the Quick Access Toolbar.

j. At the Save As dialog box, type HPhoneFind and then click OK.

k. Close the HPhoneFind macro.

2. Use the Action Catalog to create a macro to close the current database and exit Access by completing the following steps:

a. Click the Create tab and then click the Macro button.

b. Click the box right of the search text box in the Action Catalog task pane to clear *Run* from the search text box and redisplay all the Action Catalog categories.

c. Click the expand button (which displays as a white triangle) next to *System Commands* in the *Actions* list in the Action Catalog task pane.

d. Double-click *QuitAccess* in the expanded *System Commands* actions list.

e. With *Save All* the default argument in the *Options* option box, click the Save button on the Quick Access Toolbar.

f. Type ExitRSRdb at the Save As dialog box and then click OK.

3. Close the ExitRSRdb macro.

4. Double-click *ExitRSRdb* in the Navigation Pane.

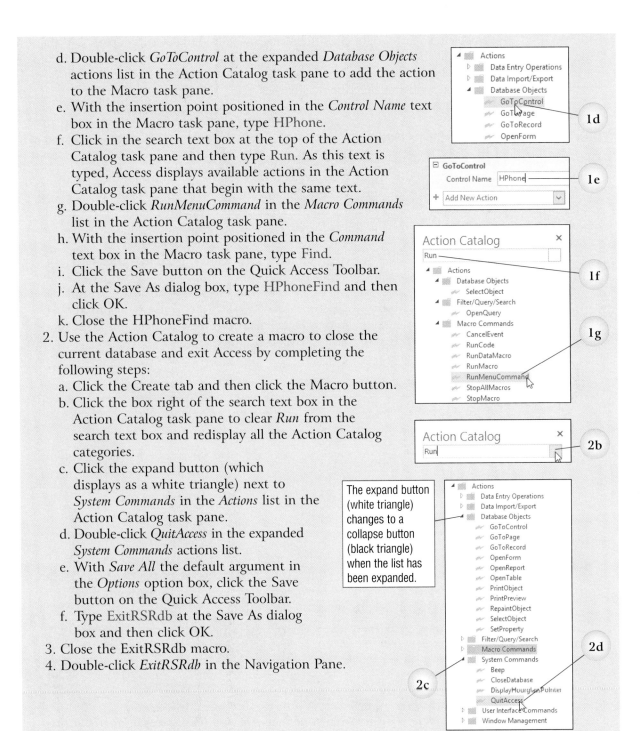

The expand button (white triangle) changes to a collapse button (black triangle) when the list has been expanded.

![Tutorial]

Editing a Macro

Editing and Deleting a Macro

To edit a macro, right-click the macro name in the Navigation pane and then click *Design View* at the shortcut menu or right-click the macro name and press Ctrl + Enter. The macro opens in the Macro Builder window. Edit an action and/or its arguments, insert new actions, and/or delete actions as required. Save the revised macro and close the Macro Builder window when finished.

To delete a macro, right-click the macro name in the Navigation pane and then click *Delete* at the shortcut menu. A macro can also be deleted by selecting it in the Navigation Pane and clicking the Delete key. At the Microsoft Access dialog box asking if you want to delete the macro, click Yes.

Project 1d Editing and Deleting a Macro

1. Open **7-RSRCompServ.accdb.** It has been decided that the macro to find a technician record will begin with the TechMaintenance form already opened. This means that the first macro instruction to open the TechMaintenance form in the FormFindTech macro needs to be deleted. To do this, complete the following steps:
   a. If necessary, scroll down the Navigation pane to view the macro object names.
   b. Right-click *FormFindTech* in the Macros group in the Navigation pane and then click *Design View* at the shortcut menu. The macro opens in the Macro Builder window.
   c. Position the mouse pointer over the *OpenForm* action in the Macro task pane. As an action is pointed to in the Macro task pane, Access displays a collapse indicator at the left of the action to allow the arguments to be collapsed; a green arrow at the right to allow the action to be moved; and a black *X* to delete the action.

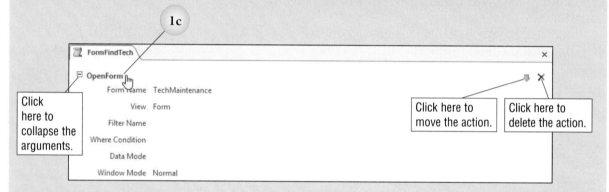

   d. Click the black *X* at the right side of the Macro task pane across from *OpenForm*. The action is removed from the Macro task pane. *Note: If the buttons at the right side of the Macro task pane disappear as you move the mouse to the right, move the pointer up so it is on the same line as* **OpenForm** *to redisplay the buttons.*

2. Save the revised macro. *Note: This macro can no longer be run by double-clicking it in the Navigation pane. As mentioned earlier, an error will occur. The macro will be assigned to a button in Projects 1e and 1f.*
3. Close the macro.
4. The revised macro contains two instructions that activate the *LName* control and then open the Find and Replace dialog box. This macro can be used in any form that contains a field named *LName*; therefore, the macro should be renamed. To do this, right-click *FormFindTech* in the Navigation pane, click *Rename* at the shortcut menu, type LNameFind, and then press the Enter key.

5. Delete the FormCustMaint macro by completing the
   following steps:
   a. Right-click *FormCustMaint* in the Navigation pane and
      then click *Delete* at the shortcut menu.
   b. At the Microsoft Access dialog box asking if you want
      to delete the macro, click Yes.

Tutorial

Creating a
Command Button
to Run a Macro

 Button

Quick Steps

Create a Command Button in a Form
1. Open form in Design view.
2. Click Button button.
3. Drag to create button.
4. Click *Miscellaneous*.
5. Click *Run Macro*.
6. Click Next.
7. Click macro name.
8. Click Next.
9. Click *Text*.
10. Select current text in *Text* text box.
11. Type text to appear on button.
12. Click Next.
13. Type name for command button.
14. Click Finish.

Creating a Command Button to Run a Macro

A macro can be assigned to a button in a form so it can be executed with a single mouse click. This method of running macros makes them more accessible and efficient.

To add a button to a form for running a macro, open the form in Design view. Click the Button button in the Controls group on the Form Design Tools Design tab and then drag to create a button in any form section. When the mouse is released, the Command Button Wizard launches (if the Use Control Wizards feature is active). Recall from Chapter 4 that the Use Control Wizards button displays with a pink or gray background when the feature is active, depending on whether the latest Access 2016 Service Pack has been installed on your computer.

At the first Command Button Wizard dialog box, shown in Figure 7.3, begin by choosing the type of command to assign to the button. Click *Miscellaneous* in the *Categories* list box, click *Run Macro* in the *Actions* list box, and then click the

Figure 7.3 First Command Button Wizard Dialog Box

Figure 7.4 Third Command Button Wizard Dialog Box

Click to display *Text* or *Picture* on the face of the button.

Click the Browse button to locate a picture to display on the face of the button.

Hint An action can be assigned to a command button without using a macro. Explore the categories and actions for each category at the first Command Button Wizard dialog box.

Next button. At the second Command Button Wizard dialog box, choose the name of the macro to assign to the button. At the third dialog box, shown in Figure 7.4, specify text or a picture to display on the face of the button. When text is entered or a picture file is selected, the button in the *Sample* section of the dialog box updates to show how the button will appear. At the last Command Button Wizard dialog box, assign a name to associate with the command button and then click the Finish button.

Project 1e Creating a Button and Assigning a Macro to a Button in a Form

Part 5 of 8

1. With **7-RSRCompServ.accdb** open, create a command button to run the macro to locate a technician record by last name in the TechMaintenance form by completing the following steps:
   a. Open the TechMaintenance form in Design view. To make room for the new button in the *Form Header* section, click to select the control object with the title text and then drag the right middle sizing handle to the left until the right edge is at approximately the 3.5-inch mark on the horizontal ruler.
   b. By default, the Use Control Wizards button is toggled on in the Controls group. Click the More button in the Controls group on the Form Design Tools Design tab. If the Use Control Wizards button displays with a pink or gray background, the feature is active. If the button is pink or gray, click in a blank area of the form to close the expanded Controls group. If the feature is not active (displays with a white background), click the Use Control Wizards button to turn on the feature.
   c. Click the Button button in the Controls group.
   d. Position the crosshairs with the button icon attached in the *Form Header* section, click and hold down the left mouse button, drag to create a button of the approximate height and width shown at the right, and then release the mouse button.

e. At the first Command Button Wizard dialog box, click *Miscellaneous* in the *Categories* list box.

f. Click *Run Macro* in the *Actions* list box and then click the Next button.

g. At the second Command Button Wizard dialog box, click *LNameFind* in the *What macro would you like the command button to run?* list box and then click the Next button.

h. At the third Command Button Wizard dialog box, click the *Text* option.

i. Select the current text in the *Text* text box, type Find Technician by Last Name, and then click the Next button.

j. With *Command##* (where ## is the number of the command button) already selected in the *What do you want to name the button?* text box, type FindTechRec and then click the Finish button. Access automatically resizes the width of the button to accommodate the text to be displayed on its face.

2. Save the revised form.
3. Switch to Form view.
4. Click the Find Technician by Last Name button to run the macro.
5. Type Colacci in the *Find What* text box at the Find and Replace dialog box and then press the Enter key or click the Find Next button. Access makes record 9 active.
6. Close the Find and Replace dialog box.
7. Close the form.

Project 1f Creating Two Command Buttons and Assigning Macros to the Buttons

Part 6 of 8

1. With **7-RSRCompServ.accdb** open, create a command button to run the macro to find a record by the home telephone number field in the CustMaintenance form by completing the following steps:
   a. Open the CustMaintenance form in Design view.
   b. Click the Button button in the Controls group on the Form Design Tools Design tab.
   c. Position the crosshairs with the button icon attached in the *Detail* section below the *Service Contract?* label control object, click and hold down the left mouse button, drag to create a button of the approximate height and width shown at the right, and then release the mouse button.

   d. Click *Miscellaneous* in the *Categories* list box, click *Run Macro* in the *Actions* list box, and then click the Next button.
   e. Click *HPhoneFind* and then click the Next button.
   f. Click *Text*, select the current text in the *Text* text box, type Find Customer by Home Phone, and then click the Next button.
   g. Type FindByPhone and then click the Finish button.

2. Save the revised form.
3. If necessary, move the tab control group down so the top of the object is at the 2.25-inch mark on the vertical ruler. Create a second button below the button created in Step 1 to run the macro to find a record by the last name by completing steps similar to those in Steps 1b through 1g and using the following additional information:
   - Select *LNameFind* as the macro to assign to the button.
   - Display the text *Find Customer by Last Name* on the button.
   - Name the button *FindByLName*.
4. Select both buttons and apply the Intense Effect - Blue-Gray, Accent 3 quick style (fourth column, last row in the *Theme Styles* gallery of the Quick Styles button). Resize, align, and then position the two buttons as shown below.

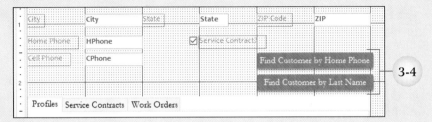

5. Save the revised form.
6. Switch to Form view.
7. Click the Find Customer by Home Phone button, type 313-555-7486 at the Find and Replace dialog box, and then press the Enter key. Close the dialog box and review the record for Customer ID 1025.
8. Click the Find Customer by Last Name button, type Antone at the Find and Replace dialog box, and then press the Enter key. Close the dialog box and review the record for Customer ID 1075.
9. Close the CustMaintenance form.

Viewing an Embedded Macro

Quick Steps

View the Macro Code for a Command Button

1. Open form in Design view.
2. Click to select command button.
3. Display Property Sheet task pane.
4. Click Event tab.
5. Click Build button in *On Click* property box.

The Command Button Wizard used in Projects 1e and 1f created an embedded macro in the Property Sheet task pane for the button. An embedded macro is a macro stored within a form, report, or control that is run when a specific event occurs, such as clicking a button.

Embedded macros are objects that are not seen in the Navigation pane. To view an embedded macro, open the command button's Property Sheet task pane and then click the Event tab. *[Embedded Macro]* will be visible in the *On Click* property box. Click the Build button (which displays three dots) at the right side of the *On Click* property box to open the Macro Builder window with the macro actions displayed. The macro and macro actions were created by the Command Button Wizard.

To delete an embedded macro, open the Property Sheet task pane, select *[Embedded Macro]* in the *On Click* property box, and then press the Delete key. Close the Property Sheet task pane and then save the form.

1. With **7-RSRCompServ.accdb** open, view the macro actions embedded in a command button when the Command Button Wizard is used by completing the following steps:
   a. Open the CustMaintenance form in Design view.
   b. Click to select the Find Customer by Home Phone command button.
   c. Click the Property Sheet button in the Tools group on the Form Design Tools Design tab or press the F4 function key.
   d. Click the Event tab in the Command Button Property Sheet task pane.
   e. Notice that the text in the *On Click* property box reads *[Embedded Macro]*.
   f. Click the Build button (which displays three dots) in the *On Click* property box. When the Build button is clicked, Access opens the Macro Builder window for the macro embedded in the command button.
   g. Notice that the name of the macro created by the Command Button Wizard is *CustMaintenance: FindByPhone: On Click*. The macro's name is made up of the form name, followed by the button name with which the macro is associated, and then the event that causes the macro to run (*On Click*).
   h. Review the macro actions in the Macro task pane. Notice that the macro action is *RunMacro* and that the name of the macro selected at the second Command Button Wizard dialog box, *HPhoneFind*, appears in the *Macro Name* option box.
   i. Click the Close button in the Close group on the Macro Tools Design tab.

2. With the Property Sheet task pane still open, click to select the Find Customer by Last Name command button and then click the Build button in the *On Click* property box on the Event tab in the Property Sheet task pane.
3. Review the embedded macro name and macro actions in the Macro task pane and then click the Close button in the Close group on the Macro Tools Design tab.
4. Close the form.

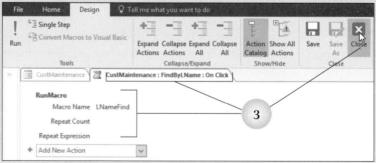

Tutorial

Converting Macros to Visual Basic for Applications

Quick Steps

Convert a Macro to Visual Basic
1. Open macro in Design view.
2. Click Convert Macros to Visual Basic button.
3. Click Convert button.
4. Click OK.

Convert Macros to Visual Basic

Converting Macros to Visual Basic for Applications

Creating and using macros enables the user to add automation and functionality within Access without having to learn how to write programming code. In the Microsoft Office suite, Visual Basic for Applications (VBA) is the programming language used to build custom applications that operate within Word, Excel, PowerPoint, and Access. The macros used so far in this chapter have been simple enough that they do not need VBA programming. However, when automating more complex tasks, a developer may prefer to write a program using VBA.

A quick method for starting a VBA program is to create a macro and then convert it to VBA code. To do this, open the macro in the Macro Builder window and then click the Convert Macros to Visual Basic button in the Tools group on the Macro Tools Design tab. Access opens a Microsoft Visual Basic window with the VBA code for the macro. When converting an embedded macro, Access also changes the property box in the Property Sheet task pane for the form, report, or control to run the VBA procedure instead of the macro.

Project 1h Converting a Macro to Visual Basic for Applications   Part 8 of 8

1. With **7-RSRCompServ.accdb** open, convert a macro to Visual Basic for Applications (VBA) by completing the following steps:
   a. Right-click *HPhoneFind* in the Macros group in the Navigation pane and then click *Design View* at the shortcut menu. The Macro Builder window opens with the macro actions and arguments for the HPhoneFind macro.
   b. Click the Convert Macros to Visual Basic button in the Tools group on the Macro Tools Design tab.

   c. At the Convert macro: HPhoneFind dialog box with the *Add error handling to generated functions* and *Include macro comments* check boxes selected, click the Convert button.
   d. At the *Convert macros to Visual Basic* message box alerting that the conversion has finished, click OK.

2. Access opens a Microsoft Visual Basic for Applications window when the macro is converted and displays the converted event procedure below the expanded *Modules* folder in the Project pane. If necessary, drag the right border of the Project pane to the right to expand the pane so the entire converted macro name is visible and then double-click the macro name to open the event procedure in its class module window.
3. Read the VBA code and then close the Converted Macro-HPhoneFind (Code) window.

4. Click File on the Menu bar and then click *Close and Return to Microsoft Access* at the drop-down menu.
5. Close the HPhoneFind Macro Builder window.

Project 2 Create a Navigation Form   2 Parts

You will create a Navigation form to be used as a main menu for the RSR Computer Services database.

Tutorial

Creating a Navigation Form

Creating a Navigation Form

Database files are often accessed by multiple users who use them for specific purposes, such as updating customer records and entering details related to completed work orders. These individuals may not know much about database applications and may want an easy method for completing data entry or maintenance tasks. Users can open the forms and reports needed to update, view, and print data using a Navigation form as a menu. A Navigation form has tabs along the top, left, or right. It can be set to display automatically when the database file is opened so users do not need to choose which objects to open from the Navigation pane.

Quick Steps

Create a Navigation Form

1. Click Create tab.
2. Click Navigation button.
3. Click form style.
4. Drag form or report name to *[Add New]* in Navigation Form window.
5. Repeat Step 4 as needed.
6. Click Save.
7. Type form name.
8. Press Enter.

Navigation

To create a Navigation form, click the Create tab and then click the Navigation button in the Forms group. At the Navigation button drop-down list, choose the type of form to be created by selecting the option in the drop-down list that positions the tabs where they are to appear. A Navigation Form window opens with a title and a tab bar. Access displays *[Add New]* in the first tab in the form. To add a form or report to a Navigation form, drag it from the Navigation pane and drop it into the to *[Add New]* tab in the Navigation Form window. Continue dragging and dropping form and/or report names from the Navigation pane into the *[Add New]* tab in the Navigation Form window in the order they are to appear. Figure 7.5 illustrates the Navigation form to be created in Projects 2a and 2b.

Figure 7.5 Navigation Form for Projects 2a and 2b

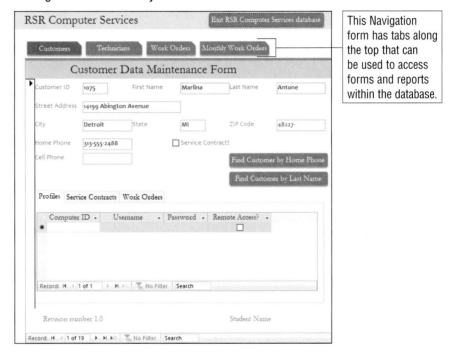

This Navigation form has tabs along the top that can be used to access forms and reports within the database.

Project 2a Creating a Navigation Form

Part 1 of 2

1. With **7-RSRCompServ.accdb** open, create a Navigation form with tabs along the top for accessing forms and reports by completing the following steps:
   a. Click the Create tab.
   b. Click the Navigation button in the Forms group.
   c. Click *Horizontal Tabs* at the drop-down list. Access opens a Navigation Form window with a Field List task pane at the right side of the work area. The horizontal tab at the top of the form is selected and displays *[Add New]*.

d. Position the mouse pointer on the *CustMaintenance* form name in the Navigation pane, click and hold down the left mouse button, drag the form name to *[Add New]* in the Navigation form, and then release the mouse button. Access adds the CustMaintenance form to the first tab in the form and displays a new tab with *[Add New]* right of the CustMaintenance tab.

e. Drag the *TechMaintenance* form name from the Navigation pane to the second tab (which displays *[Add New]*).
f. Drag the *WorkOrders* report name from the Navigation pane to the third tab (which displays *[Add New]*).
g. Drag the *WorkOrdersbyMonth* report name from the Navigation pane to the fourth tab (which displays *[Add New]*).
2. Close the Field List task pane at the right side of the work area.
3. Click the Save button on the Quick Access Toolbar. At the Save As dialog box, type MainMenu in the *Form Name* text box and then click OK.
4. Switch to Form view.
5. Click each tab along the top of the Navigation form to view each form or report in the work area. Leave the MainMenu form open for the next project.

Tutorial

Adding a Command Button to a Navigation Form

A Navigation form can be edited in Layout view or Form view using all the tools and techniques discussed in Chapter 4 for working with forms. Consider changing the title, adding a logo and/or a command button, and renaming tabs to customize the Navigation form.

1. With **7-RSRCompServ.accdb** open and the MainMenu form displayed in the work area, add a command button to the Navigation form by completing the following steps:
   a. Switch to Design view.
   b. Select the *Form Header* section bar and then click the Form Design Tools Format tab. Change the shape fill color of the *Form Header* section to Blue-Gray, Accent 3, Lighter 80% (seventh column in the second row in the *Theme Colors* section).
   c. Resize the title control object in the *Form Header* section to align with the right edge of the object at approximately the 3-inch mark on the horizontal ruler.
   d. Click the Button button in the Controls group on the Form Design Tools Design tab and then drag to create a button in the Form Header section the approximate height and width shown below.

   e. At the first Command Button Wizard dialog box, select *Miscellaneous* in the *Categories* list box, select *Run Macro* in the *Actions* list box, and then click the Next button.
   f. With *ExitRSRdb* already selected in the *Macros* list box at the second Command Button Wizard dialog box, click the Next button.
   g. At the third Command Button Wizard dialog box, click *Text*, select the current entry in the *Text* text box, type Exit RSR Computer Services database, and then click the Next button.
   h. Type Exitdb at the last Command Button Wizard dialog box and then click the Finish button.

2. Click to select the logo control object left of the title in the *Form Header* section and then press the Delete key.
3. Change the text in the Title control object in the *Form Header* section to *RSR Computer Services*.
4. Relabel the tabs along the top of the Navigation form by completing the following steps:
   a. Click to select the *CustMaintenance* tab and then click the Property Sheet button in the Tools group on the Form Design Tools Design tab.
   b. Click the Format tab in the Property Sheet task pane, select the current text in the *Caption* property box, and then type Customers.
   c. Click the *TechMaintenance* tab, select the current text in the *Caption* property box in the Property Sheet task pane, and then type Technicians.
   d. Click the *WorkOrders* tab, click in the *Caption* property box, and then insert a space between *Work* and *Orders* so the tab name displays as *Work Orders*.
   e. Click the *WorkOrdersbyMonth* tab, select the current text in the *Caption* property box, and then type Monthly Work Orders.
   f. Close the Property Sheet task pane.

5. Select the four named tabs plus the [Add New] tab and then make the following formatting changes:
   a. Change the shape to Snip Single Corner Rectangle.
   b. Apply the Intense Effect - Blue-Gray, Accent 3 quick style.
6. Select the Exit RSR Computer Services database button and apply the Intense Effect - Blue-Gray, Accent 3 quick style.

Tab names were changed and formatting options were applied in Steps 4 and 5.

7. Save and close the revised form.

Project 3 Configure Database Options   7 Parts

You will configure database options for the active database and configure error-checking options for all databases. You will also customize the ribbon and Quick Access Toolbar.

Preview Finished Project

Tutorial

Customizing the Access Environment

Customizing the Access Environment

Quick Steps

Set a Startup Form
1. Click File tab.
2. Click *Options*.
3. Click *Current Database* in left pane.
4. Click arrow next to *Display Form*.
5. Click form.
6. Click OK.

Specify an Application Title
1. Click File tab.
2. Click *Options*.
3. Click *Current Database* in left pane.
4. Click in *Application Title* text box.
5. Type title.
6. Click OK.

Click the File tab and then click *Options* to open the Access Options dialog box, which can be used to customize the Access environment. Options can be specified for all databases or only the current database. The behaviors of certain keys and the default margins for printing can also be defined. Choose to set a form to display automatically whenever the database file is opened or to hide the Navigation pane for the current database. For example, if a Navigation form has been created that provides access only to a certain group of objects, hide the Navigation pane. A database can be set to open by default in shared use or exclusive use. *Exclusive use* means the file is restricted to one individual user.

Figure 7.6 displays the Access Options dialog box with *Current Database* selected in the left pane. With options for the current database displayed, define a startup form to open automatically when the database is opened. Project 3a demonstrates how to configure the current database to display the MainMenu form when the database is opened and to specify an application title to display in the Title bar when the database is open. The Navigation pane is customized in Project 3b.

Figure 7.6 Access Options Dialog Box with *Current Database* Selected

Customize the active database using options in this section.

Click this button to open the Navigation Options dialog box, where the Navigation pane can be customized.

Remove this check mark to hide the Navigation pane in the current database.

Project 3a Specifying a Startup Form and Application Title

Part 1 of 7

1. With **7-RSRCompServ.accdb** open, specify an application title to display in the Title bar and choose a form to display automatically when the database file is opened by completing the following steps:
   a. Click the File tab.
   b. Click *Options* to open the Access Options dialog box.
   c. Click *Current Database* in the left pane.
   d. Click in the *Application Title* text box in the *Application Options* section and then type RSR Computer Services Database.
   e. Click the arrow next to the *Display Form* option box (which displays *[none]*) and then click *MainMenu* at the drop-down list.
2. Click OK.
3. Click OK at the Microsoft Access message box indicating that the database must be closed and reopened for the options to take effect.

4. Close **7-RSRCompServ.accdb**.

5. Reopen **7-RSRCompServ.accdb**. The MainMenu form displays automatically in the work area and the Title bar displays the application title *RSR Computer Services Database*.

Tutorial

Limiting Ribbon
Tabs and Menus
in a Database

Limiting Ribbon Tabs and Menus in a Database

In addition to limiting users' access to objects, access to options in the ribbon and menus can be limited. Restricting users from seeing the full ribbon and shortcut menus will prevent accidental changes from being made if someone switches views and edits or deletes objects without knowing the full impact of these changes.

To limit users' access, display the Access Options dialog box and select *Current Database* in the left pane. Scroll down the dialog box to the *Ribbon and Toolbar Options* section. Click to remove the check marks from the *Allow Full Menus* and *Allow Default Shortcut Menus* check boxes and then click OK. When the database is closed and reopened, only the Home tab will display in the ribbon. The File tab backstage area will display only print options. Users will not be able to switch views and right-clicking will not display a shortcut menu.

If full access to the ribbon and menus is needed, bypass the startup options. Do this by pressing and holding down the Shift key while double-clicking the file name in the File Open backstage area when opening the database.

Tutorial

Customizing the
Navigation Pane

Customizing the Navigation Pane

When using a startup form in a database, consider hiding the Navigation pane to prevent users from accidentally making changes to other objects. To hide the Navigation pane, open the Access Options dialog box, click *Current Database* in the left pane, and then click to remove the check mark from the *Display Navigation Pane* check box in the *Navigation* section. When the Navigation pane is hidden, use the F11 function key to unhide it.

Click the Navigation Options button in the *Navigation* section to open the Navigation Options dialog box, shown in Figure 7.7. At this dialog box, choose to hide individual objects or groups of objects, set display options for the pane, and define whether objects can be opened using a single or double mouse click. For example, to prevent changes from being made to the table design, hide the Tables group.

Ǒuick Steps

Hide the Navigation Pane
1. Click File tab.
2. Click *Options*.
3. Click *Current Database* in left pane.
4. Clear *Display Navigation Pane* check box.
5. Click OK.
6. Click OK.

Quick Steps

Figure 7.7 Navigation Options Dialog Box

**Customize the
Navigation Pane**
1. Click File tab.
2. Click *Options*.
3. Click *Current
   Database* in left
   pane.
4. Click Navigation
   Options button.
5. Select options.
6. Click OK.
7. Click OK.

Click this check box to display hidden object names in the Navigation pane in dimmed text.

Remove the check mark from any object to be hidden in the Navigation pane.

Remove this check mark to hide the search bar, where an object name can be entered and searched for.

Click this check box to display the system tables that Access creates for each database.

Project 3b Customizing the Navigation Pane

Part 2 of 7

1. With **7-RSRCompServ.accdb** open, customize the Navigation pane to hide all the table, macro, and module objects by completing the following steps:
   a. Click the File tab and then click *Options*.
   b. If necessary, click *Current Database* in the left pane. Click the Navigation Options button in the *Navigation* section. (You may need to scroll down to view the *Navigation* section.)
   c. Click *Object Type* in the *Categories* list box.
   d. Click the *Tables* check box in the *Groups for "Object Type"* list box to remove the check mark.
   e. Remove the check mark from the *Macros* check box.
   f. Remove the check mark from the *Modules* check box.
   g. Click OK to close the Navigation Options dialog box.

h. Click OK to close the Access Options dialog box.

i. Click OK at the message box stating that the current database must be closed and reopened for the specified option to take effect.

2. Notice that the Tables, Macros, and Modules groups are hidden in the Navigation pane.

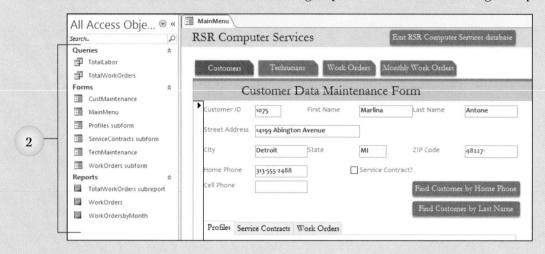

3. After reviewing the customized Navigation pane, you have decided that the database will be more secure if the entire pane is hidden when the database is opened. To do this, complete the following steps:

a. Click the File tab and then click *Options*.

b. With *Current Database* already selected in the left pane, click the *Display Navigation Pane* check box in the *Navigation* section to remove the check mark.

c. Click OK.

d. Click OK at the message box indicating that the database must be closed and reopened for the option to take effect.

4. Close **7-RSRCompServ.accdb**.

5. Reopen **7-RSRCompServ.accdb**. The Navigation pane is hidden and the MainMenu form is open in the work area.

Configuring Error-Checking Options

Recall from Chapter 5 that a green diagonal triangle displays in the Report Selector button when the report is wider than the page allows. Clicking the error-checking options button provides access to tools that can fix the report automatically. A green triangle also appears in a new label control object that is added to a report without being associated with another control object. Access flags the label as an error because it is not associated with another control object. Unchecking the *Check for unassociated label and control option* stops Access from flagging the control object.

By default, Access has error checking turned on and all error-checking options active. To configure error-checking options in Access, open the Access Options dialog box and select *Object Designers* in the left pane. Scroll down the right pane to locate the *Error checking in form and report design view* section, shown in Figure 7.8. Remove the check marks in the check boxes for those options to be disabled and then click OK. Table 7.1 provides a description of each option.

Quick Steps

**Customize Error-
Checking Options**
1. Click File tab.
2. Click *Options*.
3. Click *Object Designers* in left pane.
4. Scroll down to *Error checking in form and report design view* section.
5. Click to remove check marks.
6. Click OK.

Figure 7.8 Error-Checking Options in Access

Table 7.1 Error-Checking Options

Error-Checking Option	Description
Enable error checking	Error checking can be turned on or off in forms and reports. An error is indicated by a green triangle in the upper left corner of a control object.
Check for unassociated label and control	A selected label and text box control object are checked to make sure the two control objects are associated. A Trace Error button appears if Access detects an error.
Check for new unassociated labels	Each new label control object is checked for association with a text box control object.
Check for keyboard shortcut errors	Duplicate keyboard shortcuts and invalid shortcuts are flagged.
Check for invalid control properties	Invalid properties, formula expressions, and field names are flagged.
Check for common report errors	Reports are checked for errors, such as invalid sort orders and reports that are wider than the selected paper size.
Error indicator color	A green triangle indicates an error in a control. Click the Color Picker button to change to a different color.

1. With **7-RSRCompServ.accdb** open, assume that label control objects that contain explanatory text for users are frequently added to forms and reports. Customize the error-checking options to prevent Access from flagging these independent label control objects as errors. To do this, complete the following steps:
   a. Click the File tab and then click *Options*.
   b. Click *Object Designers* in the left pane.
   c. Scroll down the right pane to the *Error checking in form and report design view* section.
   d. Click the *Check for new unassociated labels* check box to remove the check mark.
   e. Click OK.
   f. Click OK.

   Error checking in form and report design view

   ☑ Enable error checking
   ☑ Check for unassociated label and control
   ☐ Check for new unassociated labels   **1d**
   ☑ Check for keyboard shortcut errors
   ☑ Check for invalid control properties
   ☑ Check for common report errors

   Error indicator color   🎨 ▾

Customizing the Ribbon

💡 **Hint** To save mouse clicks, consider creating a custom tab that contains the buttons used on a regular basis.

Customize the ribbon by creating a new tab. Within the new tab, add groups and then add buttons within the groups. To customize the ribbon, click the File tab and then click *Options*. At the Access Options dialog box, click *Customize Ribbon* in the left pane. Options for customizing the ribbon are shown in Figure 7.9.

Figure 7.9 Access Options Dialog Box with *Customize Ribbon* Selected

The commands shown in the left list box in Figure 7.9 are dependent on the current option selected in the *Choose commands from* option box above it. Click the arrow right of the current option (*Popular Commands*) to select from a variety of command lists, such as *Commands Not in the Ribbon* and *All Commands*. The tabs shown in the right list box are dependent on the current option selected in the *Customize the Ribbon* option box. Click the arrow right of the current option (*Main Tabs*) to select *All Tabs*, *Main Tabs*, or *Tool Tabs*.

Create a new group in an existing tab or create a new tab along with a new group within the tab. Add buttons that are regularly used to either of the new groups.

Tutorial

Creating a New Tab

Create a New Tab, Group, and Add a Button

Quick Steps

Create a New Tab and Group
1. Click File tab.
2. Click *Options*.
3. Click *Customize Ribbon* in left pane.
4. Click tab name to precede new tab.
5. Click New Tab button.

Add a New Group to an Existing Tab
1. Click File tab.
2. Click *Options*.
3. Click *Customize Ribbon* in left pane.
4. Click tab name with which new group is associated.
5. Click New Group button.

To create a new tab, click the tab name in the *Main Tabs* list box that the new tab is to follow and then click the New Tab button below the list box. This inserts a new tab in the list box along with a new group below the new tab, as shown in Figure 7.10. If the wrong tab name was selected before clicking the New Tab button, the new tab can be moved up or down in the list box. To do this, click *New Tab (Custom)* and then click the Move Up or Move Down buttons that display at the right side of the dialog box.

Figure 7.10 New Tab and Group Created in the Customize Ribbon Pane at the Access Options Dialog Box

Click to select the *Home* tab name and then click the New Tab button to create the *New Tab (Custom)* tab and *New Group (Custom)* group below Home.

Use the Move Up and Move Down buttons to change the tab order. Click a tab name and then click Move Up or Move Down.

Use the Import/Export button to import and export customized settings.

Exporting Customizations

Your educational institution may already have taken the time to customize the ribbon in Access. To ensure that these customizations can be restored after the ribbon is changed in Project 3e, the settings will be saved (exported) in Project 3d. In Project 3g, the original settings will be reinstalled (imported).

To save the current ribbon settings, click the File tab and then click *Options*. At the Access Options dialog box, click *Customize Ribbon* in the left pane. Click the Import/Export button in the lower right corner of the Access Options dialog box. Click *Export all customizations* to save the file with the custom settings. This file will be used to reinstall the saved settings; it could also be used to install the customized settings on a different computer. To import the saved settings, click the Import/Export button and then click *Import customization file*. Locate the file and reinstall the customized settings.

Quick Steps

**Rename a Tab
or Group**

1. Click File tab.
2. Click *Options*.
3. Click *Customize Ribbon* in left pane.
4. Click tab or group to be renamed.
5. Click Rename button.
6. Type new name.
7. Press Enter.

**Add Buttons
to a Group**

1. Click File tab.
2. Click *Options*.
3. Click *Customize Ribbon* in left pane.
4. Click group name in which to insert new button.
5. Change *Choose commands from* to desired command list.
6. Scroll down and click a command.
7. Click Add button.

Renaming a Tab or Group

Rename a tab by clicking the tab name in the *Main Tabs* list box and then clicking the Rename button below the list box. At the Rename dialog box, type the name for the tab and then press the Enter key or click OK. The Rename dialog box can also be displayed by right-clicking the tab name and then clicking *Rename* at the shortcut menu.

Complete similar steps to rename a group. The Rename dialog box for a group name or command name contains a *Symbol* list box as well as a *Display name* text box. However, the symbols are more useful for identifying new buttons than new groups. Type the new name for the group in the *Display name* text box and then press the Enter key or click OK.

Adding Buttons to a Tab Group

Add commands to a tab by clicking the group name within the tab, clicking the desired command in the list box at the left, and then clicking the Add button that displays between the two list boxes. Remove commands in a similar manner but click the Remove button instead.

Project 3d Exporting Customizations

Part 4 of 7

1. With **7-RSRCompServ.accdb** open, save the current ribbon settings to the desktop by completing the following steps:
   a. Click the File tab and then click *Options*.
   b. Click *Customize Ribbon* in the left pane of the Access Options dialog box.
   c. Click the Import/Export button in the bottom right of the Access Options dialog box.
   d. Click *Export all customizations* at the drop-down list.
   e. Click *Desktop* in the *Favorites* list at the left side of the File Save dialog box.
   f. Change the file name to **7-AccessCustomizations.exportedUI** and then click the Save button.
   g. Click OK two times.

1. With **7-RSRCompServ.accdb** open, customize the ribbon by adding a new tab and two new groups on the tab by completing the following steps. *Note: The original ribbon settings will be restored in Project 3g.*
   a. Click the File tab and then click *Options*.
   b. If necessary click *Customize Ribbon* in the left pane of the Access Options dialog box.
   c. Click *Home* in the *Main Tabs* list box.
   d. Click the New Tab button below the list box. (This inserts a new tab below *Home* and a new group below the new tab.)
   e. With *New Group (Custom)* selected below *New Tab (Custom)*, click the New Group button below the list box. (This inserts another new group below the new tab.)

2. Rename the tab and groups by completing the following steps:
   a. Click to select *New Tab (Custom)* in the *Main Tabs* list box.
   b. Click the Rename button below the list box.
   c. At the Rename dialog box, type your first and last names and then click OK.
   d. Click to select the first *New Group (Custom)* group name that displays below the new tab.
   e. Click the Rename button.
   f. At the Rename dialog box, type Views in the *Display name* text box and then click OK. (Notice that the Rename dialog box for a group or button displays symbols in addition to the *Display name* text box. You will apply a symbol to a button in a later step).
   g. Right-click the *New Group (Custom)* group name below *Views (Custom)* and then click *Rename* at the shortcut menu.
   h. Type Records in the *Display name* text box at the Rename dialog box and then click OK.

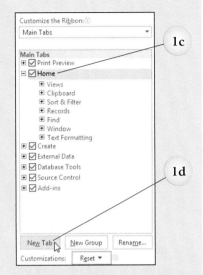

3. Add buttons to the Views (Custom) group by completing the following steps:
   a. Click to select *Views (Custom)* in the *Main Tabs* list box.
   b. With *Popular Commands* selected in the *Choose commands from* option box, click *Form View* in the list box and then click the Add button between the two list boxes. This inserts the command below the *Views (Custom)* group name.

   c. Scroll down the *Popular Commands* list box; click the second *Print Preview* option, which displays the ScreenTip *Popular Commands | Print Preview (FilePrintPreview)*, and then click the Add button. ***Note: The commands are organized in alphabetical order.***
   d. Click *Report View* in the *Popular Commands* list box and then click the Add button.
   e. Scroll to the bottom of the *Popular Commands* list box, click *View*, and then click the Add button.
4. Add buttons to the Records (Custom) group by completing the following steps:
   a. Click to select *Records (Custom)* in the *Main Tabs* list box.
   b. Click the *Choose commands from* option box arrow (which displays *Popular Commands*) and then click *All Commands* at the drop-down list.
   c. Scroll down the *All Commands* list box, click *Ascending*, and then click the Add button.
   d. Scroll down the *All Commands* list box (the list displays alphabetically), click *Delete Record*, and then click the Add button.

e. Scroll down the *All Commands* list box, click *Find*, and then click the Add button.

f. Scroll down the *All Commands* list box, click the first *New* option (which displays the ScreenTip *Home Tab | Records | New (GoToNewRecord)*), and then click the Add button.

g. Scroll down the *All Commands* list box, click *Spelling*, and then click the Add button.

5. Change the symbol for the Spelling button by completing the following steps:

a. Right-click *Spelling* in the *Records (Custom)* group in the *Main Tabs* list box.

b. Click *Rename* at the shortcut menu.

c. At the Rename dialog box click the purple book icon in the *Symbol* list box (fourth column eighth row).

d. Click OK.

6. Click OK to close the Access Options dialog box. If a message displays stating that the database must be closed and reopened for the option to take effect click OK..

7. Use buttons in the custom tab to change views and spell check a form by completing the following steps:

a. Click the Technicians tab at the top of the MainMenu form.

b. Click the custom tab with your name and then click the Print Preview button in the Views group.

c. Click the Form View button in the Views group to switch back to the form.

d. Click in the *Last Name* field and then click the Spelling button.

e. Click the Cancel button at the Spelling dialog box.

f. Click the Customers tab at the top of the MainMenu form.

8. Insert a screenshot of the database window that shows the custom tab in a new Microsoft Word document using either the Screenshot button in the Illustrations group on the Insert tab or the Print Screen key and the Paste feature. Type your name a few lines below the screen image and add any other identifying information as instructed (for example, the chapter number and project number).

9. Save the Microsoft Word document and name it **7-CustomRibbon**.

11. Print **7-CustomRibbon.docx** and then exit Word.

Check Your Work

Customizing the Quick Access Toolbar

Customize Quick Access Toolbar

Click the Customize Quick Access Toolbar button at the right side of the Quick Access Toolbar to open the Customize Quick Access Toolbar drop-down list, as shown in Figure 7.11. Click *More Commands* at the drop-down list to open the Access Options dialog box with *Quick Access Toolbar* selected in the left pane, as shown in Figure 7.12. Change the list of commands that display in the left list box by clicking *Choose commands from* option box arrow and then clicking the appropriate category. Scroll down the list box to locate the command and then double-click the command name to add it to the Quick Access Toolbar.

Quick Steps

Add a Button to the Quick Access Toolbar
1. Click Customize Quick Access Toolbar button.
2. Click button.
OR
1. Click Customize Quick Access Toolbar button.
2. Click *More Commands.*
3. Click *Choose commands from* option box arrow.
4. Click category.
5. Click command in commands list box.
6. Click Add.
7. Click OK.

Remove a Button from the Quick Access Toolbar
1. Click Customize Quick Access Toolbar button.
2. Click button.
OR
1. Click Customize Quick Access Toolbar button.
2. Click *More Commands.*
3. Click command in right list box.
4. Click Remove button.
5. Click OK.

Figure 7.11 Customize Quick Access Toolbar Drop-Down List

Click *More Commands* to open the Access Options dialog box with *Quick Access Toolbar* selected.

Figure 7.12 Access Options Dialog Box with *Quick Access Toolbar* Selected

1. With **7-RSRCompServ.accdb** open, add the Print Preview and Close Window commands to the Quick Access Toolbar by completing the following steps. ***Note: The original settings for the Quick Access Toolbar will be restored in Project 3g.***

   a. Click the Customize Quick Access toolbar button at the right side of the Quick Access Toolbar.
   b. Click *Print Preview* at the drop-down list. The Print Preview button is added to the end of the Quick Access Toolbar. ***Note: Skip to Step 1d if the Print Preview button already displays on your Quick Access Toolbar.***
   c. Click the Customize Quick Access Toobar button.
   d. Click *More Commands* at the drop-down list.
   e. At the Access Options dialog box with *Quick Access Toolbar* selected in the left pane, click the *Choose commands from* option box arrow and then click *Commands Not in the Ribbon*.
   f. Double-click *Close Window* in the *Command Not in the Ribbon* list box. ***Note: The commands are organized in alphabetical order.***
   g. Click OK. If a message displays stating that the database must be closed and reopened for the option to take effect, click OK. The Close Window button is added right of the Save button.
2. Click the WorkOrders tab in the MainMenu navigation form.
3. Click the PrintPreview button on the Quick Access Toolbar to open the WorkOrders report in Print Preview. Click Close Print Preview.
4. Click the Close Window button on the Quick Access Toolbar.

Delete a button from the Quick Access Toolbar by clicking the Customize Quick Access Toolbar button and then clicking the command at the drop-down list. If the command does not appear in the drop-down list, click the *More Commands* option. At the Access Options dialog box, click the command to be removed in the right list box and then click the Remove button.

Resetting the Ribbon and the Quick Access Toolbar

Restore the original ribbon and the Quick Access Toolbar by clicking the Reset button below the *Main Tabs* list box in the Access Options dialog box with *Customize Ribbon* selected in the left pane. Clicking the Reset button displays these two options: *Reset only selected Ribbon tab* and *Reset all customizations*. Click *Reset all customizations* to restore the ribbon and the Quick Access Toolbar to its original settings and then click Yes at the Microsoft Office message box that displays the message *Delete all Ribbon and Quick Access Toolbar customizations for this program?*

To restore the ribbon and the Quick Access Toolbar to your institution's customized settings, import the settings that were exported in Project 3d. Click the Import/Export button in the lower right corner of the Access Options dialog box and then click *Import customization file* at the drop-down list. Locate the file and reinstall the customized settings.

1. Import the customization file saved in Project 3d to reset the ribbon and the Quick Access Toolbar to your institution's original settings by completing the following steps:
   a. Click the File tab and then click *Options* to open the Access Options dialog box.
   b. If necessary, click *Customize Ribbon* in the left pane.
   c. Click the Import/Export button in the bottom right corner of the dialog box.
   d. Click *Import customization file* at the drop-down list.

   e. Click *Desktop* in the *Favorites* list at the left of the File Open dialog box.
   f. Click **7-AccessCustomizations.exportedUI**.
   g. Click the Open button.
   h. Click Yes at the Microsoft Office message box that asks about replacing all existing ribbon and Quick Access Toolbar customizations.

   i. Click OK to close the Access Options dialog box.
   j. Click OK at the message that displays saying that the database must be closed and reopened for the option to take effect.
2. If **7-RSRCompServ.accdb** is open, close it.

In this chapter, you have learned techniques to automate and customize an Access database. As you gain more experience with Access, explore further customizations that allow for changing the behaviors of actions and keys while editing. Also consider experimenting with other macro actions, such as using the OpenQuery action to automate queries.

Chapter Summary

- A macro can be used to automate actions within a database, such as opening a form, query, or report.
- To create a macro, click the Create tab and then click the Macro button in the Macros & Code group, which opens a Macro Builder window. Add a macro action using the *Add New Action* option box or Action Catalog task pane.
- Action arguments are the parameters for the action, such as the object name, mode in which the object opens, and other restrictions placed on the action.
- The arguments displayed vary depending on the active action.
- Most macros can be run by double-clicking the macro name in the Navigation pane, right-clicking the macro name, or clicking the Run button in the Macro Builder window.
- A macro can also be created by dragging and dropping an object name from the Navigation pane into the *Add New Action* option box in a Macro task pane.
- Edit a macro by right-clicking the macro name in the Navigation pane and clicking *Design View* at the shortcut menu.

- A macro can be assigned to a button in a form to allow running the macro with a single mouse click.
- Use the Button button to create a command button in a form.
- Use the Command Button Wizard to create an embedded macro that tells Access which macro to run when the button is clicked. View the macro by opening the command button's Property Sheet task pane, clicking the Event tab, and then clicking the Build button in the *On Click* property box.
- Convert a macro to Visual Basic for Applications (VBA) code by opening it in the Macro Builder window and then clicking the Convert Macros to Visual Basic button in the Tools group on the Macro Tools Design tab.
- A Navigation form has tabs along the top, left, or right and is used as a menu. Users can open the forms and reports in the database by clicking a tab, rather than using the Navigation pane.
- To create a Navigation form, click the Create tab and then click the Navigation button in the Forms group. Choose the form type at the drop-down list and then drag and drop form and/or report names from the Navigation pane into *[Add New]* in the tab bar.
- A form can be set to display automatically when the database is opened. Select the startup form at the *Display Form* option box in the Access Options dialog box with *Current Database* selected in the left pane.
- Change the title that appears in the Title bar for the active database by typing text in the *Application Title* text box at the Access Options dialog box with *Current Database* selected in the left pane.
- Set options for the Navigation pane, such as hiding individual objects and groups of objects, at the Navigation Options dialog box.
- Hide the Navigation pane by removing the check mark from the *Display Navigation Pane* check box at the Access Options dialog box with *Current Database* selected in the left pane.
- Change the default error-checking options at the Access Options dialog box with *Object Designers* selected in the left pane.
- Customize the ribbon by creating a new tab, creating a new group on the new tab, and then adding buttons within the new group.
- To customize the ribbon, open the Access Options dialog box and click *Customize Ribbon* in the left pane.
- To save the current ribbon and Quick Access Toolbar settings, open the Access Options dialog box, click *Customize Ribbon* in the left pane, click the Import/Export button, and then click *Export all customizations*. This file can then be used to reinstall the customizations.
- Create a new tab by clicking the tab name that will precede the new tab in the *Main Tabs* list box and then clicking the New Tab button. A new group is automatically added with the new tab.
- Rename a tab by clicking the tab name in the *Main Tabs* list box, clicking the Rename button, typing a new name, and then pressing the Enter key or clicking OK. Rename a group using a similar process.
- Add buttons to a tab by clicking the group name within the tab, selecting the desired command in the commands list box, and then clicking the Add button between the two list boxes.

- Add buttons to or delete buttons from the Quick Access Toolbar using the Customize Quick Access Toolbar button. To locate a feature to add, click the *More Commands* at the drop-down list to open the Access Options dialog box with *Quick Access Toolbar* selected.
- Restore the ribbon to the default settings by clicking the Reset button below the *Main Tabs* list box in the Access Options dialog box with *Customize Ribbon* selected and then clicking *Reset all customizations* at the drop-down list.

Commands Review

FEATURE	RIBBON TAB, GROUP	BUTTON
convert macros to Visual Basic for Applications	Macro Tools Design, Tools	
create command button	Form Design Tools Design, Controls	
create macro	Create, Macros & Code	
create Navigation form	Create, Forms	
customize Navigation pane	File, Options	
run macro	Macro Tools Design, Tools	

Workbook

Chapter study tools and assessment activities are available in the *Workbook* ebook. These resources are designed to help you further develop and demonstrate mastery of the skills learned in this chapter.

Microsoft®
Access®

Integrating Access Data

Performance Objectives

Upon successful completion of Chapter 8, you will be able to:

1 Create and restore a backup database file

2 Create an ACCDE database file

3 View Trust Center settings

4 Import and merge data from another Access database

5 Link to a table in another Access database

6 Determine when to import or link to external source data

7 Reset or refresh a link using the Linked Table Manager

8 Import data from a text file

9 Save and repeat import specifications

10 Export Access data to a text file

11 Save and repeat export specifications

12 Create a database in an older format

Integrating Access data with other applications in the Microsoft Office suite is easily accomplished with buttons on the External Data tab. These buttons allow you to export data to and import data from Word and Excel files. Data can be exchanged between the Microsoft programs with the formatting and data structure intact. In some cases, however, you may need to exchange data between Access and a non-Microsoft program. In this chapter, you will learn how to create and restore a backup database file, how to integrate data between individual Access database files, and how to import and export data in a text file format that is recognized by nearly all applications. You will also learn how to prevent changes from being made to the design of objects.

You will back up and restore a database and secure a database by making an ACCDE file. You will also explore the default settings in the Trust Center.

Preview Finished Project

Tutorial

Review: Backing Up a Database

Quick Steps

Back Up a Database
1. Click File.
2. Click *Save As*.
3. Click *Back Up Database*.
4. Click Save As.
5. Navigate to appropriate folder.
6. Click Save.

Creating and Restoring a Backup File

Before making any major changes to a database, such as running action queries or modifying table structures, it is a good idea to back it up. Certain changes made to a database cannot be reversed. For example, if a delete query is run to remove the work orders for the month of September, the work orders cannot be reinstated. If field sizes are changed and made too small, the data truncated cannot be restored if the revised table has been saved. The data will be lost unless a backup exists.

Consider backing up your database on a regular basis to minimize any data loss that may occur due to system failures or design mistakes. Once a backup database has been created, use it to restore the entire database or to import a specific object. Project 1 will demonstrate how to restore the entire database and Project 2 will demonstrate how to import objects.

To create a backup of a database, click the File tab and then click the *Save As* option. Click *Back Up Database* in the *Advanced* section of the Save As backstage area and then click the Save As button. (Access closes any open objects.) Navigate to or create a folder to store backup databases and then click the Save button. Notice that the current date is added to the end of the file name.

To replace a database with a backup copy, copy the backup database from the backup folder and then paste it in the same folder as the database to be replaced. Delete the database to be replaced and rename the backup database.

Project 1a Creating and Restoring a Backup File
Part 1 of 3

1. Open **8-RSRCompServ.accdb** and enable the content.
2. Create a backup database file by completing the following steps:
   a. Click the File tab and then click the *Save As* option.
   b. Click *Back Up Database* in the *Advanced* section.
   c. Click the Save As button.

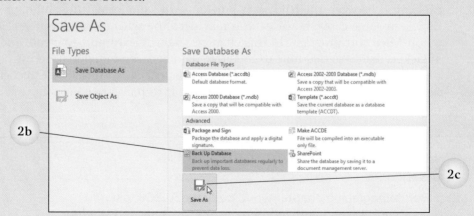

d. The backup file is named **8-RSRCompServ_yyyy-mm-dd.accdb**, where *yyyy-mm-dd* represents the year, month, and day the backup was created. (Your date will differ from the one shown below.) Notice that the default location is the AL2C8 folder on your storage medium. Instead of saving the file in this folder, click the New folder button.

e. With *New folder* selected, type DatabaseBackUps and then press the Enter key.

f. Click the Open button to open the folder.

g. Click Save.

3. With **8-RSRCompServ.accdb** open, open the Customers table in Design view, click *City*, and then change the field size from 25 characters to 5 characters. Save the table.

4. Answer Yes to the Microsoft Access message box stating that some data may be lost.

5. Switch to Datasheet view and look at the data in the *City* column. The last two letters were permanently deleted from *Detroit*. Notice that the Undo button on the Quick Access Toolbar is dimmed, indicating that this change cannot be reversed.

Customer ID	First Name	Last Name	Street Address	City	State	
1000	Jade	Fleming	12109 Woodward Avenue	Detro	MI	The field size for the *City*
1005	Cayla	Fahri	12793 Riverdale Avenue	Detro	MI	field has been changed
1008	Leslie	Carmichael	10303 Elmira Street	Detro	MI	to 5 characters. The last
1010	Randall	Lemaire	16659 Lawton Street	Detro	MI	two letters in *Detroit*
1015	Shauna	Friesen	12914 Mitchell Avenue	Detro	MI	have been permanently
1020	Kirk	Cobb	2829 Carter Street	Detro	MI	deleted.

6. Close **8-RSRCompServ.accdb** and then close Access.

7. Restore the backup copy of the database by completing the following steps:
   a. Click the Start button.
   b. At the Start screen, start typing file explorer. When the File Explorer icon displays below the *Apps* heading, press the Enter key. (Depending on your operating system, these steps may vary.)
   c. Navigate to the DatabaseBackUps folder in the AL2C8 folder on your storage medium and then right-click **8-RSRCompServ_yyyy-mm-dd.accdb**, where *yyyy-mm-dd* represents the year, month, and day the backup was created.
   d. Click *Copy* at the shortcut menu.
   e. Click *AL2C8* in the Address bar.

   f. Right-click a blank area of the content pane and then click *Paste* at the shortcut menu.
   g. Right-click **8-RSRCompServ.accdb** and then click *Delete* at the shortcut menu.
   h. Right-click **8-RSRCompServ_yyyy-mm-dd.accdb** and then click *Rename* at the shortcut menu.
   i. Delete *_yyyy-mm-dd* and then press the Enter key.
8. Open **8-RSRCompServ.accdb**, enable the content if necessary, and then open the Customers table. Verify that *Detroit* is displayed in the *City* field and then close the table.
9. Close **8-RSRCompServ.accdb**.

Tutorial

Creating an
ACCDE Database
File

Creating an ACCDE Database File

In Chapter 6, a database was split into two files to create a front-end database and a back-end database. Using this method improved the performance of the database and protected the table objects from being changed by separating them from the queries, forms, and reports. Another method to protect an Access database is to create an ACCDE file. In an ACCDE file, end users are prevented from making changes to the designs of objects. An Access database stored as an ACCDE file is a locked-down version of the database and therefore does not provide access to Design view or Layout view. In addition, if the database contains any Visual Basic for Applications (VBA) code, the code cannot be modified or changed.

To save an Access database as an ACCDE file, click the File tab and then click the *Save As* option. Click the *Make ACCDE* option in the *Advanced* section of the Save As backstage area and then click the Save As button to open the Save As dialog box. Navigate to the drive and/or folder in which to save the database, type the file name in the *File name* text box, and then click the Save button. Once the file is created, move the original database with the .accdb extension to a secure location and provide end users with the path to the ACCDE file for daily use.

Project 1b Creating an ACCDE Database File

1. Open **8-RSRNavPane.accdb** and enable the content.
2. Create an ACCDE file by completing the following steps:
   a. Click the File tab and then click the *Save As* option.
   b. Click *Make ACCDE* in the *Advanced* section of the Save As backstage area.
   c. Click the Save As button.

   d. At the Save As dialog box with the default location the AL2C8 folder on your storage medium and **8-RSRNavPane.accde** in the *File name* text box, click the Save button.

3. Close **8-RSRNavPane.accdb**.
4. Open **8-RSRNavPane.accde**.

5. At the Microsoft Access Security Notice dialog box stating that the file might contain unsafe content, click the Open button.
6. With Customers the active tab in the MainMenu form and the Customer Data Maintenance Form open in Form view, click the Home tab if necessary. Notice that the View button in the Views group is dimmed.

7. Click the Monthly Work Orders tab in the MainMenu form to view the Work Orders by Month report. Notice that the View button on the Home tab is still dimmed. Also notice that only one view button is available in the view area at the right side of the Status bar.
8. Insert a screen shot of the database window in a new Microsoft Word document using either the Screenshot button in the Illustrations group on the Insert tab or the Print Screen key and the Paste feature. Type your name a few lines below the screen image and add other identifying information as instructed.
9. Save the Microsoft Word document and name it **8-ACCDEWindow**.
10. Print **8-ACCDEWindow.docx** and then exit Word.
11. Close **8-RSRNavPane.accde**.

Check Your Work

Viewing Trust Center Settings

In Access, the Trust Center is set to block unsafe content when a database is opened. Thoughout these chapters, the security warning that appears in the message bar when a database is opened has been closed by clicking the Enable Content button. Access provides the Trust Center to allow viewing and/or modifying the security options that are in place to protect your computer from malicious content.

The Trust Center maintains a Trusted Locations list, in which the content stored is considered to be from trusted sources. Add a path to the Trusted Locations list and Access will treat any file opened from the drive and folder as safe. A database opened from a trusted location does not display the security warning in the message bar and does not have content blocked.

Before the macros are enabled for a database, the Trust Center checks for a valid and current digital signature signed by an entity that is stored in the Trusted Publishers list. The Trusted Publishers list is maintained by the user on the computer being used. A trusted publisher is added to the list when the content is enabled from an authenticated source and the *Trust all content from this publisher*

Hint Changing the macro security setting in Access does not affect the setting in other Microsoft programs, such as Word and Excel.

option has been clicked. Depending on the active macro security setting, if the Trust Center cannot match the digital signature information with an entity in the Trusted Publishers list or if the macro does not contain a digital signature, the security warning displays in the message bar.

Table 8.1 describes the four options available for macro security. The default macro security option is *Disable all macros with notification*. In some cases, it may be decided to change the default macro security setting by opening the Trust Center dialog box. The Trust Center will be explored in Project 1c.

Table 8.1 Macro Security Settings for a Database Not Opened from a Trusted Location

Macro Setting	Description
Disable all macros without notification	All macros are disabled; security alerts will not appear.
Disable all macros with notification	All macros are disabled; security alert appears with the option to enable the content if the source of the file is trusted. This is the default setting.
Disable all macros except digitally signed macros	A macro that does not contain a digital signature is disabled; security alerts do not appear. If the macro is digitally signed by a publisher in the Trusted Publishers list, the macro is allowed to run. If the macro is digitally signed by a publisher not in the Trusted Publishers list, a security alert appears.
Enable all macros (not recommended; potentially dangerous code can run)	All macros are allowed; security alerts do not appear.

Project 1c Viewing Trust Center Settings

Part 3 of 3

1. To explore current settings in the Trust Center, complete the following steps:
   a. Click the <u>Open Other Files</u> hyperlink at the bottom of the Recent list and then click *Options*.
   b. Click *Trust Center* in the left pane of the Access Options dialog box.
   c. Click the Trust Center Settings button in the *Microsoft Access Trust Center* section.

d. At the Trust Center dialog box, click *Macro Settings* in the left pane.

e. Review the options in the *Macro Settings* section. Notice which option is active on your computer. The default option is *Disable all macros with notification*. **Note: The security setting on your computer may be different from the default option. Do not change the security setting without the permission of your instructor.**

f. Click *Trusted Publishers* in the left pane. If any publishers have been added to the list on your computer, their names will appear in the list box. If the list box is empty, no trusted publishers have been added.

g. Click Trusted Locations in the left pane. Review the path and description of any folder in the Trusted Locations list. By default, Access adds the folder created when Microsoft Access is installed that contains the wizard database templates provided by Microsoft. Additional folders that have been added by a system administrator or network administrator may also appear.

h. Click OK to close the Trust Center dialog box.

2. Click OK to close the Access Options dialog box.

Project 2 Import and Merge Data from External Sources   4 Parts

You will link and import data from a table in another Access database and a comma delimited text file. You will also save import specifications for an import routine that you expect to repeat often.

Preview Finished Project

Tutorial

Importing Data from Another Access Database

Importing Data from Another Access Database

Data stored in another Access database can be merged with data in the active database by importing a copy of the source object. Multiple objects can be copied, including the relationships between tables. When importing, specify to import only the definition or both the definition and the data.

In Chapter 3, an append query was used to merge data from tables that contain the same fields by adding selected records to the end of an existing table. Earlier in this chapter, Project 1 stressed the importance of backing up a database before making any major changes to it (such as merging the data) because some changes cannot be undone. If problems arise as a result of making changes to a database, either restore the entire database or import only the damaged table from the backup copy that was created.

Quick Steps

Import Objects from an Access Database

1. Open destination database.
2. Click External Data tab.
3. Click Import Access database button.
4. Click Browse button.
5. If necessary, navigate to drive and/or folder.
6. Double-click source file name.
7. Click OK.
8. Select import object(s).
9. Click OK.
10. Click Close.

 Import Access Database

Hint If an object with the same name as an imported table already exists in the destination database, Access does not overwrite the existing object. Instead, it adds *1* to the end of the name of the imported object.

To begin an import operation, click the External Data tab and then click the Import Access database button (which displays the text *Access*) in the Import & Link group to open the Get External Data - Access Database dialog box, shown in Figure 8.1. Specify the source database containing the object(s) to be imported by clicking the Browse button to open the File Open dialog box. Navigate to the drive and/or folder containing the source database and then double-click the Access database file name to insert the database file name in the *File name* text box. With the *Import tables, queries, forms, reports, macros, and modules into the current database* option selected by default, click OK. This opens the Import Objects dialog box, shown in Figure 8.2. Select the objects to be imported, change options if necessary, and then click OK.

Figure 8.1 Get External Data - Access Database Dialog Box with the Import Option Selected

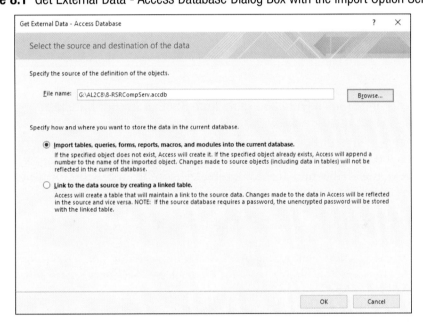

Figure 8.2 Import Objects Dialog Box

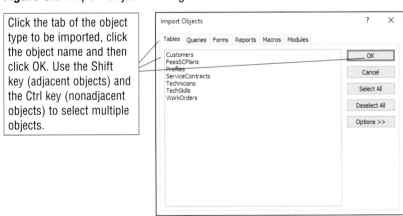

Click the tab of the object type to be imported, click the object name and then click OK. Use the Shift key (adjacent objects) and the Ctrl key (nonadjacent objects) to select multiple objects.

Click the Options button to display the *Import*, *Import Tables*, and *Import Queries* sections, shown in Figure 8.3. By default, Access imports relationships between tables as well as their structure definitions and data. Access also imports a query as a query, as opposed to importing a query as a table. Select or deselect the options as necessary before clicking OK to begin the import operation.

Figure 8.3 Import Objects Dialog Box with Options Displayed

The default import options are displayed here. Select or clear options before clicking OK to import selected objects.

Project 2a Importing a Form and Table from Another Access Database

Part 1 of 4

1. Open **8-RSRTechPay.accdb** and enable the content.
2. Merge the RSRCompServe database with the RSRTechPay database by importing the WorkOrders table and TechMaintenance form from **8-RSRCompServ.accdb**. Import the two objects by completing the following steps:
   a. Click the External Data tab.
   b. Click the Import Access database button (displays the text *Access*) in the Import & Link group.
   c. At the Get External Data - Access Database dialog box, click the Browse button.
   d. At the File Open dialog box, double-click **8-RSRCompServ.accdb**. *Note: Navigate to the AL2C8 folder on your storage medium, if necessary*.
   e. With the *Import tables, queries, forms, reports, macros, and modules into the current database* option already selected, click OK.

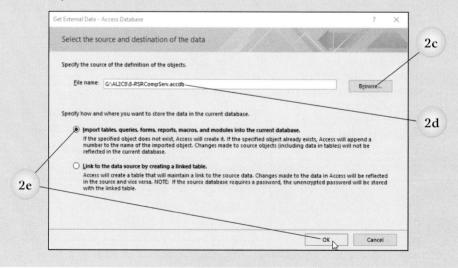

f. At the Import Objects dialog box with the Tables tab selected, click *WorkOrders* in the list box.

g. Click the Forms tab.

h. Click *TechMaintenance* in the list box and then click OK.

i. At the Get External Data - Access Database dialog box with the *Save import steps* check box empty, click the Close button.

3. Access imports the WorkOrders table and TechMaintenance form and adds the object names to the Navigation pane. The form will not be operational until after Project 2b because the tables needed to populate data in the form do not yet reside in the database. The dependent tables were not imported in this project because the tables that contain the records are to be linked in a later project.

An object can also be copied by opening two copies of Access: one with the source database opened and the other with the destination database opened. With the source database window active, right-click the source object in the Navigation pane and then click *Copy*. Switch to the window containing the destination database, right-click in the Navigation pane, and then click *Paste*. Close the Access window containing the source database.

Tutorial

Linking to a Table in Another Access Database

Linking to a Table in Another Access Database

In Project 2a, a copy of a form was imported from one database to another. If the source form object is modified, the imported copy of the form object will not be altered. To ensure that the table in the destination database will reflect any changes made to the source table, link the data in the object when it is imported.

Link to a Table in Another Database
1. Open destination database.
2. Click External Data tab.
3. Click Import Access database button.
4. Click Browse button.
5. If necessary, navigate to drive and/or folder.
6. Double-click source file name.
7. Click *Link to the data source by creating a linked table.*
8. Click OK.
9. Select table(s).
10. Click OK.

To create a linked table in the destination database, click the External Data tab and then click the Import Access database button. Click the Browse button, navigate to the drive and/or folder in which the source database is stored, and then double-click the source database file name. Click the *Link to the data source by creating a linked table* option at the Get External Data - Access Database dialog box and then click OK, as shown in Figure 8.4.

The Link Tables dialog box, shown in Figure 8.5, contains the list box, from which the tables to be linked are selected. Use the Shift key or the Ctrl key to select multiple tables to link in one step. Linked tables are indicated in the Navigation pane with blue right-pointing arrows.

Figure 8.4 Get External Data - Access Database Dialog Box with the Link Option Selected

Click here to create a new table in the destination database by linking to the source table.

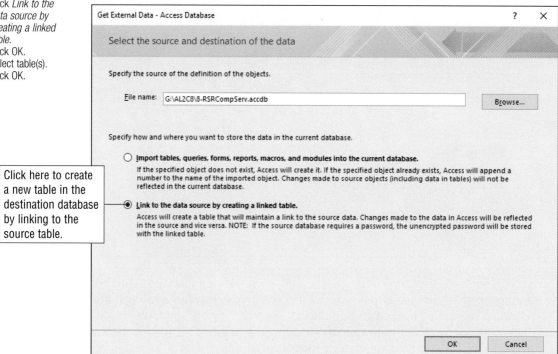

Figure 8.5 Link Tables Dialog Box

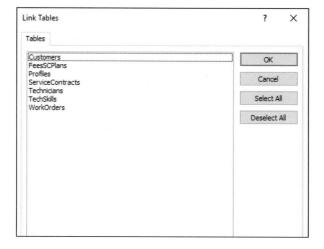

1. With **8-RSRTechPay.accdb** open, link to two tables in **8-RSRCompServ.accdb** by completing the following steps:
   a. With the External Data tab still active, click the Import Access database button.
   b. Click the Browse button and then double-click *8-RSRCompServ.accdb* in the AL2C8 folder.
   c. Click the *Link to the data source by creating a linked table* option and then click OK.

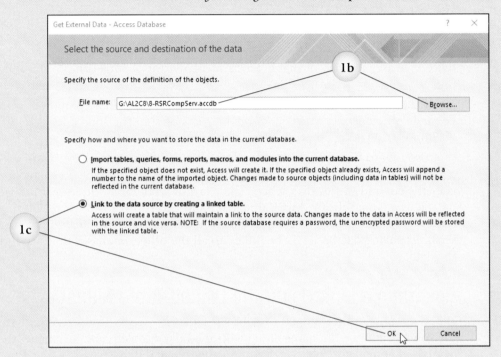

   d. At the Link Tables dialog box, click *Technicians* in the list box.
   e. Press and hold down the Shift key, click *TechSkills* in the list box, and then release the Shift key.
   f. Click OK. Access links the two tables to the source database and adds the table names to the Navigation pane. Each linked table displays with a blue right-pointing arrow next to the table icon.

2. Double-click *TechMaintenance* in the Forms group in the Navigation pane to view the form with the first record displayed. Close the form.

   > At the end of Step 1f, each linked table displays with a blue right-pointing arrow next to the table icon.

3. Double-click *Technicians* in the Tables group in the Navigation pane to view the table datasheet and then close the datasheet.
4. Double-click *TechSkills* in the Tables group in the Navigation pane to view the table datasheet and then close the datasheet.

Quick Steps

Refresh a Link
1. Click External Data tab.
2. Click Linked Table Manager button.
3. Click Select All button or click check boxes for specific links.
4. Click OK.
5. Navigate to drive and/or folder.
6. Double-click source database file name.
7. Click OK.
8. Click Close button.

When a table is linked, the source data does not reside in the destination database. Opening a linked table causes Access to update the datasheet with the information in the source table in the other database. Edit the source data in either the source table or the linked table in the destination database. Either way, the changes will be reflected in both tables.

Choosing Whether to Import or Link to Source Data

If the source data is not likely to change, the table should be imported. Keep in mind, however, that because importing creates copies of the data in two locations, changes or updates to the data must be made in both copies. Making the changes twice increases the risk of making a data entry error or forgetting to make an update in one or the other location.

If the source data is updated frequently, link to it so that changes have to be made only once. Because linked data exists only in the source location, the likelihood of making an error or missing an update is reduced.

Also link to the data source file when several different databases require a common table, such as an Inventory table. To duplicate the table in each database is inefficient and wastes disk space. There is also a potential for error if individual databases are not refreshed with updated data. Given these risks, it makes more sense to link rather than import. In this scenario, a master Inventory table in a separate, shared database will be linked to all the other databases that need to use the data.

Tutorial

Resetting a Link Using the Linked Table Manager

Resetting a Link Using the Linked Table Manager

When a table has been linked to another database, Access stores the full path to the source database file name along with the linked table name. Changing the database file name or folder location for the source database means that the linked table will no longer function. Access provides the Linked Table Manager dialog box, shown in Figure 8.6, to allow the user to reset or refresh the link to a table to reconnect to the data source file.

Figure 8.6 Linked Table Manager Dialog Box

Click here to export a list of links and their sources to Excel. The button is grayed out because no links are currently selected.

Linked Table Manager

To refresh a link to a table, open the Linked Table Manager dialog box by clicking the Linked Table Manager button in the Import & Link group on the External Data tab. Click the check box next to the link to be refreshed and then click OK. Access displays a message box stating that the link was successfully refreshed or provides a dialog box for navigating to the new location of the data source file.

If a database contains links to many different sources, consider exporting a list of these links to Excel. This feature, which is new to Access 2016, creates a spreadsheet that lists the linked table, source file, and file type. Click the Export to Excel button in the Linked Table Manager dialog box to create this useful list.

Project 2c Refreshing a Link

Part 3 of 4

1. With **8-RSRTechPay.accdb** open, change the location of **8-RSRCompServ.accdb** by completing the following steps:
   a. Click the File tab, click *Open*, click the *Browse* option in the *Recent* section, and then locate the AL2C8 folder on your storage medium.
   b. Right-click **8-RSRCompServ.accdb** in the file list box and then click *Cut* at the shortcut menu.
   c. Double-click the *DatabaseBackUps* folder.
   d. Right-click in a blank area of the file list box and then click *Paste* at the shortcut menu.
   e. Close the Open dialog box. Because the location of the source database has been moved, the linked tables are no longer connected to the correct location.
   f. Click the Back button.
2. Refresh the links to the two tables by completing the following steps:
   a. If necessary, click the External Data tab.
   b. Click the Linked Table Manager button in the Import & Link group.
   c. At the Linked Table Manager dialog box, click the Select All button to select all the linked objects.

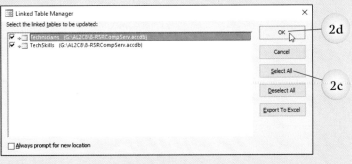

   d. Click OK. Access attempts to refresh the links. Because the source database has been moved, Access displays a dialog box for selecting a new location.
   e. At the Select New Location of Technicians dialog box, locate and then double-click **8-RSRCompServ.accdb**.
   f. Click OK at the Linked Table Manager message box stating that all the selected links were successfully refreshed.

3. Export the linked data source file to Excel by completing the following steps:
   a. With the Linked Table Manager dialog box open, click the Select All button.
   b. Click the Export to Excel button.
   c. Navigate to the AL2C8 folder, type 8-ExportedLinks in the *File name* text box, and then click the Save button.
4. Review the linked table and source information and then close Excel.
5. Click the Close button at the Linked Table Manager dialog box.

Check Your Work

Tutorial

Importing Data into a Database from a Text File

Importing Data into a Database from a Text File

Text files are often used to exchange data between dissimilar programs because this file format is recognized by nearly all applications. Text files contain no formatting and consist only of letters, numbers, punctuation symbols, and a few control characters. Two commonly used text file formats separate fields with a tab (delimited file format) and a comma (comma separated file format). Figure 8.7 shows a partial view of the text file used in Project 2d in a Notepad window. If necessary, view and edit a text file in Notepad before importing if the source application inserts characters that will be deleted.

Hint If data is needed from a program that is not compatible with Access, check the source program's export options for a text file format. Most programs can export data in this format.

Quick Steps

Import Data from a Comma Separated Text File
1. Click External Data tab.
2. Click Import text file button.
3. Click Browse button.
4. If necessary, navigate to drive and/or folder.
5. Double-click .csv file name.
6. Click OK.
7. Click Next.
8. If applicable, click *First Row Contains Field Names* check box.
9. Click Next.
10. Choose primary key field.
11. Click Next.
12. Click Finish.

Figure 8.7 Project 2d Partial View of Text File Content in Notepad

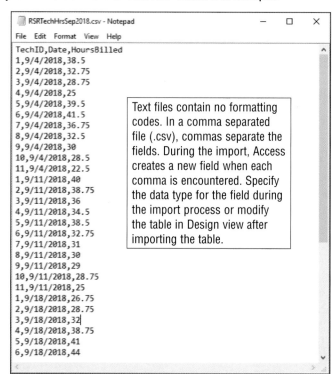

Text files contain no formatting codes. In a comma separated file (.csv), commas separate the fields. During the import, Access creates a new field when each comma is encountered. Specify the data type for the field during the import process or modify the table in Design view after importing the table.

text file

To import a text file into Access, click the Import text file button (which displays the text *Text File*) in the Import & Link group on the External Data tab. Access opens the Get External Data - Text File dialog box, which is similar to the dialog box used to import data from another Access database. When importing a text file, Access provides an append option in addition to the import and link options in the *Specify how and where you want to store the data in the current database* section. Click the Browse button to navigate to the source file and double-click the source file name to launch the Import Text Wizard, which guides the user through the import process using four dialog boxes.

Saving and Repeating Import Specifications

Quick Steps

Save Import Specifications
1. At last Get External Data dialog box, click *Save import steps.*
2. If necessary, edit name in *Save as* text box.
3. Type description in *Description* text box.
4. Click Save Import button.

Save import specifications for an import routine that is likely to be repeated. The last step in the Get External Data - Text File dialog box displays a *Save import steps* check box. Click the check box to expand the dialog box to display the *Save as* and *Description* text boxes as shown in Figure 8.8. Type a unique name to assign to the import routine and provide a brief description of the steps. Click the Save Import button to complete the import and store the specifications. Click the *Create Outlook Task* check box to create an Outlook task that can be set up as a recurring item for an import or export operation that is repeated at fixed intervals.

Figure 8.8 Get External Data - Text File Dialog Box with Save Import Steps

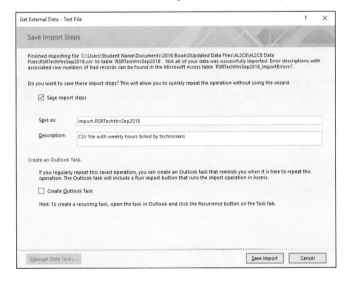

Project 2d Importing Data from a Comma Separated Text File
and Saving Import Specifications
Part 4 of 4

1. With **8-RSRTechPay.accdb** open, select a text file to import that contains the weekly hours billed for each technician for the month of September 2018 by completing the following steps:
   a. If necessary, click the External Data tab.
   b. Click the Import text file button (displays the text *Text File*) in the Import & Link group.

c. At the Get External Data - Text File dialog box, click the Browse button.

d. At the File Open dialog box, navigate to the AL2C8 folder on your storage medium if necessary.

e. Double-click the file named ***RSRTechHrsSep2018.csv***.

f. With *Import the source data into a new table in the current database* already selected, click OK. This launches the Import Text Wizard.

2. Import the comma separated data using the Import Text Wizard by completing the following steps:

a. At the first Import Text Wizard dialog box with *Delimited* selected as the format, notice that the preview section in the lower half of the dialog box displays a sample of the data in the source text file. Delimited files use commas or tabs as separators while fixed width files use spaces. Click the Next button.

b. At the second Import Text Wizard dialog box with *Comma* already selected as the delimiter, click the *First Row Contains Field Names* check box. Notice that the preview section already shows the data set in columns, similar to a table datasheet. Click the Next button.

c. At the third Import Text Wizard dialog box with the *TechID* column in the preview section selected, click the *Data Type* option box arrow in the *Field Options* section and then click *Short Text* at the drop-down list.
d. Click the Next button.

e. At the fourth Import Text Wizard dialog box with *Let Access add primary key* already selected, notice that Access has added a column in the preview section with the field title *ID*. The column added by Access is defined as an AutoNumber data type field, in which each row in the text file is numbered sequentially to make the row unique. The ID for any new record added to the table will automatically be incremented by one. Click the Next button.

f. At the last Import Text Wizard dialog box, with *RSRTechHrsSep2018* entered in the *Import to Table* text box, click the Finish button.

3. Save the import specifications, in case this import needs to be run again, by completing the following steps:

a. At the Get External Data - Text File dialog box, click the *Save import steps* check box. This causes the *Save as* and *Description* text boxes to appear, as well as the *Create an Outlook Task* section. By default, Access creates a name in the *Save as* text box and *Import* precedes the file name containing the imported data.

b. Click in the *Description* text box and then type CSV file with weekly hours billed by technicians.

c. Click the Save Import button.

4. Double-click *RSRTechHoursSep2018* in the Tables group in the Navigation pane to open the table in Datasheet view.
5. Print the datasheet with the bottom margin set to 0.5 inch and then close the datasheet.
6. Close **8-RSRTechPay.accdb**.

Check Your Work

 Saved Imports

Once an import routine has been saved, repeat the import process by opening the Manage Data Tasks dialog box with the Saved Imports tab selected, as shown in Figure 8.9. To do this, click the External Data tab and then click the Saved Imports button in the Import & Link group. Click the import name and then click the Run button to instruct Access to repeat the import operation.

Figure 8.9 Manage Data Tasks Dialog Box with the Saved Imports Tab Selected

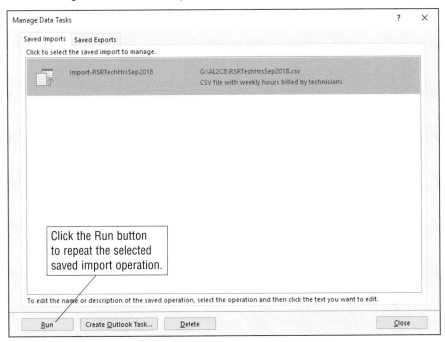

Project 3 **Export Access Data to a Text File**   **3 Parts**

You will export a query as a comma delimited text file and another query as a tab delimited text file, including saving the second export steps so you can repeat the export operation.

Preview Finished Project

Exporting Access Data to a Text File

The Export group on the External Data tab contains buttons to export Access data from a table, query, form, or report to other applications, such as Excel and Word. To work with data from Access in a program that is not part of the Microsoft Office suite, click the More button in the Export group to see if a file format converter exists for the application to be used. For example, the More button contains options to export in Word, SharePoint List, ODBC Database, and HTML Document format. (Access 2016 does not support exporting to dBase file formats.)

Export to
text file

If a file format converter does not exist for the program to be used, export the data as a text file; most applications recognize and can import a text data file. Access provides the Export Text Wizard, which is launched after an object is selected in the Navigation pane. Click the Export to text file button (which displays the text *Text File*) in the Export group on the External Data tab and then specify the name of the exported text file and where to store it. The steps in the Export Text Wizard are similar to those in the Import Text Wizard, used in Project 2d.

Project 3a Exporting a Query as a Text File

Part 1 of 3

1. Display the Open dialog box and then use the Cut and Paste features to move **8-RSRCompServ.accdb** back to the AL2C8 folder on your storage medium.
2. Open **8-RSRCompServ.accdb** and enable the content if necessary.
3. Export the TotalWorkOrders query as a text file by completing the following steps:
   a. Select the TotalWorkOrders query in the Navigation pane.
   b. Click the External Data tab.
   c. Click the Export to text file button (which displays the text *Text File*) in the Export group.
   d. At the Export - Text File dialog box, click the Browse button.
   e. At the File Save dialog box, navigate to the AL2C8 folder on your storage medium if necessary.
   f. With the default file name *TotalWorkOrders.txt* in the *File name* text box, click the Save button.
   g. Click OK.

h. At the first Export Text Wizard dialog box with *Delimited* selected as the format, notice in the preview section of the dialog box that commas separate the fields and that data in a field defined with the Text data type is enclosed in quotation marks. Click the Next button.

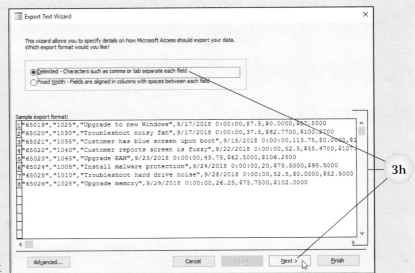

i. At the second Export Text Wizard dialog box with *Comma* selected as the delimiter character that separates the fields, click the *Include Field Names on First Row* check box to insert a check mark. Note that Access adds a row containing the field names to the top of the data in the preview section. Each field name is enclosed in quotation marks.

j. Click the arrow next to the *Text Qualifier* option box and then click {*none*} at the drop-down list. Access removes all the quotation marks from the text data in the preview section.

k. Click the Next button.

l. At the last Export Text Wizard dialog box, with *[d]:\AL2C8\TotalWorkOrders.txt* (where *[d]* is the drive for your storage medium) entered in the *Export to File* text box, click the Finish button.

m. Click the Close button to close the dialog box without saving the export steps.

4. Open Notepad and view the text file by completing the following steps:

a. Click the Start button, and then start typing notepad. When *Notepad* displays in the *Best match* section, press the Enter key. (Depending on your operating system, these steps may vary).

b. At a blank Notepad window, click the File button and then click *Open*. Navigate to the AL2C8 folder on your storage medium and then double-click *TotalWorkOrders.txt.*

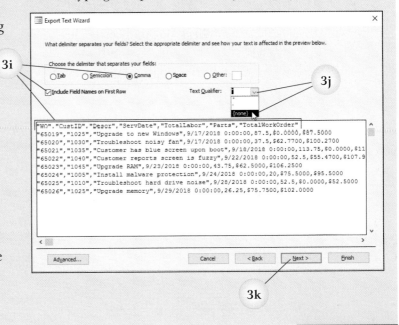

5. Click the File button and then click *Print* to print the exported text file.

6. Exit Notepad.

Check Your Work

Saving and Repeating Export Specifications

Just as import specifications can be saved for reuse, so can export specifications. The last Export - Text File dialog box displays a *Save export steps* check box. Click the check box to expand the dialog box options and display the *Save as* and *Description* text boxes. Type a unique name for the export routine and a brief description of the steps. Click the Save Export button to complete the export operation and store the specifications for later use.

Project 3b   Exporting a Query as a Text File and Saving the Export Steps   Part 2 of 3

1. With **8-RSRCompServ.accdb** open, double-click the TotalLabor query in the Navigation pane. Notice that only the work orders for the month of September are retrieved. Switch to Design view and see that *DatePart("m",[ServDate])* has been added right of the *TotalLabor* field and that *9* displays in the *Criteria* row. With this criteria, the query returns only the results for September, the ninth month. Close the query.

2. Export the TotalLabor query as a text file using tabs as the delimiter characters by completing the following steps:

   a. With the TotalLabor query selected in the Navigation pane, click the External Data tab and then click the Export to text file button in the Export group.

   b. With *[d]:\AL2C8\TotalLabor.txt* (where *[d]* is the drive for your storage medium) entered in the *File name* text box, click OK.

   c. Complete the steps of the Export Text Wizard as follows:

      1) With *Delimited* selected in the first dialog box, click the Next button.

      2) At the second dialog box, choose *Tab* as the delimiter character, click the *Include Field Names on First Row* check box to insert a check mark, change the *Text Qualifier* option to *{none}*, and then click the Next button.

      3) Click the Finish button.

d. At the Export - Text File dialog box, click the *Save export steps* check box to insert a check mark.

e. Click in the *Description* text box and then type TotalLabor query for RSR Computer Service work orders as a text file.

f. Click the Save Export button.

2. Start Notepad.

3. At a blank Notepad window, open **TotalLabor.txt**.

4. Print **TotalLabor.txt** and then exit Notepad.

Check Your Work

Saved Exports

Quick Steps

Repeat Export Steps
1. Click External Data tab.
2. Click specific saved export.
3. Click OK.
4. Click Close.

Once an export routine has been saved, repeat the export process by clicking the Saved Exports button in the Export group on the External Data tab. This opens the Manage Data Tasks dialog box with the Saved Exports tab selected, as shown in Figure 8.10. Click the export name in the dialog box and then click the Run button to instruct Access to repeat the export operation. Be careful not to override any previous exported files because the file name and location will be the same.

Figure 8.10 Manage Data Tasks Dialog Box with the Saved Exports Tab Selected

Click the Run button to repeat the selected saved export operation.

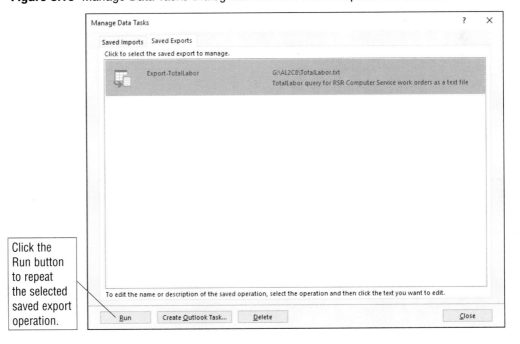

1. With **8-RSRCompServ.accdb** open, change the location of **TotalLabor.txt** by completing the following steps:
   a. Click the File tab, click *Open*, click the Browse button, and then locate the AL2C8 folder on your storage medium.
   b. Click the *Data Type* option box that currently displays *Microsoft Access (*.accdb;*.mdb...)* and change the option to *All Files (*.*)*.
   c. Scroll down, right-click *TotalLabor.txt* in the file list box, and then click *Cut* at the shortcut menu.
   d. Double-click the *DatabaseBackUps* folder.
   e. Right-click in a blank area of the file list box and then click *Paste*.
   f. Close the Open dialog box. The Export procedure can now be run without overwriting the data for the month of September. Click the Back button.
2. Export the results of the TotalLabor query for October by completing the following steps:
   a. Open the TotalLabor query in Design view.
   b. In the *Criteria* row of the *DatePart("m",[ServDate])* field, change the *9* to a *10*. Changing this number will return the data for the month of October.
   c. Save, run, and then close the query.
   d. Click the External Data tab.
   e. Click the Saved Exports button in the Export group.
   f. With *Export-TotalLabor* selected, click the Run button.
   g. Click OK.
   h. Click the Close button.

3. Click the Close button in the upper right corner to close Access.

Check Your Work

You will create a database in an older format.

Tutorial

Creating a Database in an Older Format

Creating a Database in an Older Format

Hint If most of your databases need to be created in an earlier version of Access, consider changing the default file format to an earlier version. The default can be changed in the *Default file format for Blank Database* option box in the General section of the Access Options dialog box.

Recall from Level 1, Chapter 7 that Access 2016, 2013, 2010, and 2007 databases save with the file extension *.accdb* and cannot be opened with earlier versions of Access. If a user needs to open one of these databases in an earlier version of Access, the database will need to saved in an earlier version by clicking the *Microsoft Access Database (2002-2003)(*.mdb)* button or the *Access 2000 Database (*.mdb)* button in the *Save Database As* section of the Save As backstage area. The database saves with the .mdb file extension. If it is known before the database is created that it needs to be saved using the .mdb file extension, the database should simply be created in an older format rather than resaved later.

To create a database in an older format, open Access. At the Access 2016 opening screen, click the *Blank desktop database* template, click the *Browse* button, and then navigate to your storage medium. Type the name of the database and then click the *Save as type* option. Choose *Microsoft Access Databases (2002-2003 format)(*.mdb)* or *Microsoft Access Databases (2000 format) (*.mdb)* from the options list. Click OK.

Project 4 Creating a Database in an Older Format   Part 1 of 1

1. Open Access.
2. At the Access 2016 opening screen, complete the following steps to create a new database in the 2002-2003 format:
   a. Click the *Blank desktop database* template.
   b. At the Blank desktop database window that displays, click the Browse button, navigate to the AL2C8 folder on your storage medium, select the current text in the *File name* text box, and then type 8-RSR2003.
   c. Click the *Save as type* option, click *Microsoft Access Databases (2002-2003 format)(*.mdb)*, and then click OK.
   d. Click the Create button below the *File Name* text box.
3. Close Access.

In this chapter, you have learned to back up and restore data, secure an Access database, import and merge data from another Access database, and import and export using a text file format to exchange data between Access and non-Microsoft programs. Finally, you have learned how to create a database in an earlier version of Access.

Chapter Summary

- Use options at the Save As backstage area to create backup database files on a regular basis. This will help to minimize any data loss due to system failures or design mistakes.

- Create a backup copy of a database before making any major changes to it.

- An ACCDE file is a locked-down version of a database, in which users do not have access to Design view or Layout view and therefore cannot make changes to the design of objects.

- Create an ACCDE database file at the Save As backstage area.

- Open the Access Options dialog box, click *Trust Center* in the left pane, and then click the Trust Center Settings button to view and/or modify Trust Center options.

- An object in another Access database can be imported into the active database using the Import Access database button in the Import & Link group on the External Data tab.

- If the source object is a table, choose to import or link to the source table.

- When a table is linked, the data is not copied into the active database; it resides only in the source database.

- Edit source data in a linked table in the source database or the destination database; the changes will be reflected in both tables.

- Import the table if the source data is not likely to change.

- Link to a data source file that is updated frequently so changes have to be made only once; this reduces the potential for making data entry mistakes or missing updates.

- Link to a source table that is shared among several different databases within an organization.

- When a table has been linked to another database, Access stores the full path to the source database. If the location of the source database is moved or the file name is changed, the links will need to be refreshed.

- A text file is often used to exchange data between dissimilar programs because this file format is recognized by nearly all applications.

- Import a text file into an Access database by clicking the Import text file button in the Import & Link group on the External Data tab.

- When a text file is selected for import, Access launches the Text Import Wizard, which guides the user through the steps to import the text into a table.

- If an import routine is repeated often, consider saving the steps so the routine can be run without having to perform each step every time.

- Open the Manage Data Tasks dialog box to run a saved import by clicking the Saved Imports button in the Import & Link group on the External Data tab.

- Export Access data in a text file format using the Export Text Wizard by clicking the Export to text file button in the Export group on the External Data tab.

- Within the Export Text Wizard, the user is prompted to choose the text format, delimiter character, field names, text qualifier symbols, export path, and file name.

- To repeat an export routine, first save the export steps at the last Export - Text File dialog box.
- Click the Saved Exports button in the Export group on the External Data tab to run a saved export routine.
- Create a database in a previous version of Access using the *Save as type* option at the File New Database dialog box.

Commands Review

FEATURE	RIBBON TAB, GROUP	BUTTON
create ACCDE file	File, *Save As*	
export data as text file	External Data, Export	
import data from text file	External Data, Import & Link	
import or link data from Access database	External Data, Import & Link	
Linked Table Manager	External Data, Import & Link	
saved exports	External Data, Export	
saved imports	External Data, Import & Link	

Workbook

Chapter study tools and assessment activities are available in the *Workbook* ebook. These resources are designed to help you further develop and demonstrate mastery of the skills learned in this chapter.

Unit assessment activities are also available in the *Workbook*. These activities are designed to help you demonstrate mastery of the skills learned in this unit.

Index

embedded macro, viewing, 221–224

Enable Content button, 250

Enforce Referential Integrity, 33–34

Enter Parameter Value dialog box, 56

entity, 5

error-checking options, configuring, 233–234

exclusive use, 228

exporting
    data to text file, 266–267
    ribbon customizations, 236
    saving and repeating export specifications, 268–270

Export Text Wizard, 266–267

Export to text file button, 266

External Data tab, 253, 256, 265

F

Field List task pane, 87, 116, 132, 164

field names
    abbreviation of, 6
    spaces in, 6

field properties
    captions, adding, 9–12
    creating custom format for text data type fields, 12–13
    Default Value property, 20
    requiring data in field, 10
    size property to restrict field length, 7–8
    Validation Rule property, 20
    Validation Text property, 20
    zero-length string, 10–12

fields
    adding
        calculated field to report, 154–155
        to custom form, 87–89
        to custom report, 132–133
    to answer questions, 5
    assigning data types for, 6–7
    Attachment data type field, 23–25
    calculated from other fields, 5
    changing tab order of, 94–95

data redundancy, 5

designing for new database, 4–9

diagramming databases, 5–6

foreign key, 30

lookup values in another table, 40–43

primary key, 5

restricting data entry/display with properties, 9–20

that allows multiple values, 43–46

Field Size property
    default settings, 7
    to restrict field length, 7–8

files, attaching to records, 23–25

filter
    saving as query, 54–55
    uses of, 54

Filter by Form feature, 54

Find button, 121

Find feature, 120–122
    wildcard character used with, 121

finding, records in forms, 120–122

first normal form, 49

Force New Page property, 156

foreign key, defined, 30

Format property, custom format for text data type field, 12–13

formatting
    chart in report, 162–164
    controls, 91, 93–94

Form Design button, 84

Form Design Tools Arrange tab, 105, 106, 111

Form Design Tools Design tab, 84–85, 87, 91, 217

Form Design Tools Format tab, 108

Form Design view window, 84

forms
    adding to Navigation form, 225
    adjusting objects for consistency of appearance, 105–108
    anchoring controls to, 110–111

Blank Form tool for creating, 116–120

calculations, adding, 103–105

command button to run macro, 217–221

creating
    new form, using Application Parts blank form layout, 184–186
    user-defined form template, 186–188
    using Application Parts template, 182–183

custom form creating in Design view, 84–102, 130–140
    adding fields to, 87–89
    adding tab control to, 95–99
    applying theme, 91
    bound, unbound and calculated control objects, 85
    changing tab order of fields, 94–95
    connecting table to form, 87–89
    creating titles, 85–87
    formatting controls, 91, 93–94
    label objects, 85–87
    moving and resizing control objects, 90–92
    overview of, 84
    subform, creating, 96–102

datasheet form creation, 113–115

finding and sorting records in, 120–122

function of, 83

graphics, adding, 108–110

importing from another Access database, 254–255

list box and combo box, adding to, 116–120

macro to open and find record, 212–213

main form defined, 96

restricting form actions, 113–115

set control defaults option, 186–188
startup form, specifying, 229–230
subforms, 96–102
Form Selector button, 87, 100
Form tool, 84
Form Wizard, 84
front-end database, 197
functions, adding to group in report, 150–153

G

Get External Data-Access Database dialog box, 253, 256, 261
GoToControl action, 211
graphics, adding
  to form, 108–110
  to report, 144–146
Group, Sort and Total pane, 148, 150, 156
Group Footer section, 130
Group Header section, 130
groups
  adding functions to, 150–153
  grouping records in reports, 147–149
Group & Sort button, 148

H

Hidden mode, 211
Hyperlink button, 165
Hyperlink data type, 7
hyperlinks, adding to report, 165–169

I

Icon mode, 211
IF function, 70
image, adding
  to form, 108–110
  to report, 144–146
Immediate IF (IIF) function, 70
Import Access Database button, 253, 256
Import/Export button, 236
importing

choosing to import or link to source data, 258
data from another Access database, 252–255
data from text file, 260–265
form and table from another database, 254–255
linking table in another Access database, 255–260
saving and repeating import specifications, 261–265
Import Objects dialog box, 253–254
Import text file button, 261
indexes, creating, 47–48
Indexes button, 47
inner join, 59, 61
input mask
  commonly used codes, 18
  creating custom, 18–20
  defined, 17
  restricting data entry using, 17–20
Input Mask Wizard, 17
Insert Chart button, 158
Insert Hyperlink dialog box, 165
Insert Image button, 108, 144
inserting, chart in report, 158–161
Insert Page, 96
Insert Picture dialog box, 108

J

Join Properties dialog box, 59
join properties in query, 59–66
  defined, 59
  inner join, 59, 61
  left outer join, 59, 60, 62
  outer join, 59
  right outer join, 60, 63–64
  self-join query, 64–66
  specifying, 59–62
junction table, 38

K

Keep Together property, 156

L

Label button, 85
label control object, 85–87
  adding fields to forms, 87
  moving and resizing, 90–92
  moving to another section in custom report, 134–135
left outer join, 59, 60, 62
Line button, 108
Linked Table Manager button, 259
Linked Table Manager dialog box, 258–259
linking
  choosing to import or link to source data, 258
  resetting link using Linked Table Manager, 258–260
  table to another Access database, 255–260
Link Tables dialog box, 256
list box, adding
  to form, 116–118
  to report, 164–165
List Box button, 116, 164
List Box Wizard, 116
logical functions, 70
logo, adding
  to form, 108–110
  to report, 144–146
Logo button, 108
Long Text data type, 7
  Append Only property, 21
  commonly used format codes for, 12
  custom formatting for, 12
  enabling rich text formatting, 21–23
  maintaining history of changes in, 21–23
lookup field
  assigning multiple values to lookup list, 46
  create relationship with Applications Parts template, 180–181
  data from another table, 40–42
  modifying lookup list properties, 42–43

composite key, 39
defining multiple-field primary key, 39
in one-to-many relationship, 30
Primary Key button, 39
primary key field, 5
diagramming databases, 6
set as Required property, 10
printing, relationships, 36
Priority buttons, 148
Property Sheet task pane, 64, 87, 96, 155–156

Q

queries, 53–80
action queries, 74–80
adding records to table using, 78–79
creating new table with, 75–76
deleting group of records, 77
modifying records using, 79–80
adding/removing tables from, 62–64
alias for table, 64
append query, 74, 78–79
Cartesian product query, 66
conditional logic in, 70–71
creating using Application Parts template, 182–183
cross product query, 66
delete query, 74, 77
exporting query as text file, 266–267
join properties in, 59–66
inner join, 59, 61
left outer join, 59, 60, 62
outer join, 59–60
right outer join, 60, 63–64
self-join query, 64–66
specifying join type, 59–62
make-table query, 74, 75–76
multiple-value fields in, 72–73
parameter query, 56–58
prompting for criteria using parameter query, 56–57

running with no established relationship, 66
saving a filter as, 54–55
select query, 54–58
subqueries, 67–69
update query, 74, 79–80
Query Design view, 54
Query Tools Design tab, 62, 74
question mark, as wildcard character with Find feature, 121
Quick Access Toolbar
customizing, 240–242
resetting, 242
Quick Start options, 180–181, 203–204

R

records
adding, using query, 78–79
attaching files to, 23–25
deleting, using query, 78
finding and sorting in forms, 120–122
grouping in report, 147–149
macro to open form and find record, 212–213
modifying, using update query, 79–80
orphan records, 34
preventing deletion of, in forms, 114–115
selecting using multiple-value field, 72–73
Record Source property, 132
Record Source property box, 87
referential integrity, activating, 34–35
relational database, 5
Relationship Report button, 36
relationships, building, 30–38
with Applications Parts template, 180–181
diagramming, 31
editing, 33–35
foreign key, 30
junction table, 38
many-to-many, 37–38
one-to-many, 30–33
one-to-one, 36–37

printing, 36
referential integrity, 34–35
Relationships button, 30
Remove Field button, 148
Remove Layout button, 184
removing, attached file, 25
Rename button, 236
Rename dialog box, 236
renaming, objects, 201–203
Report Design button, 130
Report Design Tools Design tab, 135, 136
Report Footer section, 131
Report Header section, 131
date and time control objects, 141
reports
adding
calculated field to, 154–155
functions to a group, 150–153
to Navigation form, 225
Application Parts template to create, 182–183
Blank Report tool to create, 164–169
adding hyperlinks to report, 165–169
adding list box and combo box to report, 164–165
adding subform to, 165–169
adding tab control, 164
changing shape of control object, 165
changing tab order of fields, 165
charts, inserting and editing in, 158–164
custom report creation in Design view, 130–140
adding fields, 132–133
adding title and label object, 131–132
applying a theme, 135–136
connecting table or query to, 132–133
inserting subreport, 136–140
moving control objects to another section, 134–135

Table Analyzer Wizard, 191–194

Table Analyzer Wizard dialog box, 191

tables
adding records to, using query, 78–79
adding/removing from query, 62–64
alias for, 64
attaching files to records, 23–25
connect to form, 87–89
connect to report, 132–133
copying table structure to create new table, 188–190
create relationship with Applications Parts template, 180–183
creating new, with query, 75–76
designing for new database, 4–9
diagramming databases, 5–6, 31
as entity, 5
evaluating using Table Analyzer Wizard, 191–194
importing from another Access database, 254–255
junction table, 38
linking to another Access database, 255–260
Long Text data type fields, 21–23
with multiple-field primary key, 39
normal forms and, 49
restricting data entry/display using field properties, 9–20
splitting with Table Analyzer Wizard, 192–194

tab order
changing
in form, 94–95

in report, 165
defined, 94

Tab Order button, 94, 165

Tab Order dialog box, 94, 165

Tab Stop property, 103

templates
available templates at New backstage area, 174–175
to create database, 203–205
creating
new database with, 174–178
objects using application parts template, 180–186
user-defined form template, 186–188
deleting custom template, 180
saving database as, 178–180
using custom templates, 180

Text Box button, 103

text box control object
adding fields to forms, 87
moving and resizing, 90–92

text file
exporting data to, 266–267
importing data from, 260–265

Text Format property, changing from plain text to rich text formatting, 21–23

theme, applying in custom report, 135–136

Themes button, 91, 135

third normal form, 49

time, adding to reports, 140–144

title, creating for custom form, 85–87

Title bar, specify application title on startup, 229–230

Title button, 85

Toggle Filter button, 54

Totals option box, 150

Trust Center, viewing setting for, 250–252

Trusted Locations list, 250–251

Trusted Publishers list, 250–251

U

unbound objects, 85, 103

Union query, 74–75

Update button, 74, 79

update query, 74, 79–80

Use Control Wizards button, 96–97, 136

user-defined form template, 186–188

V

Validation Rule property, 20

Validation Text property, 20

Variance function, 150

viewing
contents of attached file, 24–25
embedded macros, 221–224

Visual Basic for Applications (VBA), 223
ACCDE files and, 249
IF function, 70

W

wildcard character used with Find feature, 121

Window Mode argument, 211

WODate field, 17

Y

Yes/No data type, 7

Z

zero-length string, using and disallowing, 10–12